AMERICA,
NEW
MEXICO

AMERICA,

NEW

MEXICO

ROBERT LEONARD REID

THE UNIVERSITY OF ARIZONA PRESS
TUCSON

The University of Arizona Press
© 1998 Robert Leonard Reid
All Rights Reserved

∞ This book is printed on acid-free, archival-quality paper
Manufactured in the United States of America
First printing

Library of Congress Cataloging-in-Publication Data
Reid, Robert Leonard.
America, New Mexico / Robert Leonard Reid.
p. cm.
Includes bibliographical references (p.   ).
ISBN 0-8165-1851-3 (alk. paper). —
ISBN 0-8165-1876-9 (pbk.: alk. paper)
1. New Mexico—Description and travel.   I. Title.
F801.2.R45   1998
917.904'53—dc21   97-21238
                                                                    CIP

British Cataloguing-in-Publication Data
A catalogue record for this book is available from the British Library.

Publication of this book is made possible in part by the proceeds of a
permanent endowment created with the assistance of a Challenge
Grant from the National Endowment for the Humanities, a federal
agency.

For my brother, Bill

CONTENTS

ACKNOWLEDGMENTS

I owe a deep debt of gratitude to Nat Sobel, without whom this book would not have been written. Some years ago Nat suggested the idea for the book to me. He hounded me until I began writing and remained a guiding light until I was finished. To him goes my profound thanks for his faith in me, his unwavering support, and his generosity.

A number of people took time to speak to me at length about their experiences of New Mexico. Their names appear throughout these pages, but I want to single them out here for special thanks, for their stories and observations are central to this book: D. Ray Blakeley, Judy Chicago, Max Córdova, Martin Kelleher, Jean LeMarr, Jorge León, Lupe León, George López, Mimi López, Kathy McKesson, Eddie Montoya, Sabinita Ortiz, Peter Simonson, Frederico Vigil, and Manny Vildasol.

Sometime in midvoyage this project and its captain struck an iceberg. Many friends came to our aid, lending support and encouragement, and managing somehow to keep us afloat. I can never repay these stalwart souls, but I want to acknowledge their help, for which I shall forever be grateful: Ed Albright, Richard Araiza, Michael Berger, Bain Chadsey, Bob Faxon, Sascha Feinstein, David Hertz, John Miller, Ivan Manson, Charlie Moss, Joe Petulla, Ed Shirkey, Jonathan Strong, the Reverend Brian Taylor, and Bill Thielen.

For not altogether different reasons, I want to thank Joanne O'Hare of the University of Arizona Press. Arriving as a light in a very dark darkness,

Joanne has since served variously as wise counsel, staunch advocate, sympathetic sounding board, and understanding confidant. I'm deeply grateful. I'm grateful, too, to Joanne's colleague Sally Bennett, for locating my antecedents, rehanging my participles, and as anyone who has ever knowingly committed a murky metaphor will understand, helping me to discover what I was really trying to say.

I would like to thank the many people who shared stories about New Mexico with me, pointed me toward not-to-be-missed destinations, or, in a few cases, not wishing to miss those destinations, climbed into the car and came along. My thanks to Saraj Cory, Julie and Alan Cota, Michael DeLapa, Betty and Jim Dimmick, Suzanna Fastabend, Priscilla Grano, Al Hawkinson, Mary Mandeville and Peter Chase, Jane and David McGuire, John and Verena McMahan, Pam McNamara, Marcia Miller and Marty Lee, Wilbur Miller, Steve and Trish Shelly, Linda Solomon, Mimi Weinberg and Dan Clark, and Wilbur Woodis.

For their quick, expert, and gracious responses to my requests for information or technical assistance, I would like to thank Larnetta Buck of the American Bar Association; Bob Crisman of the naturalists staff at Carlsbad Caverns National Park; Guy Dameron of the University of New Mexico Bureau of Business and Economic Research; Wallace Ford of the New Mexico Council of Churches; Mary J. Grzeskowiak, Historic Preservation Planner for the City of Santa Fe; Don Hancock of the Southwest Research and Information Center; Aaron Handler of the Indian Health Service; Bonnie Hughes, Hank Hughes, and the staff of St. Elizabeth Shelter for the Homeless; Dorothy Indyke of Through the Flower; Rafael Mieszala and Eleanor Milroy of the Albuquerque Border City Project; Janet Mygatt of the University of New Mexico Herbarium; Janet Saiers of the Albuquerque Cultural and Recreational Services Department; Jackie Seidenwurm of Saint Joseph Rehabilitation Hospital; Magoo Shoulderblade of the University of New Mexico Native American Studies Program; Delos Smith of the Conference Board; Rita Spillenger of the American Civil Liberties Union; Marcia Starr of the New Mexico Office of the Medical Investigator; Nano Takuma of the Albuquerque

Parks and General Services Department; and Wayne Treers of the U.S. Bureau of Reclamation.

Several of the people about whom I have written spoke to me at some risk to themselves. I am profoundly grateful to them for doing so. To protect their identities, I have told their stories with a few names, dates, and places changed.

Most of all, I want to thank my wife, Carol, and my son, Jake, for their constancy, their resiliency, and the innumerable sacrifices they made so that I could explore New Mexico.

INTRODUCTION

In the summer of 1859 the American artist Frederic Edwin Church set sail for Newfoundland in search of light. Church belonged to the so-called luminist school of painting, whose adherents through the precise depiction of atmospheric light strove to portray in their art the spiritual nature of the American landscape. Big, grand, hauntingly silent, the best works of Church, Thomas Moran, Albert Bierstadt, and other members of the school create a cathedral-like effect, a sense of sunlight pouring through stained glass. In a luminist painting, Barry Lopez tells us in his own exceptionally luminous *Arctic Dreams,* light "is like a creature, a living, integral part of the scene. The landscape is numinous, real. It ceases to be, as it was in Europe, merely symbolic."

In the tumbled ice of the northern seas Frederic Church found what was for him the essence of light in nature. *The Icebergs,* the huge painting he executed upon his return to New York, is a magnificent radiance of ice and snow and mist. The scene is sublime: too big, too grand, and—despite the stormy sea and the giant bergs—too *quiet* for Earth. To the first viewers who saw it, the work appeared to depict a place that was not merely remote, it was unreachable—more celestial, perhaps, than earthly.

It was a failure. In seeking to subordinate himself to the authority of nature, a primary aim of the luminist artist, Church created a work to which few viewers could respond. Like nonrepresentational painting, which appeared half a century later, *The Icebergs* tested the limits of human sympathy and understanding. The initial public reaction was, fittingly, ice-cold.

Church understood the reason at once. Returning to the studio, he added to the foreground of the painting a portion of the main topmast of a wrecked ship—a human thumbprint. When the work was exhibited again it soared in popularity; today many authorities regard *The Icebergs* as an essential work of American art. Barry Lopez explains Church's decision to alter the painting: "Try as we might, we ultimately can make very little sense at all of nature without resorting to such devices. Whether they are such bald assertions of human presence as Church's cruciform mast or the intangible, metaphorical tools of the mind—contrast, remembrance, analogy—we bring our own worlds to bear in foreign landscapes in order to clarify them for ourselves." Lopez continues, asserting an intimate relationship between land and mind: "To inquire into the intricacies of a distant landscape is to provoke thoughts about one's own interior landscape, and the familiar landscapes of memory. The land urges us to come around to an understanding of ourselves."

Newfoundland is a long way from New Mexico, but reading Lopez's story of the creation of *The Icebergs* recently, I found myself thinking of New Mexico and, especially, of the reasons that led me to write this book. I lived in New Mexico for eight years, from 1987 to 1995. During that time I traveled extensively and restlessly throughout the state, poking into its recesses, enjoying its singular pleasures, kicking up the dust that has settled onto the creaking floorboards of its past, and most important, contemplating its significance, both to residents and to those who live beyond its borders.

What I found in that sprawling country of mountains, deserts, and plains was a luminist painting come to life. New Mexico is big, grand, and hauntingly silent—famously so, as countless numbers of people have discovered and as I have tried to show in these pages. For many artists the state shimmers in a light as essential as that which drew Frederic Church to the North Atlantic, a light I refer to often, beginning on the first page of the first chapter of this book. At frequent and unexpected moments during my odyssey I observed events that seemed to possess spiritual or supernatural elements, events that, as I found out, are as common in New Mexico as jackrabbits. To me they illustrate the luminist paradox that Barry Lopez describes simply as "numinous, real." I've written about some of them in these pages.

My travels brought me familiarity and occasionally even intimacy with a unique and unforgettable land, one whose memory remains as strange, as beautiful, and as humbling as the icebergs of the Labrador Sea must have seemed to Frederic Church. At last, however, I grew restless. A family tradition stirred, a kind of genetic wanderlust. Soon I was studying maps and writing to friends in other exotic locations, just as I had before immigrating to New Mexico, and before that California, New York City, Maine, and a half-dozen other places. In the spring of 1995 my family and I packed our bags, loaded our belongings into a rented truck, said goodbye once again to friends and to a plot of earth that we knew and loved, and moved on.

Today, a thousand miles distant, I see that I was destined from the beginning to be merely a visitor to New Mexico; I see, too, that this book was meant to be something more than a portrait of an alluring place in which to live. Ever shifting in character and in hue, New Mexico became during my eight-year sojourn that faraway landscape—that crash and tumble of icebergs—for which I had long been searching. New Mexico was the canvas upon which I could begin to delineate my interior landscape and to discover its essential light.

So it is that the issues I write about in these pages are issues of more than regional interest—violence, homelessness, militarism, immigration, censorship, racism. Long concerned with these issues, I had lacked a fitting context in which to view and to write about them. In New Mexico I discovered my context: sun, sky, wind, clouds, star-studded night. Here was a confident and exacting medium with the power to search out and illuminate solutions to the most intractable and most urgent of problems—travelers without papers, men and women without homes, children without hope. It was a medium of endless promise.

And the themes I explore are universal themes: the vision and resilience of the human animal, the power of land and tradition, the juxtaposition of opposites that so dependably characterizes our everyday experiences—

grandeur and ugliness, triumph and tragedy, hope and despair—and, most of all, the centrality of the natural world to the human condition and to any effort to improve it.

Helping me to make sense of all this are some of the men and women I encountered on my travels. Few remain in view for more than a page or two; most play supporting roles behind desert, wind, and sky. All, however, are essential, for this lustrous cast of characters testifies to that intimate connection between people and land which we must learn to understand if we are to understand either people or land. A gang member in Albuquerque, a customs agent on the Mexican border, an Indian filmmaker, a small-town radio news reporter, a drifter by the side of the road: these are the thumbprints I have added to my canvas in an effort to bring my stories down to earth. Anchored there, perhaps they can provide fixes on two haunting and elusive landscapes which we spend a fair portion of our days seeking, striving to know, and struggling to make peace with—our selves and the ancient rocks and hills.

AMERICA,
NEW
MEXICO

In this land there is a graveness, of color and heart. . . .

—Jimmy Santiago Baca, "In My Land"

TUMBLEWEEDS

To persons standing alone on a clear midnight such as this, the roll of the world eastward is almost a palpable movement.

—*Thomas Hardy,* Far from the Madding Crowd

Begin with the morning and the light. Begin with the crack of dawn, that sudden, silvery occasion of the horizon when the first chill sliver of day slips beneath the shell of night and blinks on far away and silent, like a porch light in a fog. Begin with belief in a place that is still mostly earth and sky, a time-scented garden where nature is foremost and rocks are truth, and where dawn is a paean to fresh starts and reckless plans—new lives, first dates, opening pages of books. Begin in Truchas, Cordova, or any of a score of villages scattered over the northern mountains, where the rude walls of old adobe churches shimmer in the pearly flicker of dawn, while in hushed interiors men and women born to brightness and faith utter soft rosaries in Spanish, then light candles of propitiation and give thanks.

Or begin in Dulce, Zuni, or some centuries-old pueblo just waking on the still-black river, where Indians greet the sun with plainsong, then stoop to kindle fires of home-grown piñon for their morning bread. Or on the arid flatlands of the south among communities of mesquite and ocotillo, where yellow lamplight beckons in windows of houses lining the new underground railroad, welcoming weary travelers of the night seeking refuge after the harrowing crossing from Mexico. Or on some remote landscape where icy beams from headlamps or flashlights open pathways through the shadows for early-rising workers off to do business with the earth: on ranches moored in buffalo grass; in oil fields hissing with pumpjacks and gas flares; in coal pits or molybdenum mines; on chile, cotton, or alfalfa plantations.

Or begin to see New Mexico on the threadbare plain that the first Spanish explorers christened Jornada del Muerto—"dead man's march"—at a crossroads called Trinity Site by a whimsical cloud-seeder of nuclear times, where each day at 5:29 A.M. a low flame licks out of the dust, the inextinguishable memory of a thousand suns called Fat Man.

The crack widens, the shell lifts cloud by cloud. Boisterous light spills in to fill the void. Sleepy and irresolute, I angle against a fender of the old Dodge sipping coffee and observing the swift execution of New Mexico's peerless Sistine sky. Surrounding me are the sounds, the smells, and the feel of the start of the journey—the dogs and roosters howling like orphans, the apples rotting under the Jonathan trees, the budding light, the cry of geese echoing off the luster of the sky, the consecration of cedar wafting down from my neighbor's chimney, the small wind loping off the sandhills and tripping the leaves on the cottonwoods, the flooding light, the rosy cast on the lingering patches of late snow, the old man draped over the fence at the end of the road, his dreamy eyes frozen in the breath of his horses.

The violent light. As I gaze east the sun lunges into a notch on the ridge below Sandia Peak and detonates over the valley. Blinded, I spin away. Then, shading my eyes, I turn to witness the crowning strokes—the relentless stripping of the last of night from behind the trees and under the rocks, the nailing down of the great arch, the filling in of the last touches of day. Craning my neck, scanning the blue and the radiance and the fearfulness of it all, I wonder if I may be gazing into the eye of God.

Then I sever the ties, catch the soft curve of a slowly ascending breeze, and bound into the sky. . . .

I'm off!

Off for the land of roadrunners and chile love! Off for the snow-mantled mountains and the cattle-studded plains! Off for the rainbow-thatched badlands and the high, not-at-all-unpleasant desert! Off for Aztec, Angel Fire, and Apache Creek, for inscrutable Chaco Canyon and all-too-obvious Truth or Consequences! Off for towns that barely rate zip codes and counties that barely rate towns! Off for the state that is quirkily, lustily tricultural, where Indians hold seniority and Latinos plurality, and where all others from Australians to Zulus parade under a many-colored umbrella called Anglo. Off to view rituals strange and wonderful—four hundred lavishly tasseled corn dancers bursting the tiny square at Santo Domingo; bearded men of the Penitente Brotherhood bearing crosses along country roads and scourging themselves with cactus spines; dashing pilots commanding six hundred hot-air balloons into the wee hours over Albuquerque; cowboys and cowgirls in a no-name cantina holding each other like distant hopes and two-stepping smooth as saddles.

Off for the land where you're never far from a view the size of Portugal and a town negotiating with a county in New Jersey for the right to dispose of its toxic waste! Off for America's oldest towns, newest weapons, dustiest dust storms, and flashiest flash floods! Off for the fifth largest, fourth youngest, first most misunderstood state, the state identified by *Junior Scholastic* magazine in 1990 as New Mexico Territory and by an endearing portion of the American public as a foreign country! Off for the state that annually ranks with the highest per capita in highway deaths, divorces, crime, and single mothers; tops in numbers of Ph.D.'s and alcoholics; first in infant mortality and annual number of sunny days; unsurpassed in lightning deaths and poverty; unparalleled in numbers of premium wine drinkers, FM classical music listeners, and child murderers; cream-of-the-crop in artists, writers, scientists, and high-school dropouts. Bottom-of-the-barrel in teachers' salaries, teen employment, and percentage of citizens carrying health insurance.

Best in sky.

Off for the state about which has been asked most profoundly, If it's not new and it isn't Mexico, then why do they call it New Mexico?

Off to discover this enormous green-chile-stew-of-a-state and perhaps something more, a vestige of morning and light in the grand aching country of which it is a part.

So vast, so diverse, so singular is New Mexico that long after I began searching diligently through its searchless nooks and crannies, I still felt like a dazed immigrant stepping off a stagecoach, hand-drawn map and letter of introduction clenched tightly in my fist. Before moving to New Mexico I put in ten years in Manhattan and twelve more in the San Francisco Bay Area. What, then, was I to make of downtown Albuquerque streets festooned in empty parking spots, twenty-minute rush hours, Federal Express couriers who called me "podner," and newspapers that treated an appearance by Senator Pete Domenici on *Face the Nation* as front-page news? By which corollary to the principles of late capitalism was I to account for the liquor store owner so despairing of his inability to fulfill my request for empty boxes that he locked the door to his store, plunked down in an aisle, and opened and emptied a dozen cartons for me? To which authority on the art of civic buffoonery should I have turned to interpret the truly exquisite form practiced in New Mexico, a distinguished portion of whose elected officials are regularly arrested for embezzlement, fist-fighting, or drunken driving; whose largest city was governed until recently by a mayor who disappeared for such long periods of time that an Albuquerque radio station offered a prize to anyone who could find him; and whose highway department, apparently lacking anything better to do, announced one random Tuesday afternoon that it had decided to change the route number of every road in the state?

With only jaded, tough-minded, ultrasophisticated New Yorkers and Californians to compare them with, how could I explain New Mexicans, normal, everyday New Mexicans, who drive off the road to admire sunsets, who proudly reproduce Georgia O'Keeffe poppies and hollyhocks on their lowriders and Winnebagos, who collar passersby to rhapsodize over sublime weekend discoveries—salsa hot enough to brand with, bizarre acts of geology, ghost towns reverberating with noble aspirations and ragtime, dirt roads to infinity? Who blithely toss aside the day's itinerary when a more fanciful one happens along, and who take it for granted that there is something mysterious, something certifiably hyperphysical about their state?

During my stay in New Mexico I met not a single resident who doubted that space aliens landed northwest of the town of Roswell in 1947, or that New Mexico is the most logical place on the planet for such an occasion. Not long ago I watched an unworldly twilight steal over the vast expanses northwest of

Roswell—no, *felt* it—and I can testify without reservation that, yes, the extraordinary visitation took place.

Each journey in New Mexico is a test of convention, and I have learned well the cardinal rule of travel: when setting out for a new land, whether over the ocean or just to the other side of town, pack a light bag, leave behind your foolish romances and preconceptions, and set your spirit to the local time. If your destination is New Mexico, that may mean carrying no bag at all and approaching with all the speed and urgency of a full moon sailing over the Rio Grande.

Drive west from Texas, take the train south from Colorado, travel east from sprawling Phoenix, and you will discover in each direction an exact location where the land transfigures, the wind shifts, the sky stretches higher and farther than you had ever thought possible; and an oddly familiar feeling will seize you, a sense of embarking once more, happily, into uncharted terrain. From the east the moment occurs when the legs are suddenly jerked out from under the relentless Texas tableland and the surface collapses to reveal the rudimentary framework beneath, a primordial landscape of time-burnished craters and buttes. From the north it happens at Raton Pass, where the Colorado roller coaster reaches its high point and the horizon before you unfurls into ten thousand square miles of storied American frontier. Cresting the pass you emerge onto a breathtaking hundred-mile slope, then begin the slow run downward and backward in time, past Cimarron, Wagon Mound, Fort Union, Pecos, and on to Santa Fe. From the west the critical spot appears as you climb into the cool pine and piñon forests of Catron County, a county the size of Connecticut and Rhode Island combined, with a single traffic light to its name. The vastness and the emptiness strike a distantly remembered chord, and you may hear an echo of what it means to begin life anew.

"Something soft and wild and free" is how Willa Cather described the spell of this place, something that "released the prisoned spirit of man into the wind, into the blue and gold, into the morning." Wrote D. H. Lawrence, "New Mexico liberated me from the present era of civilization."

I was twelve when I first experienced morning in New Mexico. My parents and I drove from our home in Pennsylvania to visit friends recently emigrated to Albuquerque.

Alas, our bags were too heavily packed. The month was June and the direction staunchly southwest, so we prepared for suntans, cactus, and jackrabbits. Instead, we encountered snow and elk. In place of saguaro cactus and petrified forests (we had made the common and, to New Mexicans, unforgivable mistake of confusing New Mexico with Arizona), we found majestic mountains and ponderosa pines. Surely something ordinary must have occurred during the days that followed, but what I remember most is what passes for rebirth for a twelve-year-old: the soothing realization that the dreaded decline into adulthood does not necessarily await one, that the dazzle and enchantment of childhood can continue forever. Here were blue corn and dust devils, rodeos and *meep-meep*ing birds I knew from cartoons, summer snow and Indians, foreign tongues and dictionary-sized dinner rolls with the sweetness and density of cotton candy. Most astonishing of all was the vast sky that each day at sunset began trembling and twittering as though altitude-sick, then shimmering in the colors of butterfly wings. Back home in Pennsylvania I told my friends that I had been vacationing in South America.

I didn't return for more than thirty years. When I did so, it was to stay, I thought, at least till the wind freshened once more and the moment arrived to cut my tethers one more time. As it was, busted and burned-out in California, recently remarried after a calamitous divorce, I needed something bright and new and probably amazing to restart my engines. Carol and I discussed transcendental meditation and skydiving but settled on New Mexico.

We drove from California. It was August and the Mojave was afire. We traveled at night to avoid incineration. Even so, the temperature in Barstow hit a hundred degrees at midnight. The streets were jammed with Barstownians. They must have thought it was noon. Our cat, Magoo, sprawled limply in his travel cage, panting alarmingly and uttering a terrible rasping sound. His top lip was pulled back to expose his teeth; he seemed to be drying up. Barstow is an excellent argument for air-conditioning, but we had none, so we were reduced to issuing cool words of encouragement to the cat and patting his forehead with wet napkins. With his bare teeth and his sopping head he looked woeful—like an exhausted beaver.

We slept through the morning at a motel in Arizona. At an early-afternoon breakfast in a restaurant with table tops so shiny they called for sunglasses, the world seemed scrambled along with the eggs. Carol and I made small talk at a window opening on the east. What are we doing? Whose idea was this? Will they speak English?

The road was straight and endless, a slow gateway to the dizzying sky. Arizona was a grand threshold running its course beneath our wheels. The calm, the altitude, the majesty mounted with every mile. As the sun dipped below the rearview mirror and twilight flew in, low and brilliant, to illuminate the country ahead, I could make out the shape of the earth, its grace and sparkle, the way it is like a star.

We crossed into New Mexico in gathering darkness. Clouds rolled in, the wind quickened, the air grew brisk. In the sky ahead a quartet of lightning storms lifted into the evening over Albuquerque 150 miles away. It was a welcoming committee, up late to entertain us through the final hours.

I aimed the car at the fracas and punched my foot to the floor. Even at night New Mexico was a lighthouse signaling on the horizon. Signs flew by, pointers to new and splendid destinations. Zuni! Bluewater! Lava Beds! Sky City! I lowered the window to allow the scent of a new herb—part sage and part electricity—to float into the car. By the time we passed the sign for Laguna Pueblo, half the sky was bursting in fireworks every few seconds, thunder hectored and raved on all sides, and a hard wind socked us each time we emerged from the shadow of a protecting mesa. What was going on had the clear earmarks of an all-out gully-washer except that not a drop of rain had fallen. It was a thunderstorm without the storm. It was New Mexico's way of doing things.

Albuquerque lies long and narrow in the valley of the Rio Grande several thousand feet below a high tableland to the west. The traveler approaching from that direction, knowing that a city of half a million people lies just ahead but unable to see it, begins to wonder if he may have taken a wrong turn somewhere.

Then without warning the table ends and a gulf appears, and the city suddenly and spectacularly opens out before one's eyes. At midnight after a long journey under a wild sky, the effect is stunning and unforgettable. Navigating the blackness we hit table's edge and rocketed out over the valley of lights. It was as though we had happened onto a reverse eclipse, as though in the dead of night the sun had burst over us without warning, signaling our arrival in a distant country where day breaks at midnight and where rules and fashions are not highly valued, where the best bet is to hold onto one's hat and see what happens.

For the price of a toolshed in California we bought a rambling adobe house and an acre of weeds in Corrales, a small agricultural community along the Rio Grande. Among the thistles and thorns we could sometimes locate the residents that shared the land with us—rabbits, quail, roadrunners, many lizards and black widow spiders, a dozen fruit trees. Magoo, a licensed killer in California, was less ambitious than most of his potential victims in New Mexico. He relaxed in the role of underdog. He purred more, became peaceable.

Carol and I spent several summers battling the vegetation. At last we managed to slip in among the goatheads and pigweed a croquet-sized lawn of native grasses. One spring the wind was especially hale, the peach and apricot trees bloomed as though they were moonstruck, and a brace of ring-necked pheasants scratched out a nest among the tumbleweeds. In June Carol and I had our first child, Jake, a tiny, slippery, red-faced kid with the same look of wonder and expectation on his face that I had worn on my arrival in New Mexico. I was forty-seven and a father for the first time. I had struck out in search of something bright and new and probably amazing, and I had succeeded beyond my wildest dreams.

In its current edition, Corrales and the land grant of which it is a part were given by the king of Spain to one Francisco Montes y Vigil in 1710. A few descendants of the original inhabitants farm the same plots of land their ancestors worked two and a half centuries ago.

But the human story here, as in all of New Mexico, reaches deep into an unknown past shrouded by mystery and time. Francisco Vásquez de Coronado and his legions spent the winter of 1540 just north of town. Native peoples inhabited villages beside the Rio Grande for centuries before that. Today on the far side of the river just a mile or two from Corrales, Indians of Sandia Pueblo tend fields that were ancient when Coronado arrived. At certain moments of the moon, young men of the pueblo are initiated into the rites of the kiva and their elders dance the corn dance.

Much of what is bright and new and amazing to a newcomer to New Mexico is also beyond reach. Thinking about the enduring mystery of the kiva or about those day-long solemnizations of the summer harvest, I sometimes despaired that more than a few miles separated me from the people of the river. The deep roots that allow the people of Sandia Pueblo to understand the earth as creator, provider, and friend had, for me, scarcely begun to sprout. It was then that I felt most like the hapless immigrant, bewildered and never to belong.

I felt it too among New Mexico's Hispanics as I observed the smooth integration of tradition into their daily lives, the strength and presence it affords, the effortless self-knowledge. I have suggested that New Mexico is a land of wonder and curiosities, but in so doing I reveal myself as a bedazzled visitor standing in the doorway, peering in at what appears to be an entertainment in progress. To the residents of the house it is merely life.

Yet awaiting the buds on the fruit trees in spring or the first flakes of snow in the fall, I sometimes experienced a moment of serenity and light that perhaps was like a corn dance. And I wondered if it might be the passion and clarity of New Mexico discovering me at last, or the knowing touch of the grand sweep of time.

Today's Corrales is rapidly changing from the agricultural community it has long been to a bedroom community for professionals who work in Albuquerque. Fittingly, the name *Corrales* means "corral." There may be as many horses here as people. It was a rare day when I didn't spot a party of riders trotting along the irrigation ditch behind my back fence, or when someone didn't turn up at the post office on the back of a fine Arabian or old cloudy-eyed Cheyenne. However much the village may change, it remains intimately connected to all that came before, through the reverence of its people for the land and the horse and by an endless succession of sensual pleasures that cycles through the year like spins of a prayer wheel—newly turned earth in spring, freshly cut alfalfa, chiles roasting through the crystalline days of fall.

The new Corraleños arrive home at 6 P.M. and sequester themselves behind locked doors. They raise salad gardens and purchase season tickets to the New Mexico Symphony. Saturday mornings they recycle. Many have huge barking dogs with names like Ammo and Thug. At night Corrales is a symphony of deranged curs. Since most of the dogs spend their lives snarling and snapping in cages or behind chain-link fences, the animals' purpose is unclear. Surely it is not companionship. These are mean, unpleasant beasts. Nor can they be designed for protection, for there is little here that one needs to fear.

More likely they're chosen to accord with an image of ruggedness, toughness, and individuality that still infects New Mexico and, indeed, all of the West. Store clerks who pack sidearms, four-wheel-drive vehicles used mostly for grocery shopping, cruel jokes about Indians, antigovernment invective, pathetic prairie-dog shoots: these are today's version of the wild and woolly West. Like much of the whimsy that clouds our understanding of the region, they celebrate a place that never existed. Along with their counterparts throughout the West, New Mexicans have always exhibited admirable independence and resourcefulness, but rarely in the Herculean proportions that legend suggests.

Without the protection of the army during the settlement decades of the nineteenth century and the largess of the Defense Department during the past fifty years; without cheap land, cheap timber, cheap water, cheap mineral leases, and cheap grazing lands, all courtesy of the federal government; without tax breaks, subsidies, incentives, price supports, and cozy arrangements of wondrous richness and imagination, every tough-talking, tall-walking lone gun who ever stalked New Mexico would have been on welfare. New Mexicans pretend to hate the federal government, but without the federal government New Mexico would still be run by the Indians. Success here and in all the West, as each of our millionaires can attest, consists of outfitting oneself in a buck-skin jacket, braying impressively about self-reliance and free enterprise, then meeting the fellow from Washington in a dark alley to collect a suitcase full of money.

Romance is America's bread and butter. Where would we be without our noble pioneers misty-eyed before the beauty of the land, our scalping Indians descending on a party of helpless immigrants, our wild horses thundering over the plain? Never mind that land-loving pioneers and their descendants destroyed half of America's topsoil, that scalping was invented by white men, and that wild horses hail from Spain. That kind of talk is plain subversive. Who needs it! My backyard is a veritable Camelot of fantasy and romance. Sagebrush, the scent of which can make you see covered wagons. Railroad ties, salvaged from a trunk line to the turquoise mines. Best of all, tumbleweeds—huge, carefree, irresponsible things that remind you of what it was like to be eighteen.

In spring when the wind is tameless, these marvelous creations cut loose from their moorings and go bounding across New Mexico in great, giddy sine curves, skidding down interstates into oncoming traffic, taking off on brief Wright brothers flights into the jet stream that screams along at thirty feet . . . on and on and on into cowboy songs, into sunsets, into our hearts and souls and myth. Tumbleweeds symbolize both the happy-go-lucky American spirit and the man of principle who goes it alone—Randolph Scott against the Clanton gang, Jimmy Stewart versus the system. Who can watch a tumbleweed taking off for the stratosphere and not get a king-sized lump in the throat?

Regrettably, tumbleweeds are not American by birth, and most of them aren't free, not for long at least. Tumbleweeds are Russian thistles. They arrived in the West in 1873 or 1874 in a sack of flax seed packed somewhere in central Asia. After a hop, a skip, and a jump, the typical Russian thistle crashes into a fence and that's that. The mad adventure is over. It was there, lynched on a fence post, where tumbleweeds no doubt made their strongest impression on Russian peasants and where, if anyplace, they entered the brutal mythology of the steppes. And where here in America they may serve as an equally vivid reminder to whoever truly goes it alone—the longhair, the whistle blower, the rebel, the eccentric, the cultist, the uncloseted gay or lesbian, the dissident, the voice crying in the wilderness. Freedom is a grand idea, but like many of our grand ideas we enjoy it most in the abstract, where it is removed from the grave business of getting on with our lives and accumulating profits. It is better to embalm our noblest principles in symbols like flags and tumbleweeds, which are easier than the real thing to extol, idealize, and defend.

This is not a grouchy appeal for an end to myth, merely a proposal that we take a harder look at the reality that lies behind it. I wouldn't have my New Mexico without its brave pioneers, its rugged individualism, and its tumbleweeds. Like all myths they began in truth. Examined with sympathy and care, they provide important clues to our past and valuable starting points for judging and interpreting history.

Moreover, they impart a feeling about this place which for a visitor is indispensable. Anyone who spends time among New Mexico's Apaches, for example, without listening for the echoes of drums and war cries, without watching the shadows for signs of the legendary Apache warrior, has missed a great deal.

Yet, too often, Geronimo is as far as we go, and it's not far enough. Geronimo is ninety years in his grave. Many of his descendants have been robbed of their spirit. Their despairing teenagers are today taking their own lives, and their newborns are poisoned by alcohol. A visit to the Apache must include not only an embracing of legend, which is essential, but a vow to overcome it.

When I returned to Zuni, Bluewater, Lava Beds, and Sky City, it was to revel in the mystery and romance of New Mexico and, at the same time, to search for something that stood out so boldly and guilelessly I would recognize it at once as truth. And one thing more: to search for signs of a fresh wind tossing with dreams and possibilities that I remembered soaring across America when I was young. The night I drove into the valley of lights I could scarcely remember what that wind had been like. I knew it had been a grand, astonishing thing, something that could get you up in the morning—a feeling of hope and common purpose, an assurance that it was all right to believe in plain, old-fashioned things like equality, community, justice, and freedom.

But the strength and promise it had conveyed, the sense of purpose and direction, of miraculous spring—those I could no longer recall. Through three decades of adult life I had felt the wind diminish year by year, till the time came when I could no longer tell if it had been a childhood illusion or if I had simply grown old and tired and cynical, resigned to a winter without dreams.

Yet something about New Mexico gave me hope that a spirit of possibility was still to be found. Like America when it was new and the air clear and each of us wide-eyed and confident, New Mexico remains a stronghold of exuberance and expectation. Sometimes on my bounding journey across mountains and plains I caught sight of a cluster of tumbleweeds sailing across the sky, wild and beautiful and free. Sometimes at night I looked east and imagined the old footloose sun tumbling through the darkness toward its rendezvous with dawn.

JOURNEYS THROUGH
SPACE AND TIME

The Creating Power gave the people the pipe. "Live by it," he said. He named this land the Turtle Continent because it was there that the turtle came up with the mud out of which the third world was made.

"Someday there might be a fourth world," the Creating Power thought. Then he rested.

—Leonard Crow Dog, Brule Sioux legend

L ong after dark, one blustery evening in early March, I found myself in Gallup, New Mexico. It was still winter there at an elevation of nearly seven thousand feet in the heart of New Mexico's geological rust belt, the sprawling landscape of shattered red rock and worn-out hogbacks and buttes that composes the state's northwest corner. The temperature was eighteen degrees. A surly wind kicked a pair of sickly-yellow food wrappers along old Route 66, the long, grim fantasy in neon that is Gallup's signature after dark.

At night Gallup is seven miles of rhinestones. G. K. Chesterton observed of Times Square after dark that a man who couldn't read might think he was in paradise. The strip in Gallup is a long way from paradise: fast-food joints, pawn shops, dilapidated motels ("No train noise"), food marts dealing cigs at the cash register for ten cents apiece, saloons, liquor stores, more saloons, more liquor stores. No, the rhinestone fantasy is closer to hell for anyone unlucky enough to land here on a cold winter night.

I parked near Fourth Street, zipped up my jacket, stepped into the wind. Despite the cold there was a brisk trade at a package liquor store half a block away. A steady stream of Indians passed through the door in both directions. Outside, a group of young men, hatless, coal-black hair shining eerily in the amber light, huddled near the curb. They were smashed—struck down in midsentence. Silent and immobile, they appeared to be frozen in time.

Two women paced nearby. They complained hoarsely, waved their arms. A male friend approached. The women turned on him, scolding him angrily. Then the three stepped smartly into the store.

Propped against the door of my car I observed from twenty yards away. No one seemed to notice or to care. The scene unfolded with ghastly proficiency, too carefully scripted to admit a new player. Smiles were desperate, laughter uncontrolled. Drinking is serious business in Gallup. Binges can last for days. On this night it was Coors and Richard's Wild Irish Rose. On Sunday when liquor sales are banned, the drinkers will turn to hair spray and household cleaner.

A few steps from the door stood a tall, frail, ghostly figure, a Navajo—or Diné ("the People"), as many prefer to be known. He was framed by a wide window hung in an assortment of frayed ads for cheap beer and wine. The man was alone, limned by a silver glow from inside the store. He wore a blue watch-cap, a brown, tattered, thigh-length belted jacket, jeans, and brown leather shoes. His gaunt frame curved in a smooth thin line from head to foot—a crescent moon fast slipping toward the horizon. He appeared to be in his sixties, though he could have been much younger. His face was long and bony, his eyes unfocused.

He was floating.

Several minutes passed. The old man turned and shuffled to a new spot a little farther from the door. To propel himself along he clenched his fists, raised his forearms parallel to the ground, and swung his arms jerkily, like rusted pendulums. When he settled into his new position his eyes were nearly closed. His face was contorted as though he were in pain.

Patrons came and went, oblivious to the man by the window. Beside the building stood an empty lot, a pissing-and-puking place littered with paper and broken glass. A bare bulb high on the wall cast a septic glow over the area. The old man shuffled into the middle of the lot, then turned to face the street. He appeared lost, a lonely figure adrift in an immensity of space. For a few seconds he struggled for balance. Briefly anchored, he opened his eyes wide and for a long moment seemed to be at peace.

Rapt in watching the old man I failed to hear the police van pulling up in front of the store. There was a sudden commotion as the Indians on the sidewalk scattered in all directions. The dreadful, earsplitting sound of a bullhorn rent the night.

"ALL RIGHT, GET A MOVE ON!"

An expression of alarm crossed the old man's face. Curiously, he made no effort to escape. Instead, he broke into a slow-motion trot toward the van.

An officer stepped out to greet him. The Indian smiled self-consciously, his eyes lusterless. Then he lifted his hand slightly, index finger extended, as though he were hailing a waiter.

The officer stepped to the rear of the van and threw open the door. The man attempted to step up gracefully but missed his footing. With a huge effort the officer seized him like a side of beef and hoisted him through the opening.

I was ten yards behind, gazing into the dark interior of the van. On either side there was a long seat, the seats facing each other separated by a narrow aisle. The old man was on his hands and knees in the aisle; above him on both sides hung drooping heads. The van was full of Indians. The officer stepped back, and for a moment the vehicle appeared to be stuffed with corpses. Then the door slammed and the van sped off into the night.

Like many of New Mexico's cities, Gallup resists easy classification, for it has two sides: one handsome and inviting, the other almost unbearably repellent. By day it is a bright and agreeable place, a leathery, upbeat community of nineteen thousand steeped in the history, culture, and feel of the Old West. Set in a valley of enormous beauty, the city is a natural destination for travelers. Navajo, Zuni, and Hopi reservations are nearby. This favored location has made Gallup one of the nation's premier trading centers for Native American arts and crafts. For the nature-oriented visitor seeking gems of another kind, Gallup is the perfect jumping-off point for excursions to iridescent deserts, ornamented canyons and mesas, turquoise lakes, black-rock volcanoes collapsed in huge, glittering heaps, and jewels of Anasazi culture, cliff dwellings set like diamonds in stone.

At night, however, the allure disappears, and the city's downtown area is transformed into a bleak and joyless place. At night, Gallup is where the Indians come to drink. Gallup is the county seat of McKinley County, the poorest county in the second poorest state in America. Forty-three percent of the county's residents, most of them Native Americans, live below the poverty line. For children under the age of six the poverty rate is fifty-two percent. Twenty-nine percent of the county's residents are on food stamps. Liquor is not sold on the nearby reservations, so many Indians who want to drink come into Gallup to do so. Local police lock up eighty or ninety of them a night. New Mexico's highways are the nation's most dangerous, largely because of alcohol. Prudent New Mexicans steer clear of McKinley County roads, especially at night and on weekends and holidays.

The state's Indians are not always among the prudent. The slaughter of Indians on New Mexico's highways proceeds with a kind of historical inevitability. Some of the victims die conventionally in car accidents. Others are hit as they stagger along streets or country roads. During the 1980s, 668 Indians died in car wrecks in New Mexico. Another 347 Indian pedestrians, whose blood coursed with alcohol at levels averaging three times the legal limit, were struck and killed by vehicles in the state. Of the Indians who escaped the roads and crawled into alleys or culverts, 166 froze to death. One was Shannon Garnenez, a thirteen-year-old Diné girl found in a ditch behind a Gallup grocery store on December 17, 1989.

During the early 1990s, widespread publicity about Gallup's alcohol-related problems led a coalition of community and Indian leaders to take remedial steps. Prevention programs were implemented in schools, new treatment centers were opened, drive-up liquor windows were shut down, and DWI patrols and arrests were beefed up. Early indications give cause for hope: alcohol-related deaths have dropped markedly. Yet the central question remains: Why does this distressing state of affairs exist at all? In New Mexico, whose Indian population at nine percent of the state's total population is second in proportion only to that of Alaska, one hears a multitude of answers. Some theorists postulate a defective gene that makes certain Indians unusually susceptible to alcoholism. Others argue that joblessness and poverty are to blame, while still others credit a broken spirit. A few, ignorant and surely broken in spirit themselves, say that this is the best that Indians can do.

I had my own theory. To test it, I drove three hundred miles from beleaguered Gallup in New Mexico's tumbledown red-rock badlands to placid Fort Sumner on the state's lyrical eastern plains. As closely as roads would allow, I followed the route of the Long Walk, the forced march that in 1864 took the vast majority of the Diné from their ancestral homelands in Arizona and New Mexico into captivity at a place called Bosque Redondo. In 1863, following years of hostilities between Diné and the encroaching white population, General James H. Carleton had issued an ultimatum to the Indians: surrender or die. Those who turned themselves in would be resettled and converted to the white man's ways.

Like many of his contemporaries, Carleton had a simplistic notion of the ease with which such a transformation could be achieved. The Diné were savages, he reasoned, but like naughty children could be taught to behave. Take them far from their homes, Christianize them, show them the superiority of the life of the gentleman farmer to their own uncivilized ways, administer a little encouragement as necessary, and all would soon be well.

To implement his plan, which would serve as a prototype for the Indian reservation system, Carleton oversaw the construction of Fort Sumner on the banks of the Pecos River, at a spot known as Bosque Redondo—"round grove of cottonwoods." A scanty oasis in the midst of drop-dead plains, haunted by wolves, coyotes, and marauding parties of Comanches and Kiowas, the spot was fearfully isolated and almost comically ill-contrived for teaching the joys of farming. Nevertheless, Carleton pronounced it "a fine reservation." There, "old Navajos would soon die off, and carry with them all the latent longings for murdering and robbing; the young ones would take their places without these longings; and thus, little by little, the Navajos would become a happy and contented people, and Navajo wars would be remembered only as something that belongs entirely to the past." Not incidentally, Carleton had a second motive in wanting to remove the Diné to Fort Sumner. Like many before him, he believed that the tribe's homelands were storehouses of vast amounts of mineral wealth. Carleton dreamed of seizing the Diné's lands and opening them to plunder by whites.

Few Diné turned themselves in. When the deadline passed, Carleton attacked with every weapon in his arsenal. Army troops invaded Diné lands, determined to bring the Indians to their knees. Methodically moving from one habitation to the next, soldiers burned fields, slaughtered sheep and horses, and destroyed homes. Diné who refused to submit were slain or were captured and released quietly for the Indian slave trade that flourished in New Mexico. (Some five hundred Diné slaves served white owners in Santa Fe alone.)

The Diné resisted with amazing tenacity and courage. But they were hopelessly outgunned. When brutal snows hit late in 1863 and food supplies gave out, the game was up. The majority of the people, many of them starving, stumbled into Fort Defiance and Fort Wingate, army outposts near today's city of Gallup. There the Indians were told to say goodbye to the land where they had resided for centuries, where their creation story affirmed that their ancestors had emerged from beneath the ground, and where tradition held that their world was bounded by a circle of sacred mountains. Early in 1864 in deep snow and freezing cold, tribal members set out in several huge contingents for Bosque Redondo, accompanied by officers of the First New Mexico Cavalry.

Most of the Diné were clothed in rags. They slept in the open and subsisted on brutally low rations. Issued white flour they had never before seen and had no idea how to use, some of the Indians tried to eat it raw. Others made a paste of it with water. Many doubled up in cramps and were unable to walk. Hundreds of Diné died of dysentery, exposure, and starvation. Those who could not keep up were shot. Eight thousand Diné walked across New Mexico to Fort Sumner. There, General Carleton determined, they would learn prosperity and peace.

And there I found confirmation of my theory. It lay not in hard science or in masses of carefully marshalled sociological data but in legend, which— along with chiles and sunsets—is one of New Mexico's finest products. Science and data give us facts, which are useful in establishing truth; legend gives us melody, redolence, and hue, which are essential to that end.

New Mexico is bursting with such resources. Before Carol and I ever thought of moving here from California, she visited a friend in Albuquerque. The two spent an afternoon at the pueblo of Acoma, and there Carol experienced what she and I have come to understand as an enchantment—an awakening to a vivid transcendental truth which lay beyond the grasp of reason, hers or anyone else's. When she returned home she managed to convey to me the fact if not the nature of her encounter; a short while later we emigrated to New Mexico.

The catalyst for her inexplicable apprehension, the fertile ground from which it sprang, was the *Indianness* of New Mexico, the central and overwhelming affective resource of the state. It is alive here more than it is anywhere else that I know in the United States. I'm speaking not simply of the richness of the native culture or the splendid achievements of New Mexico's native peoples, though those are parts of it. But more important, New Mexico (a state with a greater concentration of scientists, engineers, and other nononsense rationalists than any other) bears witness at every turn to a critical wisdom preserved doggedly by Indians in the face of massive denial by whites: the world has a mystical, spiritual nature that is absolutely inaccessible to reason.

"The facts may help us to feel sure about our control of circumstances," observes nature writer John Hay, "but they are a poor substitute for the deeper equations of earth and human life. The American Indian saw the Word behind all manifested things, the primal, creative power." The Indian's sovereign intuition, I am convinced, is essential to our survival as a nation. Today the native peoples of this continent hold it in trust for us all. I hope that one day we will thank them for their trouble.

As a man who once earned a degree in mathematics from Harvard (by the skin of my teeth, I should admit), I for a long time looked at truths as something like genial trout lollygagging in the sun and waiting patiently for some passing logician to throw in a line and haul them out. Today I suspect I was only about half right. Climbing mountains for two decades softened me up by revealing the melodies and hues of the natural world; opening my heart to the possibilities of New Mexico finished the job. I do not argue for a rejection of reason in favor of transcendence, rather for an incorporation of both in any effort to understand the world. Surely, scientists should strive to answer every question. They are well advised, too, to read self-help manuals on how to handle disappointment and failure, to prepare themselves for the day when they complete their grand explication of the universe and discover that half of its pages are still blank.

In America only the Indian has consistently shown a keen understanding of the duality of nature. The great Lakota warrior Tasunka Witko—Crazy Horse—provides a fascinating example of a man who not only understood this duality but learned to control it and to use it for his own ends. Crazy Horse believed that we live in a shadow world, a sort of limbo parallel to another more fully realized abode. His genius was that he learned to pass from one world to the other, perhaps through the use of meditation techniques similar to those employed by Buddhist masters and other mystics. His powers enabled him to achieve what Thomas Merton, referring to the ultimate goal of Buddhism, called a "metaphysical intuition."

Crazy Horse took his horse with him into the parallel, fully realized world. The animal was happy there. It danced and leapt about in a very undignified fashion, and that was why Crazy Horse took the name that he did. He was in that parallel world, too, at the Battle of Little Bighorn, and he was there fifteen months later at Fort Robinson when he was arrested. As Dee Brown tells the story in that essential volume of American history *Bury My Heart at Wounded Knee,* Crazy Horse stood outside the jail and looked into the shadows behind the bars where men were chained like dogs, and where all was madness; and he knew he could never go inside. He chose the freedom of the fully realized world, and for that he was killed.

We have photographs of every great Indian leader from the mid nineteenth century onward, save one: there are no photographs of Crazy Horse. Perhaps the science of photography is inadequate for capturing certain images.

In the mountains and deserts of New Mexico, however, it is possible to see a world no photograph can ever depict (leave your camera at home). It is a world oblivious to comment, interpretation, judgment, or conclusion—Thomas Merton's obstacles to metaphysical intuition—a world inaccessible to those whose antennae are unresponsive to enchantments. Cautions Annie Dillard: That we are much informed does not mean that we are well informed.

To the much-informed, New Mexico proclaims, unplug your computers, toss out your guidebooks, and retune your antennae for some truly eye-opening information.

An hour from Gallup I left the interstate and rambled up to Acoma. I'd been there at least a dozen times, never tiring of the place. Residents call it Sky City, for the pueblo is built atop a tall mesa that overlooks a broad, peaceable valley of indescribable splendor. From the streets of Sky City one looks down, as if from the sky, on the woebegone rest of the world. The pueblo is well over a thousand years old—some say it's the oldest continuously inhabited settlement in North America. Information like that might get you to Acoma, but what will bring you back are the tumbling, juniper-scented wind and the sensation of lusty adventure the place invariably imparts, dizzy and mysterious, like a kiss from a beautiful stranger.

Not far from the village stands a formation called Enchanted Mesa. Its walls are vertical; there is no safe or easy route to the summit. According to legend the Acoma once lived atop Enchanted Mesa. A storm arose, destroying the stairway carved in the rock. Villagers who were stranded at the top died of starvation.

Historians say that there is no evidence to substantiate the legend. Geologists tell us that the mesa is built of Dakota sandstone. Surveyors have calculated that it is 430 feet tall. Guidebooks point out that it is nearly three times the height of the Statue of Liberty.

A swirling wind surrounded me as I stood beneath the mesa, utterly alone, struck both by the poverty of the facts and the richness of the legend. I had no doubt that what I was observing was a 430-foot-tall chunk of Dakota sandstone. But it was equally clear to me that as a means for understanding the mesa—for grasping its essential nature—the facts are hilariously inadequate. In the cry of the wind I picked out an anguished call for help floating down from the hidden recesses far above me. I listened, then searched the forbidding walls for signs of vanished stairs.

Back on my way I picked up old U.S. Route 66, a good place to see legend in the making. The myth of Route 66 keeps a good many New Mexicans busy these days, long after Interstate 40 replaced what had been the country's favorite east-west highway.

But Route 66 was more than a highway: it was a song ("Get your kicks on Route Sixty-Six"), a television show *(Route 66)*, a gas station logo (Phillips 66), a player in countless books *(On the Road)* and films *(The Grapes of Wrath)*. Route 66 was the twentieth-century embodiment of the nineteenth-century dream of going west. Steinbeck called it "the Mother Highway."

Since the creation of the interstates, Route 66—through the arcane workings of mass psychology—has been widened from a cramped two-lane road into an expansive sixteen-lane myth. Citizen groups erect reverent markers where the highway passed through their towns ("You're driving historic Route 66," gushes a sign on the strip in Gallup). Tourists go home clutching Route 66 T-shirts and coffee mugs to commemorate their visits to the hallowed pavement. In Albuquerque the Route 66 Diner on Central Avenue—old 66—is an affectionate period piece done up in the style of the 1950s. Route 66 clubs conduct weekend pilgrimages to remote spots where their archaeologists have discovered crumbling strips of asphalt languishing among the weeds. Back and forth over the storied ruins drive club members in their '57 Chevies and Rocket-Powered Oldsmobiles, visions of Chuck Berry and poodle skirts dancing in their heads.

On my first visit to New Mexico in the mid 1950s, my parents and I drove Route 66 to Albuquerque. My memories of the highway, no doubt colored by the passage of more than forty years, are considerably less romantic than the myth. We blew a tire near Tucumcari. I clearly recall that the problem occurred on the left side of the car because to this day I can see my father's rear end sticking out onto Route 66 while he changed the tire. I remember other drivers swerving and honking and shaking their fists, and I remember my mother standing with me in a clump of rabbitbrush beside the road, wailing that my father was about to be killed.

As it turned out, my father was not killed; he suffered a pair of grimy hands but that was all. In short order the tire was changed and we were on our way. But my mother was shaken by the incident and took some time to recover her normal color. My father spent the rest of the day muttering the facts about Route 66, and they were anything but romantic: Narrow. Bumpy. Dangerous. Murder on tires. Certainly none of us—and only the most prescient of our millions of fellow travelers, I am sure—even remotely imagined that we were driving into history, that one day the eyes of small children would widen and beautiful women would draw near as I related the tale of my fantastic journey, long ago and far away . . . on Route 66!

At Correo I turned southeast toward the town of Belen and made for Abo Pass, the cut in the Manzano Mountains that opens the way to the tenacious plains. I was following a route sketched on an old map but without much confidence that the line on the map marked the exact route of the Long Walk. The official U.S. Army record of the walk is almost nonexistent. Several dozen military personnel accompanied their Diné captives on each of the marches to Bosque Redondo, but few left details of their several weeks on the trail. Almost everything we know from the army's point of view stems from a single long letter (dated May 12, 1864) written by Captain Francis McCabe, the leader of one of the marches.

Most narratives of the walk are based on McCabe's letter. But a rich storehouse of little-known material can be found in the stories passed down from the Diné who were there. Twenty years ago students in the Navajo and Indian Studies Program at Navajo Community College in Tsaile, Arizona, under the direction of coordinator Ruth Roessel, collected many of the stories from older Diné, who had heard them from their parents and grandparents. The recollections were published by Navajo Community College Press in 1973 under the title *Navajo Stories of the Long Walk Period*. The book will provide vivid and compelling reading for anyone accustomed to bloodless bureaucratic and academic history. In the Diné stories, it seems to me, fact and legend combine in exactly the right proportion.

Said Howard W. Gorman, 73, born into the Bitter Water Clan:

On the journey the Navajos went through all kinds of hardships, like tiredness and having injuries. And, when those things happened, the people would hear gun shots in the rear. But they couldn't do anything about it. They just felt sorry for the ones being shot. Sometimes they would plead with the soldiers to let them go back and do something, but they were refused. This is how the story was told by my ancestors. It was said that those ancestors were on the Long Walk with their daughter, who was pregnant and about to give birth. Somewhere beyond *K'aalógii Dził* (Butterfly Mountain) on this side of *Bilín* (Belen), as it is called, south of Albuquerque, the daughter got tired and weak and couldn't keep up with the others or go any farther because of her condition. So my ancestors asked the Army to hold up for a while and to let the woman give birth. But the soldiers wouldn't do it. They forced my people to move on, saying that they were getting behind the others. The soldiers told the parents that they had to leave their daughter behind. "Your daughter is not going to survive, anyway; sooner or later she is going to die," they said in their own language.

"Go ahead," the daughter said to her parents, "things might come out all right with me." But the poor thing was mistaken, my grandparents used to say. Not long after they had moved on, they heard a gunshot from where they had been a short time ago.

"Maybe we should go back and do something, or at least cover the body with dirt," one of them said.

By that time one of the soldiers came riding up from the direction of the sound. He must have shot her to death. That's the way the story goes.

Gorman's story and others in the book preserve human feelings, a critical component of history ignored or downplayed by many historians. Gorman is regarded as an unreliable source, not only because he heard his story secondhand but because he is emotionally engaged in it.

Yet Captain McCabe was engaged in the story too (and who could have avoided becoming engaged?), and he brought his own biases to his report.

Nevertheless, because of his putatively superior status, he has become the source of nearly all that we "know" about the Long Walk. Here, then, is a dose of supposed truth from McCabe:

> On the 29th I reached Fort Wingate where I obtained a fresh supply of rations for the indians; but only in the proportion of half a pound of flour, and half a pound of beef to each. Apprehensive that this unexpected diminution of their rations would have the effect of shaking their faith in the government, and of creating mistrust and suspicion which if not promptly removed might lead to serious consequences I called the principal chiefs and warriors together, and told them that I believed they would receive their full amount of rations at Los Pinos; and that the present diminution was but a temporary arrangement occasioned by the scarcity of provisions. This seemed to satisfy them, and they assured me that they would travel forward to the reservation cheerfully; and that they had every confidence in the word of the Genl. Comdg. Department, and in the Justice of the Government. They further remarked that their minds were now firmly settled and that on arriving at the reservation they were determined to go diligently to work, and with the assistance of the Government establish themselves and their descendants forever in that location—which they regarded of all others peculiarly adapted to their present and future condition.

The wide, easy miles leading to Abo Pass revealed New Mexico at its most beguiling. Bright vagabond spring had arrived, the sun was soft, the slightly frayed countryside was a tattered picnic blanket waiting for customers. Above the evergreen-dotted foothills, Manzano Peak gleamed in a feathering of fresh snow. The road jogged left and right, sprang with the lilt of first love from one rounded destination to the next. It was midmorning in midweek in early March in New Mexico; the brooks were dawdling, the roadrunners were walking. There wasn't a cloud in the sky, and I was poking along at forty miles an hour with the windows wide open and the road to myself.

In scruffy fields beside the road slept more than the usual portion of those melancholy New Mexico staples: crumbling adobe walls, sad foundations, burned-out Chevies and Fords. Great plans gone to seed. At Salinas National Monument, more of the same. Here one can mourn the centuries-old ruins of once-grand pueblos and the long-abandoned Spanish structures that replaced them. Among the latter is the church of San Gregorio de Abo, which dates from 1629.

I passed with a wave. No sackcloth today, thank you. Beside a bridge over the Santa Fe Railroad tracks I parked the car and hiked to midspan to await a freight train sweating toward the pass. Five awful engines thundered beneath me like an earthquake, shaking the bridge so hard I wondered if it was going to collapse along with everything else around here. I leaned over the railing and exchanged greetings with the engineer. After him, appearing one by one from between a pair of dusty hills, pounded a steady rhythm of boxcars bound for the pass. I was listening to the train, but I was thinking of lost homes and the rigid, unavoidable plains.

The circle of sacred mountains passes through parts of New Mexico, Arizona, and Colorado. Traditional Diné believe it is wrong and even hazardous to travel beyond the perimeter. To go to Bosque Redondo in 1864, even today for some Diné to journey to Albuquerque or Phoenix to see friends or to look for jobs is to violate profoundly held religious beliefs.

It is unlikely that James Carleton knew of this proscription or, if he knew of it, that he granted it any importance. Utterly convinced of the rightness of his mission, he saw himself as the savior not only of New Mexico's whites but of the Diné as well. He would never have allowed the niggling concerns of a people he deemed inferior to himself—and pagan to boot—to interfere in his designs.

Carleton's supreme self-assurance illustrates a problem that has perennially plagued relations between whites and Indians, the disinclination of whites to listen quietly and respectfully to Indians, to hear what they say, and to act on it. New Mexico in particular suffers from this syndrome, perhaps because of its large Indian population. A few years ago, to cite one of many recent examples, the federal government proposed the creation of a national monument on some hauntingly beautiful volcanic badlands which happen to include grounds the Acoma Indians have used for religious purposes for hundreds of years. The Acoma protested. Hearings were held. The Interior Department accused the Indians of stalling, obfuscating, negotiating in bad faith—everything but what they were doing, which was to state clearly and explicitly that they wanted to retain exclusive rights to their traditional worship sites. At one point the Indians were told that they would be permitted to worship on the lands and that they would need only to apply to the park superintendent for a pass when they wanted to do so. One Acoma wondered how the superintendent would feel if he needed only to apply to the Acoma for permission to attend church on Sunday.

In the end, El Malpais National Monument was created on lands that include the traditional religious sites. The Acoma may visit the sites without the superintendent's permission. But because the locations of the sites are a closely guarded secret, when the Indians arrive they may find campers or sightseers already in possession of the sites.

At its most inexcusable and most easily rectified, white misunderstanding of Indians stems from mere ignorance or laziness. A 1992 column on Indians by Andy Rooney is a notable but far from atypical example. "American Indians were never subjected to the same kind of racial bias that blacks were," Rooney wrote. "The impact on the world of their culture has been slight. There are no great American Indian novels, no poetry. There's no memorable music. There's no American Indian art, except for some good craft work." About religion Rooney had this to say: "They hang onto remnants of their religion and superstitions that may have been useful to savages 500 years ago, but which are meaningless in 1992."

One hesitates to respond to such a statement for fear of dignifying it. But I cannot help quoting the distinguished art historian Vincent Scully, who, unlike Rooney, came to the Southwest to observe and to listen, and to study indigenous cultures. Scully was deeply impressed by what he found. Of

Pueblo dance he wrote: "The dances themselves I believe to be the most profound works of art yet produced on the American continent."

As for novels, Rooney can no more demand of Indians great examples of this recent Western European innovation in order to establish their cultural credentials than Japanese can demand of the Irish great Kabuki to establish theirs. But never mind: let him read *House Made of Dawn*, the 1969 Pulitzer Prize–winning novel by the Kiowa N. Scott Momaday. Poetry, music, art— listen to Pueblo myth, study the Diné Blessing Way, attend the Corn Dance at Cochiti or the Fiesta de San Gerónimo at Taos. It simply makes no sense to trivialize such achievements.

At their most intractable, misunderstandings involve clashes between wildly differing views of such concepts as space, time, and, as I have already mentioned, nature, which whites and Indians perceive in markedly differing ways. As cultural anthropologist Edward T. Hall has amply documented, whites often take such disparities as evidence of Indian inferiority or defectiveness, rather than as mere differences of points of view.

As part of General Carleton's plan to bring down the Diné, army troops under the command of the legendary Kit Carson destroyed some five thousand peach trees on Diné lands. Before the conflict began, Carson had been a longtime friend of the Indians. Dee Brown states that of all the atrocities committed by Carson against his old friends, the one act for which they never forgave him was the destruction of their peach trees. To Carson the trees were simply a component of the Diné economy, one that, ironically, had been introduced to the Diné by European settlers. To the Diné, for whom the origin of the acquisition mattered less than its essential nature, the trees were sacred. Lupita Johnson, a Diné of the Towering House Clan and a ranger in Arizona's Canyon de Chelly (where the peach trees were destroyed), turns to white legend for a comparison to what her people suffered when they lost their trees, their land, and their way of life. It was, she says, the equivalent of Adam and Eve being expelled from the Garden of Eden.

More than a century later the divergent viewpoints are little changed. To many whites, the destruction of the peach trees is a subject of historical and perhaps anthropological interest. To many Diné, it is an unforgettable blasphemy—prayer books tossed into a cesspool, communion wafers fed to pigs.

Below Abo Pass, through a stratum of old snow, the town of Mountainair popped up beside the road like a bed of crocuses. This was the shoreline. Beyond lay a new world—the Great Plains, an ocean of treeless earth.

Few of the Diné could ever have seen such a thing. The monstrous upending of convention, even for a people intimate with the huge scales of the West, must have amazed and disturbed them. Bosque Redondo lay dead ahead, a hundred miles in the interior of that strange and forbidding country.

The road before me was a cartographer's delight, a quick flick of the pen against a ruler and then on to the next latitude. The road was mostly empty. Now and then a truck rolled by. I approached and passed a retired couple in a motor home, whiling away the precious years in as blissful a manner as I can imagine.

Beside the road on the gray horizon stood a windmill. With nothing to do but hold my toe to the floor, I made a reckless guess at the windmill's distance. Sometimes I subject long-suffering guests from New York or Boston to this game when we are out exploring New Mexico's endless open roads. The general rule is that the likelihood of success in the game is inversely proportional to the amount of time one has lived east of the Mississippi River. In the windmill game, lifers from those parts would weigh in at three or four miles. I came west at the age of thirty-two, and though in the years since then I've labored diligently to craft the westerner's perspicacity, I'll never get it exactly right. Nine miles, I said to the dashboard, none too confidently.

Nine miles came and went. At ten I shook my head. At twelve I whacked the odometer to see whether it might be malfunctioning. At thirteen point six the windmill glided by, clattering derisively. Not many miles later (I'm guessing), I stopped at a convenience store. While paying for coffee and gas, I mentioned the windmill to the clerk. A flat-earth native, she related the legend of the greenhorn easterner. It seems that the man hopped off a bus somewhere near here during a rest stop and decided to hike to the top of a nearby hill. Two hours later he was back, having missed his bus and the top of the hill, which seemed no closer to him when he finally turned around than it had when he set out.

While he waited for another bus he took a stroll around town and came to a sneaker-deep irrigation ditch. The police caught him there taking off his clothes.

"I've learned a thing or two here already," he boasted in explanation. "If it's as far across that lake as it was to the top of that mountain, I'm going to be swimming for a *long* time."

Too many years in the East may partially explain the greenhorn's short-comings and my poor showing in the windmill game, but the full truth is more sobering. I don't do space well; few of us do. As close as the sounds and smells of breakfast, as common as small talk, space is invisible and impalpable—void of the kind of data we're good at processing. And so it remains unreal. The surest proof of our insensibility to space is that we tend to think of it as something far away, when in fact it is everywhere. The greatest loss we suffer in our ignorance is knowledge of the space around us, surely our most intimate and constant companion. Unknown, it becomes an obscuring envelope that clouds our view of the world. Perhaps it is the mysterious nature of this envelope that makes it so difficult for human beings to see one another as they really are.

Of all the wonders of the plains, surpassing even the width and textures, the always-springtime odors, the greatest wonder is the opportunity afforded us to sense our extended architecture—to see and feel the tiny room in which we live. Somewhere near the Lucy Ranch the road and the land suddenly abandon the horizontal and tilt upward a few degrees. This was a major event, and great consequences ensued. Around me lay a pale dash of snow on the land. Ahead loomed a wispy white sky. As I rocketed upward the whites of snow and wisp met and melted together and became one.

I stopped and stood by the road. And there alone, suspended in a fullness of white, I suddenly got it. The sky isn't *up there*. It's down here, all around me. I live in it. That stuff beside me and in front of me: it's sky.

"Before me is beauty, I am walking," sing the Diné, even as they sang while they walked to Bosque Redondo. "Behind me is beauty, I am walking." What power that refrain conveys, its tidings of the earthly heaven that surrounds us, its celebration of the nexus between Mother Earth and Father Sky that is life.

And time. As we know from Einstein, that old trickster, it is as baffling as space. Near a shallow salt pond where paleo–New Mexicans gathered spice for their banquets, time was a grand white horse. He was alone, magnificent, side-lit into ivory, patient as the dark earth awaiting spring. Does another creature know the hours so well? As I made my way across a tawny esplanade dotted with mesquite, the animal looked on in silence. Not a muscle moved.

Then with a magic that I couldn't fathom he took us both into a new world, one that was all peacefulness and light. He shifted his weight and tossed his head, and then he began to dance. Stepping forward he cocked his ears in a gesture of barely contained glee.

In the clear sky we were friends at once. I stroked his long nose, rubbed the miraculous softness where he took in the wind. He mesmerized me with his pleasure and his heart. As I gazed eastward toward my destination, my view unobstructed by mountains or trees, my timepiece an animal unhurried by plans or concerns, time and landscape seemed suddenly to melt away. That distant moment when my ancestors wagoned west and for the first time came face to face with the people who called the mountains sacred no longer seemed so remote. The grove of cottonwoods beside the Pecos suddenly seemed close enough to touch.

Said Curly Tso of the Many Goats Clan:

A majority of the Navajos didn't know the reason why they were being rounded up, and different stories went around among the people. There were reasons like: The government in Washington had ordered that all Navajos be rounded up and bunched together at *Tséhootsooí* [Fort Defiance] and then taken to *Hwééldi* [Fort Sumner] where they could be put to death eventually— killing them by means of subjecting them to different diseases, starvation and exposure, as well as using every other possible way to kill all of them. The government's reason seemed to be that the white people, coming this way, needed more land, and Navajos were scattered out too far and lived on some of the best lands; so, in order to give the white people the land, plans were made by the government to kill most of the Navajos and send the rest to *Halgai Hatéél* (Wide Plains or Oklahoma), or, perhaps, to round them up and force them to live close together like the Hopis.

Personally, I often wondered, after I became aware of white men's laws, why our ancestors were treated so unjustly. White men make and preach about all kinds of laws, laws that protect individual rights; and where were these laws then? At the time, the Navajo people were ignorant of the fact that if an individual does something wrong that individual is punished according to the laws for his wrong doings, but the laws do not say to place blame and have innocent people suffer the consequences; and such was the case that the Navajo people went through.

A group of Diné chiefs met with General Carleton at Fort Sumner. They reported that he had fierce eyes and the mouth of a man without humor. He was also fatally bullheaded. His plan to civilize the Diné was a disaster. Despite warnings from the field that he had vastly underestimated the number of Indians who would be coming in, he readied the fort for five thousand prisoners. To count the captives, soldiers regularly lined them up, and then, jabbing them with bayonets, sent them running through a gate like sheep. In the late fall of 1864 the tally showed 8,354 Diné, plus 405 Apaches whom Carleton had rounded up in the further conceit that he could smooth relations between these long-standing enemies. Before the experiment ended, more than nine thousand Diné would be quartered at Fort Sumner.

Few of them had adequate shelter. For twenty miles up and down the Pecos, most lived in holes in the ground covered with woven grass or discarded tent sections. The Pecos itself was alkaline; many prisoners became ill from drinking the water. Fort Sumner was so far from army supply lines that there was never enough food to eat or material for improving living conditions. Diné and Apache stayed on constantly low rations. Barefoot and in tattered clothing, they set to work building several miles of irrigation ditches. Carleton could come up with only fifty spades and a few hoes, so most of the workers were forced to dig with rocks or sticks or with their bare hands.

Despite the hardships, the Indians brought in three thousand acres of corn, wheat, and beans the first year. Within weeks, cutworms destroyed the corn; floods and tornadolike winds finished off most of the rest. Rations were further reduced. Deaths mounted from starvation, pneumonia, and tuberculosis. Venereal disease spread as desperate Diné women sold themselves to soldiers for food. Nighttime Comanche and Kiowa raids against the defenseless prisoners became common. Firewood gave out. Near the end, Indians were walking twenty miles to find mesquite to burn. When the branches were gone the Indians unearthed the roots with their fingers.

Despite the dangers of setting out onto the open plains alone, captives began slipping away. On the night of November 3, 1865, almost the entire Apache contingent escaped. With the Civil War ended, Congress began looking into the huge cost of interning nine thousand Indians at Fort Sumner. General William Tecumseh Sherman quipped that the government could save a great deal of money by putting up the Diné in New York City hotels.

White New Mexicans who only a few years earlier had seen Carleton as their savior began to have second thoughts. Cattle and sheep interests looked covetously on the Pecos bottomlands. Citizens who merely coveted safety recognized that the vast majority of the Diné rounded up by Carleton were peaceful; the tribe's few troublemakers were still at large. A call went out for Carleton's ouster. As for the Diné, most New Mexicans suggested sending them to Arizona.

Carleton was relieved of command in the fall of 1866. Two years of controversy ensued. The Indians remained at Bosque Redondo. Costs mounted; the suffering continued. On June 15, 1867, the principal Diné chief, Herraro Grande, spoke to A. Baldwin Norton, the superintendent of Fort Sumner:

I am thinking more about my old country than ever before, because there I could secure myself from my enemies; here we have not that chance. . . . We are all the time thinking of our old country, and we believe if the government will put us back, they could have us the same there as here.

Notwithstanding the cold and heat we have worked and we will work, but as poor as we are we would rather go back to our country. What does the government want us to do—more than we have done? Or more than we are doing?

I think in the world, the earth, and in the heavens we are all equal and we have all been born by the same mother—what we want is to be sent back to our own country. Even if we starve there, we will have no complaints to make.

A year passed. Peace talks began between the Diné and the United States government.

The Diné chief Barboncito said: "I hope to God you will not ask us to go to any other country except our own. It might turn out another Bosque Redondo. They told us this was a good place when we came here, but it is not."

The Diné chief Ganado Mucho said: "Let us go home to our mountains. Let us see our flocks feeding in the valleys, and let us ride again where we can smell the sage and know of hidden hogans by the smell of piñon smoke. Let us go where we can build our homes in solitude and privacy and live again as men, not animals. Let us be free to build a better way of life and learn to live in peace where the red buttes rise from the desert sands, and eagles sweep across the sky. Let us go home. We have learned not to kill and not to steal from the flocks of others. Here we have nothing. Our children grow up in ugliness and death. Let us go home."

The town of Fort Sumner stands by the Pecos at the edge of the Llano Estacado—"the staked plain"—the high, dry, treeless tableland that connects New Mexico geographically with the Texas panhandle. On his search for Quivira in 1541, Coronado crossed the Pecos a short distance to the north.

"It is impossible to find tracks in this country," wrote Coronado's chronicler Castañeda, "because the grass straightened up again as soon as it was trodden down. In 250 leagues was seen not a hillock which was three times as high as a man. The country is like a bowl, so that when a man sits down, the horizon surrounds him all around at the distance of a musket shot."

It was not exactly a ringing endorsement, but much has changed since Coronado passed this way. On the balmy spring afternoon when I reached Fort Sumner, the countryside appeared gentle and giving. Green fields bordering on the east and broad cottonwoods crowding the river's edge provided a luxuriant setting for the town. Cattle grazed beside narrow lanes emanating from the river. A light breeze drifted in off the plains. Fort Sumner seemed more like a midwestern town than any other place I had visited in New Mexico.

I drove south a few miles to Fort Sumner State Monument. Practically nothing remains of what scornful post–Civil War New Mexicans began calling "Fair Carletonia." Most of the fort was washed away in floods in 1932 and 1941. The visitor will find a few markers, a foundation, some artifacts. Perhaps understandably, the town plays down this chapter in its history. It is Billy the Kid who gets the notices around here, providing a cottage industry for purveyors of Wild West souvenirs and plenty of work for painters of garish signs. The notorious outlaw was killed at Fort Sumner in 1881. Local residents claim he is buried here, though some historians and champions for a competing site dispute the claim.

The tranquil Pecos, in March just a wisp of a stream, snaked north and south out of town. I pushed through the dense vegetation lining the river and jumped down a steep bank to water's edge. Like many New Mexican rivers during the sensible, sober months leading up to spring blowout, the Pecos is easy to take personally. The far side isn't far—two quick skips of a flat-backed stone. The water is so shallow it's mostly sandbars; long and fat, they stuff the river like a herd of hippos. The Pecos tiptoes around them carefully, as though it's afraid of waking them up.

Under a slow and peaceful midafternoon sun I started downstream, tracing a zig-zag path. It was quiet enough to hear the whispers of the rivulets beside me. A red-winged blackbird called from a nearby bush, then catapulted across the river like a rock, scarcely lifting its wings. The muddy flats were stamped with hand-sized asterisks—duck prints, as I quickly made out. The Pecos is a major flyway for migratory birds. Herons, snow geese, sandhill cranes, and now and then a rare whooping crane hot-rod it up this old highway. My approach startled a party of ducks snacking in ankle-deep water. They were airborne at once, wings pumping like pistons. The birds leveled off at ten feet, deployed as meticulously as navy jets, banked left, filtered through the bony arms of a scrawny cottonwood.

I padded along, suddenly suffused in melancholy. At a bend in the stream I knelt and dipped my hand into the water. The inexorable Pecos parted and trickled on.

Like the creation stories of most North American Indian peoples, that of New Mexico's Jicarilla Apaches tells us that in the beginning the earth was covered with water. The Jicarilla say that great storms rolled back the waters in each direction to form oceans at the edge of the world. To preserve water in the middle for people to drink, the beaver built a dam, creating a lake. The Jicarilla visited each of the oceans in turn but decided to return to the lake at the center of the world, near Taos, and there they remained.

The creation story of science tells us that the waters of the earth are formed from hydrogen and oxygen. Two atoms of hydrogen and one of oxygen combine to create every molecule of water. So vast is the number of molecules in even a drop of water that it is likely that a few of those washing over my hand each second entered Alexander the Great in the last drink of water he ever took, and a few bathed each hoof of Coronado's mount when he forded the Pecos in 1541, and a few helped clear the throat of Barboncito in 1868 when he said: "After we get back to our country it will brighten up again, and the Navajos will be as happy and peaceful as the land."

In the clear waters of the Pecos one can read both legend and fact. But which is which, and which shall we believe?

In the shimmering mirror I studied the face of the man staring back at me, the sun a flickering fire on his shoulder. The stern eyes, the straight mouth . . . the two possessed a familiarity that reached far beyond self-knowledge. In my face I saw the face of James H. Carleton, the face of my people—tough, practical, and supremely self-assured.

The median income of Indian families in the United States is less than half that of white families. The poverty rate is three times that of whites. Unemployment on reservations averages more than thirty percent; on a few reservations it has topped seventy-five percent in recent years. Indians are twelve times as likely as whites to suffer from alcoholism. The percentage of Indians who die of cirrhosis of the liver is more than five times the national average. American Indian youths have the nation's highest high-school drop-out rate and highest suicide rate.

There are three dependable sources of income for Indians today: oper-ating gambling houses for whites, working in life-threatening occupations such as uranium mining, and burying white-generated toxic wastes on their reservations. White New Age prophets ignore Indian political struggles but rip off Indian religious practices—drumming, dancing, sweat ceremonies, spirit quests, visions, talking circles—and then in glossy, no-effort-required packages hawk pale-faced imitations of these ancient rites to dispirited whites at get-rich-quick prices. Developers, lumber companies, and city planners plow roads across Indian religious sites without even saying hello. Judges who deem the administration of communion wine to Christian children an ac-ceptable violation of drinking laws shut the door on the employment of religious peyote by Indian adults. Huge numbers of justice-minded Ameri-cans greet the news that Swiss banks hold billions of dollars plundered from European Jews by the German government during World War II with a de-mand for the swift return of the money to the aggrieved parties or their descendants; no such demand is made for the swift return of billions of dollars in real estate to the descendants of Indians from whom that real estate was plundered by the United States government during the nineteenth cen-tury. Pious whites bow their heads before the majesty of the Constitution's guarantees of religious freedom, then thoughtlessly sink mine shafts into Indian sacred mountains, construct ski resorts on their slopes, and erect television towers on their summits. White fans of white-owned sports teams with racial slurs for nicknames paint sacred Indian symbols on their faces, chant sacred Indian songs, mock sacred Indian rituals. When Indians object, fans bristle in indignation. "What's the problem, for Christ's sake? It doesn't bother *me!*"

Wrote Lakota Sioux Randolph G. Runs After to the editor of the *Albuquerque Journal:*

> What words of encouragement can be said to the young Indian kids who see non-Indians jumping around drunk with painted faces when they've learned that it was a sacred religious practice? Where is the pride we are supposed to feel in watching the use of sacred Indian feathers trivialized and Indian spectators showered with obscenities at Kansas City Chiefs home games? . . . Would Catholics . . . be offended if the Lord's Prayer was chanted by a rowdy, inebriated crowd at a New Orleans Saints game during timeouts or if ashes were smeared across their faces and the "holy water throw" was the norm?

"Every nation, like every individual, walks in a vain show, else it could not live with itself," remarked Rudyard Kipling, a man who was something of an expert on national vanity. "But I never got over the wonder of a people who, having extirpated the aboriginals of their continent more completely than any modern race had ever done, honestly believed that they were a godly little New England community, setting examples to brutal mankind. This wonder I used to explain to Theodore Roosevelt, who made the glass cases of Indian relics shake with his rebuttals."

The native peoples of this continent continue to confound those of us who found them here when we arrived. Partly our bewilderment stems from our observation, continually reaffirmed, that after all of our painstaking efforts, many Indians, for reasons we cannot even remotely fathom, remain largely unimpressed by General Carleton's ways. Partly it originates in our continuing ignorance of the Indian's ways. Foolishly self-satisfied, we deprive ourselves of invaluable lessons in community, tolerance, moderation, cooperation, respect for nature, art, family values, and other matters we cannot even name, all of which we might learn from the Indian. A huge gulf continues to separate us, white and red. The result is that whites remain afraid of the people on the far side of the gulf, afraid of the spell they cast upon us and the power they hold over us.

Partly we are disconcerted because we know in our hearts that our victory over the Indian, if that is what it was, had nothing to do with moral or cultural superiority; victory, hollow thing, was an accident of gunpowder. Invented in the Far East, introduced into Europe during the thirteenth century by a Christian friar, it came to America in the guns of the conquerors. Had it traveled instead in the opposite direction, across the Bering Strait and down the North American continent, the Queen of England might today be Sioux, the Washington Redskins might be known as the Nanticoke Savage Whites.

But mostly, I believe, we are deeply troubled because the Indian reminds us of the monstrous truth in our past, which we have tried to hide behind the obscuring mists of myth and legend and which we continue to deny as vehemently as Germans and Russians until recently denied the truth of theirs. Our self-deception will continue to torment us until we bring it into the open, make it the centerpiece of a great national discussion, seek reconciliation with the Indian, and come face-to-face at last with this long repressed but central fact of our history. Perhaps we can begin by planting ten million peach trees as memorials to the ten million or so Indians who were killed in order to secure this continent for whites. However we proceed, the walk will be long. But it will certainly be worth taking.

I know a man, a Diné, who like many Indians today is succeeding brilliantly on his own scrupulously prescribed terms. He furnishes a luminous counterexample to commonly held white stereotypes about Indians. Fluent in his native language, rooted deeply in Diné culture, he joins his people in ritual and dance, in all-night celebrations of the hunt, in ceremonies of marriage, healing, and death. He knows Diné who can transform themselves into bears and wolves, and he has seen eagles fly down to contribute their feathers to the work of medicine men. My friend has described these events to me, and because I know him to be an honest man, I believe that the stories are true.

This is also the man who encouraged Carol and me to attend the Santa Fe Opera soon after we arrived in New Mexico, and who gave us a quick lesson on how to behave while we were there. He is a college graduate who knows and appreciates what is good in white culture, an understanding few whites have of his own. For a time he worked as an artist's agent representing the works of several Native American artists. Today he is a drug-and-alcohol rehabilitation counselor. He is married to an Apache woman and is nearer to the end of his walk than most of us are.

Not long ago he had a strange experience. A radio talk-show host invited him to talk about his work with alcoholics. In the midst of the interview, as my friend struggled to describe the long and painful journey his clients must make, he suddenly heard himself blurt out a Diné word with which he was completely unfamiliar. It popped from his mouth as easily as if it had been his own name. A tribal elder later confirmed that the word was an ancient one no longer in common use and that the startled speaker had pronounced and employed it with absolute precision. The word means "to travel back to oneself."

What a powerful fragment of neglected language my friend had discovered stranded on the distant shoals of his subconscious; what a grand journey it describes. For travelers marooned on the outer reaches of loss it points the way home and promises that a healing place waits at the end of the road.

On June 1, 1868, the principal Diné chiefs at Bosque Redondo signed a treaty of peace with the United States government. In return for their agreement to cease hostilities forever, the Diné gained freedom after more than four years in captivity. Two weeks later a column ten miles in length comprising some seven thousand Indians waded the Pecos and began the three-hundred-mile journey home. Two thousand Diné had died at Fort Sumner. Before the internment of these traditional shepherds a government survey estimated their holdings at around a quarter of a million sheep. As the Diné set out across the plain, the number of sheep in their care had been reduced to under a thousand. Recalled the Diné chief Manuelito:

> The days and nights were long before it came time for us to go to our homes. The day before we were to start we went a little way towards home, because we were so anxious to start. We came back and the Americans gave us a little stock and we thanked them for that. We told the drivers to whip the mules, we were in such a hurry. When we saw the top of the mountain from Albuquerque we wondered if it was our mountain, and we felt like talking to the ground, we loved it so, and some of the old men and women cried with joy when they reached their homes.

Not many years ago in a neighboring country where the earth's skin is red and where the mountains and rivers speak the language of the people, there was a beautiful meadow. Each day as the sun fell toward the mountains the people went to the meadow to tell stories and play games with their families, and to enjoy the beauty of descending night. Deer came to the edge of the meadow to graze in the lengthening shadows. Birds perched in the trees and sang their songs, and insects made their scratchy music in the grass. For a long time the voices of the people could be heard murmuring in that secluded place like a winding mountain brook.

One evening a group of strangers came and stood on the outskirts of the meadow. The strangers had stern expressions on their faces. They watched the goings-on without understanding. The birds flew away and the deer raced off into the forest and the insects crawled into their holes. Seeing the faces of the strangers, the people in the meadow grew afraid. They gathered their families together and returned quickly to their homes.

One man only remained behind. He was young and strong and handsome, a man greatly admired by his people. He stood in the middle of the meadow without fear. And while the strangers watched, the light of the falling sun became ghostly and yellow, and the soft grass beneath the young man's feet turned to rubble. His body bent over like a crescent moon, his face became sorely wrinkled, and his eyes grew vacant and dull. Instead of going to him the strangers watched from a distance. And the youth grew old and decrepit before their eyes, and his face contorted in pain.

He stands there yet, in New Mexico, in a city called Na'ní'zhoozhi. The strangers pass by each evening and see him and wonder why he is there. They do not understand that the ugly place where he stands is a beautiful meadow. They do not know that the old man is the tears they have never shed.

A SHELTER
IN THE SKY

Your house is the last before the infinite,
whoever you are.

—Rainer Maria Rilke, "Initiation"

(1)

To Londoners observant of the rhythms and patterns of nature, the autumn of 1940, that stark season of witness to the fire and madness of the blitz, must have seemed a season without a soul. No drifts of golden plane-tree leaves stirred in the evening wind; no banks of chill, fine mist brooded over the Thames at dawn. The leaves burned where they hung that dreadful fall, and the mist on the river was hot and thick, the acrid residue of parachute mines and incendiary bombs. In the sky the plaintive cry of greylag geese crossing from Iceland to their wintering grounds in southern France gave way to the drone of Heinkels and Messerschmitts rising from airfields just beyond the channel. A Londoner seeking cause for the emptiness of those soulless times might have found it in the words of Macbeth: "Now o'er the one half-world nature seems dead; and wicked dreams abuse the curtain'd sleep."

Nature was not dead. It lived, some said, in the hearts and minds of the German pilots and the men who commanded them, though I cannot accept such an allegation. Nature is baffling, but it is not cruel or evil or insane.

What was preeminently natural about the autumn of 1940 was the capacity of those beleaguered Londoners to touch us in their plight, and our irresistible need, in return, to see ourselves in their shoes. In such entanglements lies the essence of nature, which is connection from one elementary particle to the next. Connection explains the human capacity for reaching out to the oppressed and seeking common ground with them. It explains, too, why the most compelling work of art to emerge from the fearful days of the blitz was a series of drawings not of bombers or of flaming buildings but of Londoners sheltered in the tunnels of the Underground. The artist was the sculptor Henry Moore, the drawings his *Shelter Sketches*. Explicit, unsentimental, executed in dense whirlwinds of incisive strokes, they depict a people reduced to a single unifying concern: the business of being human. In our own season of fire and madness they remind us of the majesty of innocence and the resilience of all life.

Moore later recalled that during the early days of the blitz he had paid scant attention to the news that Londoners by the thousands were crowding into the tube each night to seek protection from the bombs. One evening he and his wife, Irina, found themselves without a ride after dining with friends in the West End. They returned home by Underground, exiting at Belsize Park. There they discovered that an air attack had begun. Because of the hostilities, they were unable to ascend to the surface.

"I spent the time looking at the rows of people sleeping on the platforms," Moore later wrote. "I had never seen so many reclining figures, and even the train tunnels seemed to be like the holes in my sculpture. Amid the grim tension, I noticed groups of strangers formed together into intimate groups and children asleep within feet of the passing trains."

In the nights that followed, Moore began haunting the Underground. He carried a notebook with him on his rounds, jotting down brief descriptions of scenes to flesh out later in his studio. Those scenes possessed him. In an uncanny example of life imitating art they mirrored his own pre-war sculptures—helpless, sprawling, bloated figures (Moore's subjects lay shrouded in blankets and sleeping bags), all horribly transfigured by their circumstances.

But there was a second and equally important reason for Moore's nightly visits to the underworld. Those huddled thousands, packed as he said like slaves in a ship bound from Africa to America, possessed a monumental quality. However nightmarish their circumstances, however powerless the innocents to affect their fates, they bore their condition staunchly and with dignity. In squalid shelters beneath the streets of a devastated city, the measures of life continued unabated: kindness, tolerance, selfishness and generosity, anger and amiability, community, heroism, love. Moore's sketches show us a people not beaten down by hardship but rather lifted up by it. As the site of a grand epic of human survival, the Underground became a hallowed sanctuary, consecrated by the sacrament of suffering within. To go down into that hellish place was to enshrine oneself in human history at the highest level. It was to be ennobled.

That an artist could find grandeur in such baseness should not surprise us, for shelters have always had the capacity to raise up those who inhabit them and to inspire those who look on. Think of Robert Scott and his party in their pathetic tent on the endless Antarctic ice, of Anne Frank in her secret annex, of the battered wife sleeping peacefully at last in a safe house with no address. The quality that touches us in these scenes arises from the poignancy of human confinement, often undeserved, sometimes defenseless, amid the menacing tentacles of peril. However timorous the act of taking shelter may seem, it has about it something of the intrepid and the defiant. Whether it is the house in which we live, our own familiar and essential refuge, or a storm-tossed raft at sea, a shelter is a place where gallantry reigns, where the human spirit takes wing.

A prominent and troubling exception mars this otherwise stirring history: far from the hallowed sanctuary of a Robert Scott or an Anne Frank, the homeless shelter has today descended to an ignoble level, a refuge unspeakable from blitzes unmentionable for the most detested among us. The homeless have come to represent our unfinished and perhaps unfinishable business as a society, and because they persist like a spot on the lungs we regard them not with admiration for their dauntlessness but with loathing and rage. Recently I remarked on a ragged family of four camped on an Albuquerque streetside in attitudes that in a different era might have inspired a Henry Moore to great art. A well-meaning friend assured me that the homeless did not in fact want permanent dwellings, that surveys showed they preferred—what, refrigerator cartons in picturesque alleyways with expansive views of garbage cans and graffiti-fouled walls? Against all of our experience and better judgment, this astounding discovery supposedly held for children as well, two of whom hunched somewhat dazedly beside their parents in their grand parlor over the gutter. As though entering upon one of the stages of death, we cope with the doctor's bad news by denying it. The homeless become the worthy victims of their own supposedly grossly mismanaged lives. And because they are to blame for their wretched predicaments, we irritably, piously, and apparently with clean hands consign them to street corners or dank shelters on the wrong side of town, like parents sending naughty children to their rooms. The word "shelter," uttered with a hint of scorn, becomes a wedge to drive between ourselves and the homeless, to shield us from them and from the disquieting knowledge that only a thin line may separate their fate from our own. Weighted down in that way, the word describes a place that is neither ennobling nor inspiring but instead humiliating and degrading.

Whether we can recover a full measure of respect for these sojourners on America's streets and alleys without actually joining them in their pasteboard boxes, I don't know. I think we can make at least a beginning in that direction by recognizing that theirs is not a lonely quest but one they undertake with us all. For to seek shelter is an elemental instinct, one which neither war nor arctic winds nor a ravaged economy is necessary to excite: a nagging fear, an aching heart, a failure of nerve can be enough. Shelters are safe harbors from personal storms, places that allow us fleeting moments of conviction that we matter, and we seek them throughout our lives. When we cannot find them in the world beyond, we create them within ourselves, homespun sanctuaries that promise escape and peace of mind. Within, we pray, we daydream, we delude ourselves. A porch swing becomes a stronghold against an uncaring world; an old rocking chair becomes a beacon in the night. I have turned often to such refuges. One was a cramped room with bare walls and an out-of-tune upright piano to which I retired often during a period of utter failure while I was in college. Another was a dimly lit hall in New York City's American Museum of Natural History. There among scenes of the great mountains and deserts of the American West I overcame the despair I felt as a city dweller, and there I found renewal and a settled heart.

I escape to such a place sometimes today. It is not a building or a room, not even an enclosed space, but a simple clearing by the road in the radiant upper reaches of Santa Fe. My shelter is open to the world, an unshackling place: the floor earth, the roof sky, the walls history, culture, and the rough-cast masonry of nature. The route of the old Santa Fe Trail rambles by, still echoing with the creak of buckboards and wagon springs. The Sangre de Cristo Mountains tower to the north, while westward the horizon tumbles to infinity with the peaks and mesas of the Jemez range, gray, weary things beaten down by a million years of trouble.

At the foot of the Jemez Mountains slicing a stark twenty-mile-wide plain flows the Rio Grande, the lifeblood of New Mexico: mainstay, dream maker, signifier, keeper of the faith, master of ceremonies, soul brother number one. Usually it wanders the landscape with a kind of jovial and majestic forbearance. But when the hour is late and the sun cooperative, the river sometimes catches the low-angled light and I see a ribbon of water ignite and leap up and race over the plain like wildfire—south through the valley of the conquistadors, south to Albuquerque and beyond, to the curving earth and the era before armies and before names. It is all there to see from my shelter, a panorama that I call the Great History. It is a vista of untold centuries, measured first in miles, then leagues, then cycles of the moon.

And just below, checkering a slanting esplanade of piñon and juniper, are the flat roofs of Santa Fe, surely one of the world's most welcoming and beguiling places. Santa Fe is advertised as America's oldest capital city, but aficionados are more likely to describe it as a feeling, a bedazzlement in the clouds. Wrote D. H. Lawrence: "The moment I saw the brilliant, proud morning shine high up over the deserts of Santa Fe, something stood still in my soul and I started to attend." Writer Paul Horgan called the city "intoxicating." Santa Fe literature is full of such commendations. To me, none captures the essence of the city better than this by a friend of mine: "When I think of Santa Fe, I think of kissing a beautiful woman in the snow."

For those not given to such romantic sentiments there is no shortage of more practical reasons for visiting Santa Fe. It is a city with perhaps more to see and to do (and to buy), block for block—more music and art to enjoy, more history to absorb, more games to play, more beauty to admire, more sensual pleasures to indulge in—than any other city I know. Santa Fe is a fiesta for hedonists. I visit several times a year and never fail to fall utterly under its spell. Who needs shelter in such a place!

Yet sometime during each visit I'm overcome by a feeling of stark oppression among the dark adobe walls and narrow streets of this ancient city. Gracious though Santa Fe may be, it carries a burden of history—a concentration of experience—that can be overwhelming. Visitors to Florence sometimes succumb to a malady called Stendhal's syndrome, an illness characterized by dizziness, depression, sometimes even paranoia. The cause is art poisoning, the cure a quiet day in the country beyond the inhuman demands of Ghiberti and Michelangelo. As a nexus of history, culture, and natural beauty matched by few other places, Santa Fe is capable of inducing a similar malaise that can be crushing. For me it begins as a vague feeling of unease and descends quickly to a deep and lingering despair—for Santa Fe, for New Mexico, for the condition of the world.

To gain relief I make my way upward out of the shadows into the evergreen-studded foothills rising to the east. At each intersection the sky widens and brightens, the vista expands, the patient's condition improves. In a short time I'm stationed in my shelter, my clearing by the road, immersed in an envelope of mountain air lucid and resonant as wind chimes. An exquisite silence, the silence of daybreak, meets my ears. The Great History opens before my eyes. The sorrow of an unhappy world disappears behind the sheltering walls. In my grand refuge overarched by a vault of fathomless blue, I remember myself and my place and rekindle my belief in something Henry Moore understood well, the monumental nature of humankind. The restorative powers of the place arise in the ultimate gift of every shelter, and that is hope—which is to say, trust that beyond the madness of electrons there are ordered molecules, and beyond them rivers, trees, music, poetry, and the quiet conversation of friends. And farther yet, in that epic sphere that defines, shapes, and connects us all, kindness, generosity, and the courage of the valiant, dauntless before the storm.

All of which is prelude to my purpose: on a bleak December morning I met one of the valiant seated on a curb in a parking lot in Santa Fe. His name was Thomas, and he slept in a field with prairie dogs. In a roundabout way, what follows is my effort to find him a home.

(2)

I'm not the only one to have discovered the therapeutic qualities of the mountainside high over Santa Fe. Hundreds of houses dot the nearby slopes. The old river's smooth flow into history, a rare entertainment for me, is for the occupants of those houses a feature of the property, a special touch located just over the garden wall.

But they pay fearfully for the privilege. A residence in the Santa Fe hills is not simply a home, but what the real estate brochures call "a gracious island of privacy," "a prestigious, elegant compound," "not a house but an experience." They are shelters of a sort, but what shelters! Through most of this century an occasional destination for the bored and the splendid, and second home to a few, Santa Fe has in the past decade or so undergone a tumefaction in reputation that has sent real estate prices soaring into the Sangre de Cristos. Money has arrived in bundles, much of it in the pockets of Californians. Between 1985 and 1990 the average selling price of a home in Santa Fe doubled. Million-dollar figures are now common. The quaint little town in the mountains of northern New Mexico, once notable merely for its beauty and its charm, is now notable as an ambition, one of America's highest.

The upgrade was not accidental, though the speed at which it happened and the completeness with which it took over the city surprised many Santa Feans and troubled not a few. At a certain moment in the early 1980s, the city's residents, smelling something in the wind, swept their sidewalks, filled their potholes, razed their head shops. A few moments later their town brimmed in clothing stores with branches in Carmel and Aspen.

The news spread. Stories in the national press documented the wonders of "the City Different," "Sagebrush Shangri-La," "Salzburg Southwest." Breathlessly, the *Washington Post* raised Santa Fe to number one on its list of the world's most prestigious "in" spots. Local artisans once happy to see their names tacked to telephone poles suddenly found themselves approving ad copy for the New Yorker. By 1983 the city had squeezed 100 art galleries into its tiny downtown area and had begun to bill itself as the nation's third largest art market. By 1984 it was possible to purchase Venetian pastries in Santa Fe. By 1985 the channelers, polarity mechanics, and psychic podiatrists—always omens of a trend—had arrived. One in fifty Santa Feans was said to be a healer of one kind or another. By 1986 a million visitors a year were choking city streets. By 1987 a logo of sorts had been created: a ridiculous coyote, usually rendered in some dizzy sunset hue. No ordinary varmint, this one craned its neck to the vertical, threw open its chops, and howled in apparent chiropractic agony. To the horror of old-timers, animal lovers, and the even modestly refined, the creature took over the city like an army of migrating toads. By 1988 the coyote with the neck brace was the ubiquitous symbol of Santa Fe, bellowing from every T-shirt, postcard, and shop window, drowning out more preferable, more tasteful images like the opera house and the Palace of the Governors.

All that remained to confirm the city's arrival as a destination as essential as Paris or Milan was a context in which to understand it. The context was created: style. Santa Fe Style. Originally a tribute to traditional New Mexican motifs and manners of presentation, it quickly became a tribute to the notion that you could sell anything if you said it was Santa Fe Style, even if it wasn't, even if it was a clock radio. Santa Fe Style wasn't exactly High Renaissance, but at its best it tried honestly to celebrate widely admired local design values— simplicity, earthiness, informality, all done up in traditional Indian, Hispanic, and Anglo garb. Either way it generated considerable amounts of civic pride and national attention, plus oodles of cash.

With context in place the truly important began to arrive. One heard rumors of icons: Redford! Spielberg! One winter day I dined with a friend in a tony restaurant just off the main plaza. A perfect fire of harmoniously arranged piñon logs crackled beside us in the fireplace. Polite noises interrupted the studied quiet of the place—snatches of civilized conversation, clinking crystalware, our own included, which snuggled a delightful California chardonnay. (New Mexico boasts a fledgling wine industry, but its product—earnest with just a touch too much of the common—is usually not up to Santa Fe standards.) We dined on peasant food—pinto beans, chiles, and tortillas, deployed in such a manner as to cost $14.95. Between bites, a shadow suddenly fell across me as an enormous figure came between me and the fireplace. The eclipse was caused by a celebrity moon, common in Santa Fe—the actor Jack Palance, as it happened, revolving grandly around the room as though he were in orbit. No one gaped or jabbed a tablemate in the ribs. Self-containment, too, is Santa Fe Style.

While the city prospered, a transformation equal in magnitude but opposite in direction was taking place. The poor of Santa Fe, always a presence in the city, grew poorer, and many joined their ranks. Here as in all of America during the shattering 1980s, the distance between rich and poor widened, the desire to find common ground dwindled, the mass of the faceless society grew larger and closer to critical. In opulent Santa Fe the transformations were merely more apparent, as well as more ironic. As restaurants catered to more and more exclusive clienteles, the line of Santa Feans waiting for groceries at the First Presbyterian Church food pantry grew longer by the month. As real estate values skyrocketed, so did the number of homeless seeking refuge in the city's shelters. Because they earned minimum wage or less, many of those on whose labors the city depended—salespeople, museum workers, restaurant and hotel employees—could not put together the several-thousand-dollar nest eggs they needed to move into apartments. (Buying homes, of course, was out of the question for those who supported the city at ground level.) Some crowded into lodgings with three or four companions. Some commuted from cheaper cities. Others, less fortunate or more resilient, found themselves sleeping in arroyos, under bridges, or in Pontiacs parked behind the Safeway. Competition for less and less intensified. The spirit of friendliness and community long celebrated in the city began to dissipate, replaced by a hard edge and a bitter tone. A young man hawking newspapers on a street corner put it to me this way: "The streets are the new killing fields."

(3)

Shelter: it is a theme woven thickly into the rich tapestry of Santa Fe history, an enduring motif that explains many of the city's paradoxes and idiosyncrasies. To understand why, it helps to see Santa Fe not as it is today, cluttered with tourists and traffic and pulsating with the rhythms of a modern sophisticated city, but as it was through the first two centuries of its history, a distant outpost at the nearly forgotten end of the Spanish empire in America. Perhaps comparison with Tibet is apt, for old Santa Fe shares some of Tibet's peculiarities: frightful isolation, religious zeal, certainty of purpose. It served as the capital of the province of Nuevo Mexico, part of the territory claimed by the Spanish, which extended from the Mississippi River to the Pacific Ocean.

Yet to see that enormous region as a province ruled by the Spanish would be a distinct mistake. A few hundred soldiers, merchants, and administrators in Santa Fe and perhaps a thousand settlers and Franciscan missionaries within a few days' journey of the capital: such a presence in an area twice the size of Spain does not make for an all-powerful authority. From a Spanish viewpoint the province of New Mexico was one prodigious emptiness, relieved only in a distant corner by the alluring smile of civilization.

But it is well to remember that in New Mexico there is always a second and equally persuasive point of view, and often several more. Indians lived here in great numbers, by one estimate some forty thousand in central New Mexico alone at the time of Coronado's expedition. In native terms the region was hardly empty. The many firsts of which New Mexicans boast proudly today—first capital city in North America, oldest public building, oldest continuously celebrated annual festival, first epic poem—rightly deserve to be lorded over only those puny bragging rights of nearsighted East Coast historians, whose working methods proceed directly from those of Julius Caesar ("It was not certain that Britain existed until I went there") and who have yet to grasp that a certain kind of American history, one they admire and have always pretended to command—the history of European America—began here, in Spanish America.

So much for priority. There are cities in New Mexico—Taos and Acoma to name two—that are older than Santa Fe by centuries, annual festivals older yet, epic poems already hoary when Columbus set sail for America. Little of this is known outside the Southwest because Indians, who hold all the records, rarely make a fuss over such trivia. As ancient travelers of the land they know that before Plymouth, Jamestown, Santa Fe, Taos, and Acoma there were now-forgotten kingdoms, and before them kingdoms more, and before them the kingdom of the earth itself, the ultimate title holder.

The first Spanish attempt to gain a foothold in New Mexico failed. Founded in 1598, the settlement of San Gabriel was hot, dusty, barren, and poorly defended. There was constant trouble with the Indians. Many of the settlers came seeking gold, and when they found none they felt swindled. Only the missionaries achieved success, finding in New Mexico's thousands an almost unbelievable fortune in souls to save. The friars went to work with a vengeance.

The San Gabrieleños held on till 1609. Late that year, cheered by a fresh commitment of support from Spain, they packed their wagons and moved thirty miles south to make a fresh start.

In the new location the settlers proved at once that they had learned from their earlier mistakes. Santa Fe's founders chose a beneficent place for their lonely city, a cool, well-watered spot among piñons and junipers at an altitude of seven thousand feet on the western slope of the southernmost Rocky Mountains. They laid out their main plaza on the ruins of an ancient pueblo. Around and near the square, using sun-dried bricks of soil, straw, and water, they constructed an administration building, a barracks, a church, a convent, shops, and homes for a few hundred residents. With San Gabriel no doubt in mind, they erected a wall at the edge of town to protect themselves from Indian raids, invasion by the French or English to the north, and perils of not quite definable origin that disturbed their sleep by night and fostered rumor and suspicion by day.

Those Santa Feans were quite on their own. The nearest Spanish settlement lay fifteen hundred miles to the south in Mexico. Were an envoy from Santa Fe to have set out for help, say at first snow in October, the winds of a different winter would have been blowing when he returned a year later with a relief party. A male child born the morning a supply caravan rolled into town might be a soldier defending the city before three more such caravans arrived. The expected invasion from the north (which for its entertainment value, at least, might have been welcomed by the citizenry) never came. Never mind armies: not a single Anglo entered New Mexico for almost two hundred years.

Even after Mexico won its independence from Spain in 1821 and began seeking trade with the almost-as-new nation to the north, visitors from the United States were rare. The journey over the Santa Fe Trail was long and arduous, a two-month ordeal at best. In *Death Comes for the Archbishop*, Willa Cather gave her ecclesiastic Jean Marie Latour a year to reach Santa Fe from Cincinnati. That was in 1851, mind you. It is true that certain misadventures befell Latour on his journey, delaying him more than most. But there is no denying the isolation of the settlement he was striving to reach: "New Mexico lay in the middle of a dark continent," Cather wrote. "No one in Cincinnati could tell him how to get to New Mexico—no one had ever been there."

In such a place, in a tiny shelter surrounded by gut-wrenching emptiness, European New Mexico found its start. The chronicles tell us nothing of the beauty of the location, but I cannot imagine that the river, the vastness, the great mountains splitting the clouds did not sometimes stir the hearts of those brave Spanish settlers. By day they must have thought they could see clear to Mexico. At sunset the high walls to the east shimmered in a dozen shades of gold and then red. The pastel sky bent low as though alighting, then grew soft and still, like a songbird closing its eyes. And then it was night and the sky dissolved, revealing the awful infinity fastened in radiant, unreachable stars clear to the western horizon.

It was an unworldly beauty, and a terrifying one. The city's founders called their refuge La Villa Real de la Santa Fe de San Francisco de Asis—the Royal City of the Holy Faith of Saint Francis of Assisi. However else you may judge their achievements, grant them their due: the gallantry of the intrepid, the nobility of monuments.

The choice of Francis as patron saint was both inspired and paradoxical. The home city of Christendom's perhaps best-loved saint shares much in common with Santa Fe. Assisi is hewn from the forested slope of a mountain in Umbria in central Italy. In Francis's time it was a well-fortified shelter for a people prepared to do battle at any time with enemies real and imagined. As a young man Francis himself went to war against the nearby city of Perugia. He was captured and spent a year in prison.

Like Santa Fe, Assisi is built on the ruins of an ancient city, the first-century B.C. Roman settlement of Asisium. At the center of town stands the plaza, the focus of civic activity. Radiating out from there are government buildings, shops, churches, and homes, all fashioned from native stone, a local rock as pink as a Santa Fe coyote.

From the plaza, steep, narrow streets wind upward past fine homes into the deep forests that carpet the mountainside. There in a refuge called the Hermitage, Francis retired to rest, to pray, even, it is said, to preach to the birds. It is a serene and beautiful spot, little changed today from the way it was eight centuries ago when Francis was alive, when Santa Fe was a bustling Tewa Indian village.

One can hike to the Hermitage from Assisi in an hour or so. From the road there are expansive vistas south and west across the Umbrian plain into the haze and history of the Roman Empire. Seeing the view a few years ago, I was reminded at once of the valley of the Rio Grande. Assisi and Santa Fe both impart a feeling of safe refuge in the sky. Saint Francis, I think, would have been happy in the city in New Mexico that bears his name.

It was perhaps inevitable that the teachings of the simple man who preached love, kindness, and tolerance would be perverted almost from the moment of his death. Married, as he said, to Lady Poverty, he could not be permitted by the Catholic church to serve as a spiritual representative of that institution, which was already married to the international banking system founded during the very years of Francis's ministry. The troublesome conviction of the once wealthy Francesco Bernadone that wealth corrupts and peace redeems was buried quietly along with his bones and his humble domicile beneath the sumptuous basilica erected in his honor.

Four centuries later, Franciscan missionaries fanned out from Santa Fe to Christianize the Indians of New Mexico. In the name of the man who preached the felicity of birds they practiced the brutality of tyrants, enslaving some fourteen thousand Indians. Within a few years of Santa Fe's founding, trade caravans could be seen snaking their way south to Mexico with their Diné, Apache, and Puebloan captives in tow. Men were sent into the mines, where inhuman conditions led to early deaths for many. Women and children were forced into domestic service in the homes of the nobility. If a woman had the misfortune to be beautiful she faced the alternatives of service in a brothel or in the bed of a nobleman. The only crime of these unfortunates was refusal to cooperate with the friars.

Through forced labor and tribute, the Indians who remained in New Mexico became the workhorses in the province's dismal economy. Much of the small amount of capital that was generated went to line the pockets of an endless procession of corrupt officials who sat in the Governor's Palace in Santa Fe. The traditional Indian economy was reduced to shambles, the life of the village destroyed. Franciscans had a hand in it all.

The friars saved their greatest wrath for native religion. They outlawed all traditional rites, destroyed ceremonial kivas, burned relics, profaned beliefs, condemned to death Indians who refused to submit to their teachings. In one of many such reprisals, forty Puebloans were hanged in Santa Fe in 1645 for defying the clerics. In another, twelve Acoma children were taken from their parents and sent to Mexico as slaves to pay for the bell that hangs in the tower of the pueblo church of Esteban Rey.

Today the majority of New Mexico's Indians are outwardly Christian. But in the sanctuaries of the reconstructed kivas, in secret hideaways hidden among the red rocks, many of the same worshippers who faithfully attend mass each Sunday invoke the ancient gods and practice rites unchanged since before the arrival of Coronado. Indian religion in New Mexico is an amalgam of traditional and Christian beliefs, a blending of inviolable old and acceptable new. The shape is Christian, the spirit native. The painting behind the altar at the Church of San José at Laguna Pueblo shows Christ, a cross, a crown, and the Virgin Mary; above it, stretching across the ceiling, is an enormous animal hide bearing images of the sun, the moon, a rainbow, and stars—pagan symbols of a nature-oriented religion. The work is a product of the nineteenth century, when relations between missionaries and natives relaxed and tolerance found its way back into Franciscan practice. Pondering the strange and wondrous Francis, one is moved to realize that among Christians of old, perhaps only he, who numbered among his spiritual allies brother fire and sister wind, would have stood humble and exultant before the altar at the Church of San José.

After the final words of the liturgy at Christmas Eve mass in the mission church at San Felipe Pueblo, the Catholic priest retires to the sacristy. Suddenly the music of ancient New Mexico erupts and fills the air—children chirping on whistles tuned to the melodies of the sparrow and the meadowlark. The door of the church swings open, and from a distance comes the thunder of drums pounding in electrifying unison. The drummers come closer and closer, and as they enter the mission and march down the aisle, the old walls threaten to burst from the din.

And then the dancers sweep in from the night—women magnificent in feathers, shells, turquoise, and spruce boughs, men in antlers and robes, leaping and strutting like deer. They are celebrating the birth of the Christ child and something more: strength, endurance, the everlasting heartbeat of the land. And something much of Christianity has never been able to abide—the wild swinging of the hips, the unbuckling of the soul strings, the unbridled passion for the here and now. It continues through the night, this Christmas of heaven and earth, till the first light of dawn glimmers on the horizon.

There is a power in it that the Spanish could not contain. On August 10, 1680, the northern pueblos revolted. Under the leadership of an Indian named Popé, a plan several years in the making unfolded with mathematical precision. At every pueblo and ranch, Indians swept down on the interlopers, slaying men, women, and children. Four hundred Spaniards died during the first four days of the revolution; twenty-five friars were martyred. After ransacking and burning Spanish homes, natives went into the fields and slaughtered the cattle. At the missions the assailants gutted the interiors, tumbled the walls and bell towers, destroyed every symbol of Christianity, every reminder of the hated friars.

The Spaniards who survived the first wave took refuge in Santa Fe and Isleta Pueblo, the latter of which briefly refused to join the uprising. The insurgents laid siege to Santa Fe, sacking homes, cutting off the water supply, tightening the noose street by street.

The Spanish rallied briefly. In a fierce and unexpected counterattack they came out from their hiding places and killed some three hundred Indians—but behind these hundreds stood thousands more. The leaders in Santa Fe and Isleta saw that their situation was hopeless. Within two weeks of the uprising the Spanish abandoned both refuges and headed south. Watching from the surrounding hills, the Puebloans allowed them to go.

The retreating parties, comprising some two thousand Spaniards, met near Socorro and continued south together. Within a month they were in El Paso. One hundred forty years after Coronado, seventy-one years after the founding of Santa Fe, not a single Spaniard remained in what had been the province of New Mexico.

Little known beyond New Mexico's borders, sometimes omitted altogether from American history texts, the Pueblo Revolt of 1680, when it is discussed at all, is usually called the most successful Indian uprising ever to take place on the continent. Such a characterization trivializes what was surely one of the most remarkable events of any kind—Indian uprising or otherwise—in American history. Had something similar happened in Massachusetts, had the Wampanaog Metacom (King Philip) scored an equivalent victory in the war he waged at almost the same moment, every last colonist not slain by Philip would have fled to Boston harbor, dived aboard ship, and beat it back to England. So consummate a triumph was more than a successful uprising: it was a confounding of destiny.

One might expect that Popé's glittering victory would have earned him fame as a military leader of the first rank. History was written, however, not by the Pueblos but by the Spanish, who returned thirteen years later and against little resistance recaptured the lost province. Not unexpectedly, we learn from the conquerors that Popé was a devil and a madman, and so he disappears among the soiled footnotes of history, even in the state where he engineered his breathtaking rout. New Mexico is, after all, more Hispanic than Indian. One is not surprised to learn that the exuberant Fiesta de Santa Fe celebrated each September commemorates not the revolution of 1680 but the reconquest in 1693 by don Diego de Vargas.

Today in an hour or so one can complete a short course in New Mexican history since the reconquest by wandering about Santa Fe's plaza and along a few of the side streets that emanate from it. Much of the old Palace of the Governors with its massive adobe walls stands yet, stately in a grace and stillness that belie its stormy history. It served as shelter for Popé, for scores of Spanish governors after him, for rebel Texans, imperial Americans, and usurping Confederate Army forces. And finally, and apparently permanently, for Union forces in 1862. The palace looks heavy and tired and past its prime, but you will not see a grander building anywhere. In its resplendent quiet, one cannot fail to hear the echoes and feel the beat of its turbulent history.

Near the altar at Saint Francis Cathedral, a block away, stands the statue of the Virgin Mary that don Diego de Vargas brought with him on his return from Mexico, and to which he attributed his easy, though not bloodless, victory. Few Santa Feans care to admit it, but the prominence of the statue— she was known until recently as "La Conquistadora"—firmly establishes the cathedral as a monument to New Mexico's violent past. At the entrance to the building is a plaque which notes that the state is the site of more Christian martyrdoms—thirty-eight—than any other place in the New World. It neglects to mention why.

So much for the short course. Something of the longer course in New Mexico history may be glimpsed beneath the colonnade that shambles in front of the Governor's Palace. Each morning several dozen Indians spread blankets on the sidewalk and lay out rows of handmade jewelry to sell. It is a thoroughly modern enterprise but one whose practitioners perfectly symbolize the continuity and changelessness of New Mexico history.

Those dogged Puebloans not only threw the rascals out, if only briefly, and coopted the best parts of the imposed religion; in the important aspects of their lives Puebloans remain substantially unchanged by the arrival of whites in America. Today they live in villages located exactly where they were five hundred years ago. Puebloans speak the ancient tongues, wear the ancient costumes, practice the traditions and rites of their forebears, and detect in the hard crust of this creaking land the old sure signs of affirmation and timelessness. It is no coincidence that New Mexico, home of Folsom Man (8,000 B.C.), Sandia Man (10,000 B.C.), and Orogrande Man (dated by some authorities at 25,000 B.C.), is one of the longest running shows in the Western Hemisphere.

Drive the interstate to Santa Fe in the most up-to-date vehicle you can find and you will experience landscape overpowering mind, body, and technology. Nature, you will know, is not dead. Charles Lyell, the father of modern geology, theorized that the processes that shape the land today are the same ones that have shaped it since the beginning. He applied his theory of uniformitarianism to geological history, but I think it can be adapted to human history as well. Beyond conquest and reconquest, goes my theory of human uniformitarianism, beyond random blips on the screen, beyond style . . . it is as it was.

Read the sage and the chamisa, lift your eyes above volcanic hills and fifty miles of piñon to gray shadows on the horizon, and you will know that you have seen it before. Speed across a whole county of sunlight and gaze over two counties more into a convocation of thunderstorms, three or four of them trumpeting atop the mesas, each storm visible in its wholeness and its singularity. And you will know that you have seen it before. The sky wheels and the earth tumbles and the moon comes up so big and fast you nearly jump out of your skin; and in your fine car driving the interstate to Santa Fe you may undergo a blinding conversion to a religion uniquely New Mexican, a dizzy synthesis of Puebloan harmony and joy and Franciscan tolerance and peace.

At the center of the plaza where following the Civil War the townspeople of Santa Fe erected a memorial to soldiers, some keeper of the faith has delivered a message. The original inscription on the side of the memorial facing the Palace of the Governors read as follows: "To the heroes who have fallen in the various battles with the savage Indians in the Territory of New Mexico." Armed with chisel and the hopefulness of the shelter of Santa Fe, the unknown sculptor has excised two words and written two others in their places. The inscription now reads: "To the heroes who have fallen in the various battles with our brother Indians in the Territory of New Mexico."

Perhaps it is a sentence that will one day find its way into a chapter in the Great History of New Mexico.

A few steps from this monument foreshadowing the Santa Fe of tomorrow stands a plaque honoring the origins of the Santa Fe of today. It marks the end of the Santa Fe Trail, the trade route that transformed Santa Fe from the city it was—languid, unpolished, enlivened only by the occasional spilling of great quantities of blood—into the city it is today, where "to buy" is the operative verb. Old-timers grumble over the supposedly recent transformation of their beloved hometown into a Destination, where in the correct downtown parlor, ice cream may run them three dollars a scoop.

"I feel like someone peed on my Renoir," a local merchant complained to me. It was a fairly ingenuous comment, I thought, given that his metaphor fairly sang with the very aesthetic he was seeking to discredit. In the rest of New Mexico, where a three-dollar ice cream would strike most people as depraved, there is not a lot of sympathy for Santa Feans, whose rather operatic troubles seem mostly self-induced. And there is more than a little of the opinion that the city has received pretty much what it deserved. Many New Mexicans feel that in its present incarnation, Santa Fe would be better off in California, or Colorado at least, to be welcomed home when it is ready to rejoin the community of struggle and pain. Behind all the finger-wagging and tongue-clucking, of course, there is a certain amount of raw envy. Still, when they have their emotions under control, the majority of New Mexicans, I think, would agree with the message on the bumper sticker seen occasionally around the state that reads, "I don't care how they do it in Santa Fe."

What they recognize but Santa Fe's old-timers may not is that today's "City Different" is far from an aberration; it is, rather, a logical and probably inevitable outgrowth of yesterday's city. Modern Santa Fe is said to have begun in May 1981 with a cover story in *Esquire* entitled "The Right Place to Live!" ("We've found it: great women, great weather, and plenty to do. Pack your bags!") Not long after, Christine Mather and Sharon Woods wrote a book called *Santa Fe Style*. It sold a hundred thousand copies, and a movement was born. Reports soon reached New Mexico that the situation in the rest of the country was getting out of hand. People in Pittsburgh, normal people, were said to be snacking on blue corn tortillas. Stores called Santa Fe Style and Santa Fe Collection opened in Washington, D.C., and Chatham, Massachusetts. Living rooms in Des Moines blossomed overnight in sun-bleached cow skulls and Indian drum coffee tables. Georgia O'Keeffe became everyone's favorite grandmother, the one who paints.

The merriment reached an apotheosis of sorts when Bloomingdale's in New York City declared June 1990 "New Mexico: America's Spirit" month. Cheerfully offering its patrons a taste of what was happening in the Southwest—buffalo dancers, concho belts, broomstick skirts, green chile peanut butter—the store's proprietors conferred the coveted mantle of Nowness on the city in the sky. It was only the second time in history that the New York elite had actually acknowledged the existence of New Mexico. The first was in 1988 when the *New York Times* reported that a consortium of East Coast venture capitalists had turned down a request for backing from some New Mexico businesses because the venture capitalists "did not wish to invest in a foreign country."

With all the sudden and unaccustomed attention, few people in New Mexico knew how to behave. Albuquerque newspapers swallowed their pride and covered the Bloomingdale's triumph as though it were a cotillion. Most New Mexicans were touched by all the fuss though not certain whether it signified approval or amusement. The only complaints came from a few residents of Carlsbad, whose plan to wear bat outfits at Bloomingdale's to promote Carlsbad Caverns was vetoed at the last minute by the store's management.

The pink of fashion though it may seem, Santa Fe Style is as ancient as the city itself. Santa Fe has always been a style. The city is today what it was yesterday, a fortress against the dangers of the world, an exotic and sublime haven from reality. Place Santa Fe where Willa Cather located New Mexico— in the middle of a dark continent—and you have a perfect explanation for Santa Fe Style, past, present, and future. Style evolves in isolation as finches evolve in the Galapagos, and the strange and rare species that have found shelter in Santa Fe, continually redefining and reshaping its character, constitute a life list for students of hermetic behavior: fanatic Franciscans, venal administrators, assorted climbers, reprobates, and flatterers, trappers and traders, the unwell (asthmatics, tuberculars, depressives suffering from diseases of the spirit), artists, photographers, actors, writers, gays and lesbians, political and social refugees, prophets, misanthropes, trend-setters.

And the most exotic species of all, the old-timers themselves, who were born here or came wide-eyed and innocent, and who stayed because there was something about the place that reached into them and grabbed them and wouldn't let them go, and who, however much they may protest the transmogrification of their paradise into a glorified shopping mall, happily, one and all, celebrate The Look: the mountainside of identically shaped, colored, constructed, and appointed buildings that compose modern Santa Fe, investing it with a form and a feel that could not be mistaken for those of any other city in the world.

The Look is the brainchild of the old-timers of 1957, who farsightedly and no doubt with a clear understanding of the peculiarity of what they were doing, adopted an ordinance that created for all time an immaculate tribute to adobe. (I say created, not preserved, because the Santa Fe of old was never as compulsively rendered as this one.) The code, strictly enforced and tested many times in court, prohibits throughout the central section of the city the construction of any building not in the ruthlessly defined Spanish-Pueblo or Territorial style of architecture:

> With rare exceptions, the buildings are of one story, few have three stories, and the characteristic effect is that the buildings are long and low. Roofs are flat with a slight slope and surrounded on at least three sides by a firewall of the same color and material as the walls or of brick. Roofs are never carried out beyond the line of the walls except to cover an enclosed portal, the outer edge of the roof being supported by wooden columns. Two-story construction is more common in the Territorial than in other substyles, and is preferably accompanied by a balcony on the level of the second story. Façades are flat, varied by inset portals, exterior portals, protecting *vigas* or roof beams, *canales* or waterspouts, flanking buttresses and wooden lintels.

Rough-textured and earthy, the structures that have grown up under the ordinance splay with religious fervor over the foothills of the Sangre de Cristos like a field of uprooted baking potatoes. The Look is generally agreed to be charming, if Territorial-style gas stations can be charming (much less historically meaningful).

Gazing at Santa Fe from a distance, one is amazed to realize that there exists in America a city where under penalty of law, neither lunatic nor certified public accountant—nay, not even Robert Redford himself—may erect a gin mill or a bordello of yellow and puce sandalwood. It is a considerable irony that a city sometimes praised for its progressive social policies is home to one of the most draconian measures ever enacted in the United States. Such an instrument can have only one effect, and that is to create style, which is a self-conscious, self-shaping of culture by decree rather than by evolution. Style is paternalistic, replacing choice with determinism and creativity with imitation. It is enfeebling, as homogeneous gene pools are enfeebling. It is incestuous and oppressive. Most of all it is boring. It transforms the singular, the personal, and the exciting into product, ripping out the heart in the process. No doubt today's version of Santa Fe Style, essentially a solemnization of shopping, is more banal than most. We may be grateful to know that before long it will give way to another, something perhaps a little more compatible with the Great History of New Mexico. Whatever happens, this much is certain: if it happens in Santa Fe, it will be style.

(4)

One December morning I spent several frustrating hours chasing a man named Mr. Lucero up and down the streets of America's oldest capital city. It was windy and bitterly cold in Santa Fe that day, conditions many of my East Coast friends are unable to reconcile with their notion of Santa Fe as an upscale city smack in the middle of pitiless desert—Phoenix, say, with curbside recycling. The myth is perpetuated in an endless succession of films, television shows, and advertisements, like the recent magazine ad for a product called Santa Fe cologne. In sultry desert tones it depicts an L.A. kind of couple (he shirtless and godlike, she lightly clad and dewy), reclining on a Santa Fe kind of bed, their lips locked in upscale, pitiless passion. The caption reads: "It gets pretty hot in Santa Fe."

Well, yes, and Denver, Seattle, and Boston, too, all of which enjoy higher average temperatures year-round than Santa Fe. No shirtless guys or lightly clad beauties passed me on the street that morning; the people I saw were swaddled like newborns. As for Mr. Lucero, I didn't know how he might be dressed, but I hoped to find out. He was a well-known thorn in the side of the Santa Fe City Council for his persistent lobbying efforts on behalf of the homeless, of which he was one. I wanted to track him down because I was sure he could tell me something about Santa Fe Style that I'd missed during my strolls around the plaza.

I was thwarted in my search at every turn. From the Friends Meeting House to the public library to the soup kitchen on Marcy Street, I was never more than a few steps behind my prey. At each location I was told that Mr. Lucero had been there only a few minutes earlier but had gone elsewhere. As the day wore on, Mr. Lucero came more and more to symbolize for me the faceless society I had heard so much about. I never found him, though I may have passed him a dozen times on the street.

Dashing from one dead end to the next, I suddenly thought of a man I knew in California during the early 1980s, those serene, self-satisfied years before we Americans heard much about homelessness. Gary worked as an all-night street cleaner for the city of Palo Alto. From him I learned that until one's eyes become accustomed to the dark, one cannot see the creatures of the night. I had daytime eyes. I couldn't believe my friend's reports of old men sleeping under the freeways and kids in sleeping bags and the occasional lifeless body without papers turning up in an alley or under a clump of bushes. Gary assured me they were true. There was a huge, invisible population that dwelt among us, phantoms who might be creatures from another planet except that they were human beings no different from ourselves. The only power they held over us was their invisibility.

This I realized with a start a moment after I decided reluctantly to abandon my search for Mr. Lucero. I'll drop him a note, I thought. Or phone him. Then, of course, I realized my mistake. *And what is Mr. Lucero's address? And in which room does he keep his phone? And is it a touch-tone or a rotary model?*

The deeper I dug, the clearer and more distressing the magnitude of the disaster became. Here in Santa Fe, like Palo Alto one of America's wealthiest cities, there were people sleeping on the streets. It wasn't that the residents of Santa Fe didn't care. Many did, and many were working to alleviate the problem. But here as in most American cities, there was simply no affordable housing for people of little means. What Santa Fe had to offer was temporary shelter with room for a hundred or so guests each night.

Sometimes that wasn't enough. Imagining the usual suspects I guessed the identities of these phantoms of the shelters—winos, spare-change artists, crazies. My eyes still weren't used to the dark. At the La Luz de Santa Fe Family Shelter, director Carol Luna told me that most of her guests were normal people down on their luck. Many had jobs, and many who did not were searching for work. Entire families were involved. During the coldest months of the year half of the guests at La Luz were children.

And then there were those who didn't come in to the shelters, those who slept in their cars, or worse. Their numbers could only be guessed at but certainly ran into the hundreds. Sometimes on a winter morning one of them was found somewhere frozen to death.

It was the ones who slept out without a roof over their head who began to haunt me. Perhaps my twenty years of mountain climbing and countless nights out in the rain and snow gave me a distant and admittedly simplistic understanding of their discomfort and sympathy with their plight. Needless to say, there was a world of difference between their experiences and mine. Many of them were draftees, so to speak, unwilling foot soldiers in the war against the dark, while I in my goose-down sleeping bag was a cheerful volunteer.

Still, volunteers dodge bullets along with the rest of the grunts, and in at least one respect I could claim solidarity with the draftees: on many occasions I had measured the winter night moment by moment, snowflake by snow-flake, and I knew its silence and its length. What I did not know was how much quieter and longer it might be were the long-awaited dawn to bring with it not a measure of hope, as it always had for me, but rather the prospect of continued night.

Or perhaps my link with the dwellers of endless night lay through Jake, my only child, at the time not yet two years old but a source of insight and understanding for me since the day he was born. Of the many rituals he, his mother, and I practiced together, none was more precious or vested in primal duty than the last, the tucking in at night. How urgent it was to ensure that his hours alone in the dark would be safe and contented ones. Did ever an evening pass when Carol or I did not look up from a book or a chore and ask: Do you think he's warm enough? Should I check to see if Jake's okay?

It was on Cerrillos Road well beyond the zone of architectural correctness, in a parking lot tumbled in smoky snow and reeking of exhaust fumes, where I met the embodiment of my fears. I saw him as I walked by and immediately averted my eyes, intending to continue on.

But something told me to stop, and a moment later I was walking toward the man. He was smoking a cigarette and seated on a curb in a rich pool of sunlight that had burst over the parking lot unexpectedly. He was about forty, a thin, tired figure in a black raincoat so scanty and frayed it appeared to need him more than he needed it. The rest of his outfit was equally unsuitable for winter in Santa Fe—T-shirt, wrinkled slacks, tattered Reeboks.

I introduced myself. I told him I wanted to talk. He smiled self-consciously. Then with an exaggerated gesture he motioned for me to sit down. We shook hands, and in a gravelly voice he told me his name was Thomas.

We talked for perhaps half an hour; or rather, he talked, for my simple invitation for him to tell me about himself seemed to open a reservoir of bottled-up need. He had the sheepish, self-deprecating manner of those who as kids failed to master the essentials like salad forks and long division and who never catch up. He had heavily lidded eyes, a small nose, and thin red hair that he combed straight back, a hedge against the possibility of finding himself without a mirror in the morning. His face was long and narrow, red as a sunset, and as ravaged as his poor raincoat.

He was from Kentucky. After graduating from high school he joined the navy. He completed a tour of duty in Vietnam, then returned to Kentucky, where he took up the steamfitting trade. During the next few years he enjoyed some success, saved a little money, allowed himself the hope of a brighter tomorrow.

But something went wrong. Something didn't work out as he had planned. Someone double-crossed him and jobs dried up and friends disappeared and family failed him and love did not come, and wisdom and prudence eluded him, and he made some mistakes.

He shook his head and chuckled. His story was short on dates and details, as though they no longer mattered. It was the broad sweep of the thing that occupied him and perplexed him—the inexplicable shape and direction of his life. If there were reasons behind any of it he was disinterested in them or could no longer remember them. He was like William Kennedy's Francis Phelan—"sure only that he lived in a world where events decided themselves, and that all a man could do was to stay one jump into their mystery." He went to school, he joined the navy, he worked, he played. One night he found himself on a freight train headed west.

It would be hard to invent a story more different from my own. But listening to the man, I realized that the narrative line we cherish so, those bright twists of plot we brandish like trophies are not ultimately what define or distinguish us, are not even what matter. What matters is simply that each of us is the star of an epic tale, and that every tale must be heard.

It is a useful exercise to consider that unique view of the world which each of us enjoys from birth until death, that aisle seat on the performance of our play. Mine seems to be oval-shaped, a bit wider than it is high. Glancing up now I notice a bit of eyebrow protruding on the left; downward I see the profile of my nose. Alone in these dark theaters we spend our days and nights, observing a sometimes unruly cast of characters as they perform our curious and unpredictable lives. Here we comment secretly on the turns of plot, the botched lines, the unexpected entrances. Here we guard the secrets of our hearts.

But there is more to the exercise. It is complete only when we can see the eyes of another as observation points exactly like our own, and the darkness behind as a universe of perception as unique and precious as the ones we inhabit. V. S. Pritchett, that master of the short story, writes, "They dwell—and this to me is the moving and dramatic thing about people—in a solitude which they alone can populate."

As I listened to the man's story I had no difficulty appreciating the gentle nudge that presses us to one side of the line or the other. Time passes, our paths diverge, and one day I am snug in my fine Polarguard jacket, and you are shivering in a raincoat of rags. The great secret—how little our control, how vital the cooperation of fate—goes unspoken. Before long we are strutting like ostriches, confident that we alone are responsible for our successes and our failures. It is the cornerstone of the American theology, and it is utterly false. Ours is a theology of convenience. It relieves the successful of any tiresome need to seek common ground with the failed. It is a knife in the heart of nature, for it severs connections between one elementary particle and the next.

The belief that we are masters of our fate requires more than anything a mountain of self-deception. A former Delaware governor campaigns for the presidency on an antiwelfare platform, declaring that a man must work if he expects to be paid. The governor is the beneficiary of a portion of one of America's great family fortunes, one he lifted not a finger to earn. (A good rule of thumb is that the louder a man bellyaches about welfare, the cushier the free ride he received from his parents.) A Supreme Court nominee, a man who claims to have pulled himself up by his own bootstraps, pours out tears of gratitude for the love and support of his grandmother. The nominee fails to notice the love and support of his grandmother woven into his bootstraps. During his 1996 presidential campaign, Texas senator Phil Gramm—a relentless purveyor of the bootstrap myth—warns that "we have gone too far in creating an entitlement society." His sentiment is echoed in turn by each of his opponents, who solemnly chimes in his own warnings about the grave threat to the republic posed by welfare, unemployment compensation, and any other government handout the candidate himself is not likely to need. A little research always reveals that the speaker is, in fact, hip-deep in government relief. Senator Gramm is in up to his shoulders—his expenses as a child paid for by a father on a veterans' disability pension, his tuition at the University of Georgia paid for by the War Orphans Act, his graduate education paid for by a

National Defense Education Act fellowship, his salary as a professor at Texas A & M University paid for by the citizens of Texas and as a member of the U.S. House of Representatives and Senate by the citizens of the United States.

Senator Gramm might be faulted for being unusually shameless, but not for being unusual. It's a rare one of us who does not cheerfully and unapologetically accept encouragement and inspiration from teachers, helping hands from friends, sympathetic ears from strangers, aid and comfort from family members, offers to open doors, smooth paths, and cut corners from cronies, trust-fund annuities and down payments for houses from parents (and inheritances not many years later), mortgage interest deductions and tax credits from the federal government, decades of love, understanding, and forbearance from spouses and children—and then claim to be self-made! One is grateful for the occasional blunt statement of truth, like this from Metromedia founder John Kluge, one of America's wealthiest men, on how a simple fellow goes out and makes a billion dollars: "The greatest factor in my life—and I know entrepreneurial people don't want to express it, they think it diminishes them—but luck plays a large part."

In Peru, New Guinea, and Namibia we discover men in strange hats and marvel at how different from us these people are. What should impress us is how like us they are. On Cerrillos Road on a bleak December morning, I felt a chill that had nothing to do with the weather when I began to hear my voice echoing in the voice of another man and to see the lines of my story weaving through his own.

In New Mexico, Thomas's luck failed to improve. His will began to falter. He went on the dole, drank some, drank some more, failed to find permanent work, lasting friendship, a woman to love. Not long before I met him someone stole everything he owned. It wasn't much—a bag with some clothes and a few other belongings. But the violation shook him deeply. It seemed to be the only thing that angered him.

"I just don't see how anyone could do that," he kept repeating. "Take a man's clothes practically right off his back. That's one thing I just don't understand."

He was not even bitter over the irony of being homeless in one of America's most glittering cities.

"There's good people in Santa Fe and there's bad people in Santa Fe," he reflected with a shrug. "Just like anywhere." Earlier that morning he had heard about a job, and he intended to apply for it, though he wasn't optimistic about being hired. He smiled. "I'm not as smart as the president of IBM."

I knew he wouldn't get the job, or that if he did he wouldn't keep it, because I had met him before, scores of times, on the front porch of my childhood home in Pennsylvania. Beaten, sheepish men—bums we called them. They showed up at our house asking for handouts. My mother enjoyed a kind of celebrity in those days. Her fans, if that is what they were, came from far and wide to knock at her door. When one arrived she plunked him down on the porch swing and handed him a magazine to read. Then she went into the kitchen and cooked up a hot meal of meat, potatoes, fresh vegetables, salad, bread, coffee, and homemade berry pie. She arranged this feast on her best china and carried it out to the porch as though she were serving a king. I think my mother fed bums as a way of nourishing her children. I think that she nourished herself, too, and that that was one of the reasons she lived a long and happy life.

I kicked at a block of cinder-encrusted snow. The sun slipped behind the gray overcast and froze. Tonight the temperature would plunge to zero. I asked Thomas where he had spent the previous night.

He glanced at me from a corner of his eye and laughed. He owned a few blankets, he said. He managed to stay warm. He pointed across the road to an open area slanting down to the Santa Fe Railroad tracks.

"Over there in the prairie dog town."

Thinking he was joking, I laughed. Then, realizing he was serious, I looked across four lanes of traffic toward the spot where he was pointing. My stomach turned.

"The cops don't usually hassle you but the railroad don't let you have a fire. Sometimes I go to the shelters but it's embarrassing. They run them like a military operation. There's no place that's perfect."

He tugged his raincoat tighter around him. Suddenly I wanted to be gone, to be as far away from this man as possible. We talked for a few minutes more. Then, abruptly and rudely, I told him I had to leave. I stood and shook his hand, then hurried off, leaving him seated on the curb.

As quickly as I could I returned to the center of town, where I wanted to be, among the relentlessly uniform buildings of Territorial and Spanish-Pueblo Santa Fe. And there I saw the fallacy of the Historical Zoning Ordinance of 1957 and its grand vision of a perfectly unified city. The fallacy is that perfection cannot be achieved by proclamation, and unity cannot be built with bricks. The unity of a city arises from its people, in their ability to join together in common cause, to share hopes and dreams and at least a small degree of prosperity. The oneness of Santa Fe and, no doubt, of most American cities runs as deep as stucco siding. Paradoxically, Santa Fe's entrancing design works to destroy the very harmony it is meant to promote. It is like a magnificent painting of heartbreak, whose splendor so overshadows its subject that we fail to perceive what the painting is about—or even to care. So blinded, we drift further and further from the only true source of unity that is possible, and that is the ability to see through buildings and walls into each other's eyes, and to be able to say: Those people are us. That child is my child. That person is me.

(5)

Christmas in New Mexico is a vibrant and luminous holiday, a grand synthesis of delights combining the old and familiar with the new, the exotic, and the unexpected. The combination is exactly right, for it places personal experience of Christmas at the center, where it belongs, and at the same time points toward a more universal expression of the season that is paramount, yet easily overlooked. For an old conservative in these matters, raised in the Lake Erie snowbelt, trained in the preeminence of the scotch pine in the living room and the blizzard at the door, I was alarmed not many years ago to find myself in New Mexico, my somewhat mysterious new home, with this most precisely defined of holidays approaching. Could a place that revered salsa music and pinto beans measure up to my exacting standards for Christmas?

I had nothing to fear. This is a state whose forests are deep and piney and whose ski areas boast some of the deepest and fluffiest snow to be found anywhere in the country. Through the winter the northern frontier towns crackle in delicious subzero temperatures that can make even the Lake Erie region seem temperate. (It hit thirty-eight below in the town of Dulce, New Mexico, on Christmas Eve in 1990.) Carol and I found a scotch pine at a local tree lot. On Christmas Eve the snow started flying, and by morning several inches of powder lay on the ground. To my surprise I felt at home, properly connected to family and friends, to childhood and memories, to the personally designed traditions that give Christmas its unique and irresistible character.

Along with the old I found much here that was new to heighten my enjoyment of the holiday. There was, to begin with, the geography of New Mexico. Much of the state outside the northern mountains has the look and feel of the place where Christmas began. Water is scarce. The land is harsh. Traveling a back road on a gray winter day, one has an easy time imagining the howling wastes of the Old Testament. One might even see shepherds tending their flocks on the treeless expanses of the southeast or along an arroyo on Diné lands or on the intermountain park that rolls south from the town of Chama.

Through the crisp evenings leading up to Christmas the air reels from the dreamy aromas of piñon and juniper. Then on the final night the darkness comes alive with the assembled light of untold numbers of *farolitos*. The farolito is a Spanish invention, a paper bag containing a few handfuls of sand and a tiny candle. Two or three farolitos don't amount to much. But New Mexicans set them out by the dozens in front yards, by the thousands in city plazas. Each timid glow joins the next and then the next, and soon the state where light is as essential as food and water is afire, a new star in the firmament. Planes steer by it. Satellite networks are disturbed. Lost sheep find their way home.

The Native American celebration of Christmas is an explosion of music, dance, and pageantry that lasts for days and can make visitors forget their fruitcake and their eggnog. At some of the pueblos, men fly like eagles. (This actually happens.) At San Juan, boogiemen devour naughty children. (This is only a simulation.) At several pueblos, actors perform *Los Matachines*, a four-centuries-old drama rooted partly in Aztec tradition, partly in medieval mystery play. Often, Anglos and Hispanics are invited into the homes of Indians to join in the feasting. To a person so invited, such an invitation, coming from one who might be forgiven for choosing selfishness over generosity, may come as a shock. Yet the practice only expresses the theme of goodwill toward all people, which under the circumstances ought not to be surprising. That it is may produce a second and even greater shock.

Paradoxically, the opening up of the boundaries of Christmas that is possible in New Mexico has a narrowing effect as well. By looking beyond one's personal definition of the holiday to other more challenging definitions, one begins to see what is unique to each and what is common to all. The year of my Santa Fe Christmas I caught sight of something I had forgotten long ago, an element of the holidays that is common to all traditions. It was an image of a poor carpenter and his wife far from home seeking shelter from the cold and the night. For the first time since my childhood, I wanted to frame that image and hang it on my Christmas tree.

At a little over a year of age, Jake was about to celebrate his first Christmas that would register as more than a glow of candlelight in his eyes. He delighted in the tree and quickly adopted a set of favorite ornaments on the lower branches. Several times a day he collected the ornaments and deposited them in his toy box. On Christmas morning he would learn that packages contain surprises, and he would learn to liberate the latter from the former, not always elegantly. Sometimes he asked Carol or me to lift him to view the manger scene on the mantle over the fireplace. Chipped and faded, a relic of sixty Christmases past, it seemed to speak to him like a revered member of the family. He gazed at the figures one by one—the wise men, the cow with three legs, the three figures grouped at the center whom he understood to be mother, father, and child.

Late on the afternoon of Christmas Eve, as the frail winter sky shattered and fell and the grand light of the farolitos rose up over New Mexico, we three drove to Santa Fe. It was about an hour from our house, up the storied valley that the Spanish traversed on their way to Santa Fe, where the Puebloans dwell and the river shapes the land. Clouds were moving in and the air was bitterly cold. Snow was forecast for later in the evening.

Unlike most cities, which on Christmas Eve pause for a few hours of deep breathing and introspection, Santa Fe slips into a state of heightened activity. Strollers bundled in furs and ski jackets crowd the sidewalks. Carolers gather at street corners. Cars creep bumper to bumper around the plaza, and a driver occasionally lowers a window to shout greetings to a passerby. In the nearby neighborhoods, residents kneel in their front yards to kindle *luminarias*—small fires of piñon logs, symbols of the fires of the shepherds of Bethlehem. More light and it is riveting: at each luminaria a crowd of revelers gathers to gossip or to stare into the coals, perhaps to enjoy warm drinks provided by the fire builder.

We passed through the center of town and exited the historical zone to the north. As though we had crossed a border into a new land, we saw the character of the surroundings change at once. The homes grew smaller and less imposing. Chainlink fences separated some of the lots. Old American-made cars stood in the driveways. Here and there graffiti-marred walls crowded the sidewalks. As we drove down a dark street toward our destination a Labrador retriever, lost and wild-eyed, charged past us into the night. We turned at the Praise Tabernacle and pulled into the parking lot at 804 Alarid Street—St. Elizabeth Shelter for the Homeless. It seemed a likely place to locate that shelter sketch I wanted for our tree.

St. Elizabeth's and its guests belie the myths of the homeless shelter. It is an attractive and dignified place, staffed by skilled professionals under the leadership of its imaginative and caring director, Hank Hughes. Volunteers and donations from concerned Santa Feans keep it afloat. The halls are clean and bright, lined with posters, photographs, and notices of job openings and support group meetings. One hallway leads to the dining room past an alcove containing a library and a television set. The other leads to separate men's and women's dormitories. (At another location, St. Elizabeth's maintains a complex of apartments for families.) Each evening several dozen sane, sober, hardworking men and women come through the door seeking refuge from the night. It will be temporary refuge only; guests are expected to move on after a few days.

The sun had set by the time Carol, Jake, and I arrived, and the shelter was nearly full. We wandered through the building trying to seem festive and comfortable, without much success on either score. Some guests lay on their bunks reading, napping, or staring at the ceiling. Others drifted up and down the halls, stopping to study the bulletin board or to engage friends in conversation. Half a dozen people lounged on sofas in the alcove. In the kitchen a volunteer crew readied a special Christmas Eve supper. The food, like much of that served year-round at St. Elizabeth's, was donated by several Santa Fe restaurateurs.

Not long after arriving I realized that something seemed to be missing. I had expected the atmosphere to be more frenetic. Perhaps I imagined rude, enraged, or deranged guests screaming or shoving each other in the hallways.

On the contrary, the shelter's most striking characteristic was its tranquility. No peals of laughter echoed up and down the halls, no shouts greeted new arrivals at the door. The guests were quiet and subdued—partly from exhaustion, partly from melancholy, I guessed, neither out of place under the circumstances.

Observing those around me and trying to imagine what had brought them there that night, I thought of Coronado and his mistaken belief that he would find the Seven Cities of Cíbola, a place that did not even exist. Like him, the explorers of St. Elizabeth's had been tricked into believing that by proceeding diligently in a steadfast direction they would reach their destinations—homes, jobs, financial success. The trick was that there were not enough of any of these to go around. Match up all the dwellings in America with people having the means to rent or purchase them, and thousands of Americans will still be sleeping in the streets. Fill every available job from the ranks of the unemployed, and millions will still be jobless. Divide the wealth of the nation among all of our citizens, and so long as some are millionaires, others must be paupers. It isn't that the guests at St. Elizabeth's were stupid or lazy or unworthy, though some of them may have been that; it's simply that even if all of them plus everyone else in the United States were bright, industrious, and eminently worthy, some would still be left out in the cold. In this relentless game of musical chairs, some of the players are practical, some are clever and quick, some are ruthless, some are wise. Some, like John Kluge, are lucky. And when the music stops, some, no matter what their attributes, will not find a place to sit down. I felt honored to be in the august company of a few of the latter, who persevered despite their circumstances.

My feeling of admiration grew during dinner as I spoke with some of the guests. Kathy McKesson is an articulate, animated woman with long brown curls and a brandy-smooth Louisiana drawl. A year before, after leaving a battered woman's shelter in Texas, she found herself in "a nowhere situation." With little money and no car she worked her way at one job after another to Santa Fe—"riding buses, praying a lot." She hoped that in fabulous Santa Fe she would find friends, a good job, a new beginning.

So far she had found none of it. But like everyone I spoke with that evening, Kathy McKesson had a job: she worked at Taco Bell earning fast-food wages. At Taco Bell she would earn in a year what the CEOs of several American corporations earn in an hour, what outfielder Barry Bonds of the San Francisco Giants earns every two innings he plays. If she could save the several thousand dollars she would need to move into an apartment, which she could not, she would see ninety percent of her wages eaten up in rent and utilities. It seemed clear that Kathy McKesson would not be staying long in Santa Fe.

Nor would the others with whom I spoke. Martin Kelleher is a short, stocky man with a neat mustache and a sly smile. He is a writer of short stories, a fancier of the works of Gabriel García Márquez. For the past month Kelleher had played Santa Claus at Santa Fe's Villa Linda Mall. In the morning, his employment ended, he would climb into his truck and head for Seattle, where he had friends and, he thought, the prospect of a job. Martin Kelleher was not angry over the irony of a homeless Santa Claus, but instead bemused by it. He had profited from the experience, he said, for it had given him the idea for a new story. In Kelleher's story, God will play Santa Claus and humans will sit on His knee asking for chocolates and eternal life.

Nor would the dark, intense young man who calls himself Christian Joe, a bell ringer for the Salvation Army, be staying. Nor would Patrick Cleland, a veteran of Vietnam, nor Anna Spence, a frightened, bewildered woman of sixty who arrived just as my family and I were about to depart, and who in a hollow voice told the receptionist that she needed a safe place to sleep. Surely they would not be long in Santa Fe, a city like every city in America, with a look and a feel—a style—that seem to define it and drive it and invest it with meaning and purpose but under scrutiny reveal a shattered core flying apart like fragments of an exploding star. On this night at least there was unity among the most distant and fastest flying of the particles, a brief coming together into incandescence. And on dark Alarid Street, a light as bright as a million farolitos—a light of courage, resilience, and hope—shone at Number 804.

The power of the mountains, cold and juniper-spiced, drifted down from the Sangre de Cristos and settled over the streets and houses of Santa Fe. In the magic of the evening, Carol, Jake, and I slipped and slid our way along Washington Street. Dangling at his mother's hand my son took on his first icy sidewalk like a new ride at the playground.

St. Elizabeth's was behind us, its guests safe for another night. We were out to enjoy the evening and, just as important, to put distance between ourselves and the shelter as rapidly as possible, the faster to assure ourselves that we had stepped back to our side of the line.

As we rounded a corner and entered the old plaza, a dream of perfect Christmas opened before our eyes. Kids skated in the street. Blithe walkers, frosty breath at their lips, strolled arm-in-arm under the porticos. Shop windows glowed with displays of toys, canned hams, and crisp new clothes. Remembering my friend's homage to Santa Fe, I kissed a beautiful woman in the snow. Jake looked on jealously, then asked to be picked up and carried. We slipped in among the strollers, joined them as though we were family. I found myself smiling and wishing well to strangers who caught my eye. The chill night, the antiquity of the surroundings, the passersby bundled so fastidiously—it was the wrong time and place but I couldn't help thinking of Dickens. I half expected to see Bob Cratchit hurrying by with a turkey under his arm.

In the park at the center of the plaza an unearthly radiance rose up, the aurora of a thousand farolitos. We crossed the street and entered the brightness, gathering its warmth and its strength.

It was quiet there, and beautiful. We walked slowly among the candles, taking in the light. It seemed eternal, yet somehow fragile enough to extinguish with a single breath.

And soon it was too much and we were in the car, driving higher and higher out of the city and the light, up winding streets where old men walked in the shadows, over dark arroyos harboring the sleeping millions, past battered Fords and Chevies where children slept and parents kept watch in the night.

Amid the majestic hills that adorn Santa Fe like a crown we stopped and in a small clearing beside the road stood rapt in the deep silence of Christmas Eve—even Jake, bundled to the teeth against the bitter cold. To the east, Sun Mountain glimmered in snowlight. Above, the sky roiled with the harbingers of an approaching storm.

But to the south over the benighted valley of the Rio Grande the sky was yet clear. It was spangled in stars. They were brighter, sharper, and more immediate, I thought, than I had ever seen them before. That fortune in crown jewels was fashioned in true Santa Fe Style! How clear it was to me then that the shelter I had been seeking to understand was much more than a simple clearing by the road, or a homeless refuge on the wrong side of town, or an old city in the Sangre de Cristo Mountains. Those are but tiny rooms in the only shelter we will ever know, this grand spinning planet we inhabit one and all, our lifelong refuge from the storm. Here in our hallowed sanctuary we join in the pageant of life and death, cast ourselves as heroes or tyrants, and share in a common fate. Here like Londoners in the Underground we take on the monumental task of being human and in our most solemn decision choose whether to hope or to despair.

The wind freshened, the mountain air coiled tighter around us. In the final moment before I escaped into the warmth of the car I thought of the ones we call the faceless, those stalwart souls who like the lights over Santa Fe burn with an unquenchable inner fire. I looked up and picked out a star, a silvery, blazing Christmas star, and I vowed that it would become the face of them all. From that moment till the end of time the star will shine on, unmistakable in its meaning. Whoever gazes up will see it and recognize its countenance. And the stalwart will never be faceless again.

And I gave a name to the star. I called it Thomas of Prairie Dog Town.

DEATH ON A
DISTANT PLAIN

It's more than wind.

—*Walter Van Tilburg Clark,* The Ox-Bow Incident

T he rule is a simple one, familiar to hangmen the world over: a stout victim requires a stout rope. At more than two hundred pounds the appointed victim, a brazen, compulsive train robber known as "Black Jack" Ketchum, clearly qualified as stout. Sheriff Pablo Baca of Union County, New Mexico, had never presided over a hanging, but he knew the rule. Mildly discomposed by the prospect of botching the first execution ever conducted in the county seat of Clayton, Baca (a prudent man) procured a hank of hemp beefy enough to string up a Brahma bull. Then, just to make sure, he scheduled a dress rehearsal—a kind of mock execution for beginners—the night before the event. As a stand-in for Ketchum, the sheriff chose a two-hundred-pound sack of sand.

With everything in order, Baca sprang the trapdoor. The door flew open, the sack fell, the rope held. The sheriff went home to a good night's sleep, satisfied that he had engaged the right rope for the job. The faithful sack of sand he left swinging in the wind. By morning any merciful give the hemp might have possessed when the evening began had given. The bounce was gone. The rope was stiff as a corpse.

Practically everyone in Union County turned out to witness the execution. Because the curious fate that befell Black Jack Ketchum that day has occurred only one other time in history, the date—April 26, 1901—is famous in the annals of hanging. Security was tight. The seeming impregnability of the gallows behind the walls of a closely guarded stockade didn't dampen the spirits of the crowd, which buzzed with rumors that Black Jack's gang would attempt a last-minute rescue of its leader. For the occasion, Ketchum, a handsome man with carefully coifed black hair and a thick black mustache, donned a black suit, white shirt, white bow tie, and spit-polished black shoes. Something of a blusterer, he arrived at the stockade not in the obligatory condition of melancholy but in apparent high spirits. He mounted the steps confidently and joked with the witnesses. As Sheriff Baca slipped the noose over Ketchum's head, the condemned man graciously assisted in the operation, shimmying his chin and tightening the muscles in his neck, as though he were about to shave.

"Hurry up," he growled good-naturedly. "I'm due in hell for dinner."

His gang was nowhere to be seen. The rumored rescue did not come off. All that distinguished the notorious train robber's final seconds on earth were the whistle of the wind and then, at the last moment, the deadly hush of the crowd.

The sheriff sprang the trapdoor. Ketchum plunged through the platform. Scant inches from the ground he hit the end of the stiff rope. The jolt was mighty. It flipped his head off like a cap from a bottle of Carlson's ginger beer. The awful sphere rolled toward a cluster of spectators, causing quite a stir and ruining what was supposed to be a festive occasion. Years later a Scottish authority on capital punishment determined that Ketchum was one of only two men ever to lose his head in a hanging. Since the other man suffered his dissociation somewhere in Europe, Black Jack established something of an American record for the town of Clayton, New Mexico. No one knew that at the time, of course, so no solace was provided. Most people went home that day in a foul mood.

I was reminded of Black Jack's woeful demise one afternoon when I witnessed another not far from where he came to the end of his rope so ingloriously. I was driving the byways of northeastern New Mexico, stopping in towns that now and then popped up beside the road, not much bigger than stop signs, to talk to people about guns. It seemed an appropriate place to conduct such an inquiry because the region was once raw-boned American frontier, where guns had the currency of food and water and where violence managed to find a warm spot for itself in the nation's heart. Bordering Texas and Oklahoma, it is ocean-sized rangeland inhabited mostly by cattle and spaciousness. No fences, no houses, no trees, no hills, no fuss: just buffalo grass and blue grama loping over the endless plains like an unvexed mustang in a summer rain. As a wag once said of a speech by William Jennings Bryan: You could waltz to it.

The county I was in, like each of the six counties in this corner of New Mexico, is larger than Delaware. It has no doctors, two grocery stores, and a population of 987. If the entire populace gathered at a strawberry social, there would still be room left over in the rest of the county to herd in the world's remaining residents, all five and a half billion of them, with each person getting a plot of prairie grass about the size of a picnic cloth.

People who decide to get rich by running cattle in their backyards soon discover that they need either larger backyards or smaller notions of what it means to get rich. A rancher requires forty acres of rangeland just to satisfy one cow, and many cows to make a living. For that reason, cattle ranching has never been a backyard business. Some ranches in this part of the state are more like grand duchies, a few of them topping three hundred thousand acres. Trucks, railroads, and machines do much of the work that used to fall to cowboys, but never fear: travel the back roads of northeastern New Mexico and you'll still encounter square-jawed trail riders driving herds of whiteface cattle before them, and you'll see rivers called the Pecos and the Cimarron, and you may get a sizable lump in your throat contemplating what you're witnessing. Back when it was still legal to smoke a cigarette they filmed Marlboro commercials near a stop sign called Roy. A few miles from that fabled location as I bounded along a dirt road that divided the earth into two equal portions, I spotted a glitch in the evenness ahead. One doesn't need binoculars to spot glitches in northeastern New Mexico; they display like oversexed sage grouse. But conventional rules of perspective do not obtain. The glitch surely grew larger as I approached it, but so, proportionally, did the rest of the world. When I reached the cause of all the excitement—a half-ton steer dead beside the road of an unknown cause—I stopped to pay my respects. The animal was enormous, I suppose, but in that sky-framing scene practically invisible.

The steer appeared to have died in mid-run. Its stiff legs pointed at me at weird angles, like rifles poking through the windows of a farmhouse. Black Jack Ketchum was a stout man who required a stout rope, but photographs of him taken as the noose was slipped over his neck show a curiously diminutive figure, like my steer dwarfed by his circumstances. A kind soul with a measure of respect for a man's dignity reattached Ketchum's head somehow, and a party appointed by the sheriff planted him in an unmarked grave. Standing beside a lifeless steer, gazing out over the plains, I perceived that the whole wide expanse is something of an unmarked grave. A fragment of a song floated into my mind: *Oh, bury me not on the lone prairie.* And for the first time I understood that poor cowboy's lament.

It was a sunny April afternoon. The day would have been warm but for a mean, infuriating wind that scudded over the plains and shoved me hard in the face. The powerful smell of the earth, the height of the sky, the hum and slap of the wind: I felt as frail and inconsequential as a blade of bunchgrass waving in a narrow gutter by the road. For a moment I registered a rousing feeling of kinship with Black Jack Ketchum and a mortifying side of beef. And I thought how death on the high plains can seem small and faintly ridiculous.

Of all the adversaries that grind you down out here, it's the wind that delivers the fatal blow—the wind and the bottomless silence that tails it and socks you in the gut when the wind cuts out suddenly, as it does from time to time, and you feel like you've fallen through a trapdoor. They tell a story in northeastern New Mexico about a time when the wind blew unremittingly for twenty days, and everyone feared that at last it had become a permanent ailment. And then one morning it stopped abruptly and all the chickens fell over. That's supposed to be a story about adaptability and its hazards, but it also suggests that wind has a more complex personality than we sometimes give it credit for.

The same can be said for the quietude that tags behind, a true silent partner to the wind. Pioneer women on the plains sometimes found themselves at home alone for days at a time. In some places and in some seasons there were no birds to dispel the quiet with their singing. The only insects were fleas and lice on the buffalo, and they did not sing songs. The silence was infernal. Some of the women went mad.

Of wind and silence it's probably the former that causes more suffering, if only because there's more of it. In Clayton and Roy the wind may blow three hundred days a year. Novelist Max Evans resided in northeastern New Mexico for a time, working a small ranch near the town of Des Moines. He's written often about this country. The wind lurks in the background in many of his stories. Like the chinooks of the Pacific Northwest and the foehn of the Swiss Alps, the high-plains wind affects the public behavior. Evans says it makes people restless and irritable. Sometimes it inspires them to violence.

Revisionist historians have exploded many of the myths about the American West, but one remains unchallenged: the Old West was a violent place. New Mexico saw some of the worst of the bloodshed. Historian W. Eugene Hollon conjectures that New Mexico may have indicted more men for murder and convicted fewer of them than any other state.

Well into the nineteenth century much of the area around Clayton remained a no-man's land between Anglo and Hispanic jurisdictions. When New Mexico became a U.S. territory, law enforcement was assigned to a handful of peace officers, each of whom sometimes found himself several days' ride from the scene of a crime. The Santa Fe Trail sliced through the region, providing easy pickings for marauding Utes and other native peoples of the plains. The arrival of cows and railroads in this land of opportunity produced occasions for new varieties of mischief. Almost overnight, cattle rustlers and train robbers moved into the area. Fifty or sixty of them made their headquarters at Robber's Roost, a hole-in-the-wall in the desolate canyon country north of Clayton. Disputes among various permutations of cattle, sheep, real estate, and other business interests led to minor flare-ups, and now and then to long-running hostilities, popularly and accurately known as "wars."

West of Clayton, the Colfax County War, a feud between landowners and squatters, dragged on for twenty years. In the southern part of the state a cattle war raged between the Good and Lee factions in the late 1880s. Both conflicts cost scores of lives.

The best known of the disputes, the Lincoln County War, lasted from 1878 till 1881 and may have been responsible for as many as two hundred deaths. It began as a rivalry between mercantile interests and degenerated into mob rule that eventually attracted the attention of President Rutherford B. Hayes. He sent in federal troops but failed to stop the war.

At the center of the conflict was a genial 140-pound psychopathic killer from New York City named William Bonney. Some authorities claim that the last name of this twenty-four-carat desperado was Antrim; others say it was McCarty. Whoever he was, in 1873 he emigrated to New Mexico, where he made a name for himself that everyone agrees on: Billy the Kid. He's a beloved folk hero here now, a local boy who made if not good, the kind of bad that is *so* bad that a century later you find yourself growing misty-eyed over it. Practically every town in eastern New Mexico has a legend about the Kid showing up unexpectedly and befriending a local widow or pitching horseshoes behind the feed store or casually blowing someone's brains out. Usually the stories are rendered in highly affectionate terms. Nobody knows how many people the Kid murdered, but it was a few. He himself died violently about a hundred miles south of Roy in a shoot-out with Sheriff Pat Garrett.

Most settlers on the frontier did not rob trains, and local legend to the contrary, few were murdered by Billy the Kid or anyone else. The best evidence suggests that ordinary citizens were peaceful, law-abiding men and women who preferred to die of natural causes and usually succeeded. Several authorities have concluded that the preeminent feature of frontier life was boredom. Scrupulous research has failed to document a single shoot-out at high noon anywhere in the West. The complex and thrilling mythology of the frontier was fabricated from a pitifully small stock of real people and actual events, mostly by dime novelists and Hollywood screenwriters capitalizing on the psychic needs of a nation too quickly hammered together to evolve a creation story based on trees, birds, or seasons of the sun but—no less than Egypt, Greece, or Rome—desperate to believe it was descended from gods, not all of them pure. It is undoubtedly true that because the law was likely to be a long way off, just about everyone on the frontier owned a gun. But few people ever got the opportunity to pull the trigger on anything more vital than a bottle of ginger beer.

The Old West is dead, and most of the desperadoes along with it, but in

Clayton, New Mexico, at least, one thing has not changed: practically everyone still owns a gun. Granted, one no longer sees shotguns framed in the windows of pickup trucks; in recent years, firearms have begun to prove as enticing as stereos to thieves, so pickup owners have swallowed their pride and switched to handguns in glove compartments.

But if the Clayton arsenal is no longer as visible as it once was, it is no less an object of civic pride. Outside the Rabbit Ear Cafe, a middle-aged rancher in Lee jeans and bolo tie told me he owns eleven firearms. Three are antiques, family heirlooms useful mostly for admiring; the rest he employs to hunt, target shoot, and "naturally," he said, protect himself and his family. I had judged the rancher to be a man not easily moved, but as we spoke I detected a hint of emotion creeping into his voice and a slight flushing of his cheeks. Then he looked over my shoulder into the distance, and I saw that I had touched on an affair of the heart and that merely by asking my question I had betrayed a vulgar atheism that elevated the man's pulse rate.

To one degree or another I elicited passion in everyone I surveyed. When I asked, Do you own a gun? the respondent did not immediately blurt out an answer. Rather, he or she paused in wonder at the question, as though I had asked, Do you live and breathe? Then each resolutely told all. A store owner kept a gun behind the counter to protect himself. Another kept one gun at work and two at home. Two women in a convenience store carried guns in their purses, which they were delighted to brandish in my direction. The manager of a motel opened a drawer to reveal a handgun laid out on a piece of cloth like a string of pearls. My survey was decidedly unscientific, but it turned up several distinct trends. Of the twenty or so people I polled in a town of about three thousand residents, each owned at least one gun. Each spoke of guns fearfully yet fondly. All expressed the belief that their lives were somehow in danger. And nearly every one made something approximating the following declaration: I own a gun. I would use it to kill another human being. But I am not a violent person.

At the Clayton police department I received at least presumptive corroboration of my results. I talked to an officer who estimated that ninety-nine percent of the adults in Clayton own a gun, and many of them many guns.

Unlike the police of many large metropolitan areas, the officer, a lifetime member of the National Rifle Association, opposed any kind of gun control. He could remember only two or three murders in Union County over the past decade or so. Perhaps because guns were a long-standing tradition in Clayton, people here understood them and respected them. Children were taught to use guns safely. Adults employed them only for sport and for self-defense. The officer spoke of guns as kindly instruments of peace. My impression that I had entered an armed camp was way off the mark. On the contrary, the guns of Clayton provided for a safe, happy town. It was different here than it was in New York City or Los Angeles, I learned. In Clayton, people were not violent.

In a report issued following the urban riots of the 1960s, the National Commission on the Causes and Prevention of Violence suggested that "Americans have always been given to a kind of historical amnesia that masks much of their turbulent past." Instead of gazing coldly at the record, we engage in "a process of selective recollection." Not long after I spoke to the Clayton policeman I contacted the Office of the Medical Investigator in Albuquerque, which looks into every homicide committed in New Mexico. A staff person confirmed not two or three murders in Union County in a decade, but five in eight years, a rate more than twice that recalled by the officer. Extrapolated from the county population of 4,500, the figures translate into an annual rate of 13.9 homicides per 100,000 population, nearly half the rates registered by New York City, Chicago, Los Angeles, and Philadelphia.

City dwellers convinced that if things get bad enough they can always escape to the safety of a rural area may find those numbers discouraging. Compared with the homicide rates of foreign countries, the figures are more than discouraging, they are stupefying. Guns were responsible for four of the five murders committed in Union County in eight years. By contrast, in Canada in a locality with a population equivalent to that of Union County, four gun murders will occur not in eight years but in a rather longer period of time—about three thousand years. (Three thousand years ago Moses led the Israelites out of Egypt.)

It would be a relief to know that the residents of Union County are a uniquely self-deceived citizenry suffering from delusions of peaceableness.

But delusions of peaceableness are a national disorder, not one confined to northeastern New Mexico. Historian Richard Hofstadter's exhaustive inquiry into the history of violence in America led him to conclude that our uniqueness lies not in the absolute *quantity* of our violent acts (other nations, many of whose pious citizens are today quite eager to lecture Americans about the evils of violence, have displayed masterful proficiency in organizing genocidal catastrophes whose short-term horrors dwarf anything ever visited upon the United States); what distinguishes us is the extraordinary *frequency* of our savagery, "its sheer commonplaceness in history." Equally distinctive, concludes Hofstadter, is our astonishing ability in the face of the record to see ourselves as among the best behaved and most lawful of people. If the citizens of Clayton perhaps overeagerly describe themselves as nonviolent even in the presence of houses full of guns they are entirely ready to discharge, they are no different from most of us. While most Americans would undoubtedly agree that we live in a violent nation, few of us are above indulging in the hallowed tradition of discovering the cause of the problem at least three counties away. Peering into our closets we somehow fail to notice the weapons that implicate ourselves in the crime.

Again and again in Clayton I heard a declaration based on a cherished but rarely questioned article of American faith, one that goes a long way toward explaining why our rate of bloodshed is so high. If I caught someone crawling out a window with my stereo, goes the oath, I'd kill him. In this commonplace equating of human life with an article of metal and plastic one hears a chilling casualness and thoughtlessness; there is a dead certainty about it that reveals a zealot searching for a target. One may assuredly have a moral as well as a legal right to blow away an intruder. But our readiness to do so—indeed, our pride in our readiness to do so—betrays such ardent disdain for that thief clambering through the window that it is hard not to view it in a broader context, one that appears to devalue all life while conveniently hiding behind a Supreme Court–approved code of behavior. Of course a man's home is his castle; but since when should that be the only justification one needs to put another man in his grave?

Since the era of those clever Anglo-Saxons, apparently, and their famous stereo-exalting principle that asserts that property rights are superior to the right to life. In a world growing more stereo-oriented every minute, we ought not to be surprised that the Anglo-Saxons, who bathed infrequently and ate raw meat, are routinely praised for their legal genius. But in our exultation over their sly promotion of home to castle, it would be wrong for us to forget that what they established is just what we say it is—a principle, not grounds for anarchy—and that it was laid down at a time when simply accomplished death did not lie within easy reach of every property holder. It is true that most killings in the United States are not committed by law-abiding citizens defending their stereos. They are committed by violent people with utter disregard for human life and with the weapons needed to formalize that disregard: which is to say, people not that much different from ourselves. Duplicates of their weapons are to be found in tens of millions of American homes. An echo of their disregard can be heard in every oath that equates people with property.

In my motel room in Clayton I flipped on the television set. HBO was showing *Out for Justice,* starring Steven Seagal: "A Brooklyn policeman tries to kill his partner's killer and anyone else who needs to be killed." On another channel two glistening black boxers in elemental garb pummeled each other toward premature senility, while outside the ring the crowd cheered. CNN brought news of an execution by lethal injection in Texas. Meanwhile, California was gearing up for its first execution in twenty-five years. ("He's been breathing smog his entire life," joked a comedian on a talk show, cracking up the audience. "What makes anyone think a little cyanide's going to bother him?") Polls showed that Americans favored speeding up what we call "the wheels of justice" in capital crimes. We were growing impatient over all the waiting. Tight as ropes forced to hold sandbags through the night, we were ready to snap.

"Supreme Court fed up with execution delays," headlined the *Albuquerque Journal* on my bedside table. Feverish though we were, we were like Arthur Koestler's pragmatic Rubashov, unable, due to lack of imagination, to picture the details of an execution. So when news came in from California a few hours later that a man named Robert Alton Harris was dead at last (dignity in an execution consists in referring to the deceased by his full name), we were invited into the death chamber by the media. The final meal, the last words, the tears, the cheers, the popping of the eyes. At each disclosure one's heart leapt with rapture. *We're a tough, unsentimental people. We're not violent, but we do what we have to do.*

Not far from my motel, not far from every motel, not far from every quiet street and ivy-covered home in America, a man bullied his wife and a woman threatened her child and an employer intimidated an employee and a teacher browbeat a student. A new estimate raised to 180,000 the number of Iraqis we killed in the Gulf War. Not a large number—the population of Tacoma, give or take a few bodies. Nothing to be alarmed about. Look what Hitler did! *Let's settle this man to man.* In times of crisis our resourcefulness knows no bounds. Five murder victims in Union County between 1984 and 1991, four by the pain of gunfire. The fifth, a 79-year-old man, was bludgeoned to death with a hammer. It is music, it is art, it is how we express ourselves, the blithe and brilliant manner in which we splatter the landscape with blood. Wrote Richard Hofstadter: "The old American tolerance for the violent act may have been founded on some secret sympathy for it."

And sympathy for the gun. Saints are often remembered for the folksy qualities they exhibited as mere earthlings. So too is the supreme symbol of American violence. Long after the beatification of the gun we like to pretend it is just a tool, a practical device for a practical people—not much different from a hedge clipper or a set of measuring spoons. Ironically, the National Rifle Association is even stingier in its praise, asserting that guns are not even capable of killing people: people kill people. This is a smear so uncharitable, and so zany, that many people believe it. It robs the gun of its rightful role as pure embodiment of violence, precise cognate for violent death. To assert that guns do not kill people is to assert that bread does not nourish them. To claim that a gun is not an invitation to kill is to claim that a Ferrari is not an invitation to drive. Hang a pistol on the wall during the first act, Chekhov admonished aspiring playwrights, and you'd damn well better shoot it by the third. This was not simply an observation about plotting and dramatic flow, it was an observation about plausibility. An audience simply will not believe a gun that doesn't go off.

When George Orwell was a police officer in Burma, an elephant in a state of seasonal frenzy killed a local coolie. The citizens of the town got it in mind that it was Orwell's duty to shoot the elephant. Orwell knew that the animal's fury would soon pass, and he did not want to shoot the creature. "As soon as I saw the elephant I knew with perfect certainty that I ought not to shoot him."

But the crowd was large and the excitement was great, and before long it was clear to Orwell that he had no choice but to shoot the elephant. The catalyst that caused the crowd to demand the elephant's hide, setting Orwell on his irreversible course, was the sight of a rifle in his hands. He called it "the magical rifle."

The killing ritual followed a time-honored course. First Orwell courted the rifle (a rare treat for hedge clippers and measuring spoons). The weapon was a beautiful thing, Orwell averred. German, with cross-hair sights. The crowd chattered festively, then, as the solemn moment approached, grew still. Studying the elephant through the sights, Orwell became cold, businesslike. Moments earlier he had sympathized with the elephant, telling us that it was eating peacefully, that it had a "grandmotherly" air, that to kill it would be tantamount to murder. Then the glass fell, resolving the living creature into object. In the sights Orwell saw only a target, a duty to be done. He analyzed the shot and impassively pulled the trigger.

The change that came over Orwell as he gazed through the sights paralleled the change I observed in a young man at the New Mexico Gun Show in Albuquerque. This is an annual affair that attracts thousands of firearms enthusiasts. The young man and his friend had been joking amiably. Approaching a dealer's table, they began pawing through the scores of firearms laid out for display. The young man put his hands on a rifle he seemed to like. As he inspected the weapon his jovial manner dissolved. His facial muscles tightened. He grew grim and resolute. (No man with a rifle in his hand sports a twinkle in his eye.) Raising the weapon to his cheek he peered through the sights at an object on the far side of the hall. His friend asked him a question.

"Affirmative!" he blurted out. Evidently he had lost his power of speech. His spontaneous impairment illustrated precisely the means by which the gun robs its user of freedom, putting the lie to one of the fundamental tenets of gun love. The weapon, more powerful than the shooter, indeed shares its inherent power. But in return it demands allegiance and ultimately slavery. That is why James Baldwin described Mickey Spillane's heroes as prisoners: "Their muscles, their fists, and their tommy guns have acquired such fantastic importance."

Surrendered to the irrefutable logic of the gun, Orwell poured shot after shot into the elephant. The once-conscious human no longer struggled with the vexations of reason and conscience; bullets emerged from the gun as though self-initiated. Orwell's only thought was "to put an end to that dreadful noise." Submission to the angel of violent death required of Orwell separation from the wholeness and variety of life—from himself, his wits and powers; from the elephant, which in its agony entered "some world remote from me"; and finally, when the beast was dead at last, from Orwell's own species: "I was very glad that the coolie had been killed; it put me legally in the right and it gave me a sufficient pretext for shooting the elephant."

The tie is invincible. The circle of violence widens to admit ever more of us. Grieves Macbeth: "I am in blood, / Stepp'd in so far, that, should I wade no more, / Returning were as tedious as go o'er." We are charmed by the sophistry of violence, which blinds us to the fact that it is not necessary to shoot or to kill to be violent: to prepare for violence is to be violent. To settle more and more costly accounts, more Americans die violently each year than died the year before, and the rate of increase is accelerating. It is ludicrous to mention the totals, so besotted are we by obese, unfathomable numbers. But for the fatally curious, here is one for 1994—number murdered by firearms: 15,459.

Look at it this way: an unswerving line, a rigid silence of men, women, and children laid head to toe across the lone prairie in a narrow, unmarked grave measuring sixteen miles from one end to the other. It is a stillness of bodies which like a country road divides the earth into two equal portions, separating each of us from the wholeness and variety of life.

At one time or another, D. Ray Blakeley, president of the Union County Historical Society, has looked into just about every aspect of Clayton and Union County history that is worth bothering over. Like his counterparts in small towns the country over, those cheerful volunteer keepers of the scribble of the American past, he is privileged to know the history of his hometown not so much as a subject of scholarly study as an element of daily life, like breakfast. His family has roots in Clayton dating back to the beginning of the century. Blakeley left town for college but couldn't stay away. He returned home, where he has remained, working as a reporter for the local newspaper, the *Union County Leader*, for more than twenty-five years, and more recently for Clayton radio station KLMX.

A wiry, spirited man, Blakeley coils like a hungry cat while the questioner is framing his query, then pounces with a flurry of facts, anecdotes, theories, and juicy rumors that a doctoral candidate in history would kill for. We spent an exhilarating afternoon together, me mostly listening, Blakeley pouncing. He took me minute by minute through the hanging of Black Jack Ketchum, along the way acquainting me with his (Blakeley's) theory that it was the bag of sand that stretched the rope that led to the head that Jack lost. We visited the Hertzstein Museum, a deservedly proud showcase of local history. Then, late in the afternoon, Blakeley told me there was something he wanted to show me, something best observed in the long shadows of the falling sun. We climbed into his car and drove north from Clayton, first on state highways, then on dirt roads that shot arrow-straight across the Kiowa National Grasslands.

In the spring, in the late afternoon, the countryside is sensuous and brilliant. Its width and volume call up grand visions of the past, of Indians and pioneers and the blissful anguish of journeying west. Those with a talent for conjuring can gaze even farther into the past. In 1893 a black cowboy named George McJunkin discovered relics of what came to be known as Folsom Man fifty miles northwest of Clayton. McJunkin's find, one of the great discoveries in American anthropological history, established that humans have inhabited northeastern New Mexico for some ten thousand years. Even older, by a hundred million years or so, are the amazingly well preserved dinosaur footprints unearthed beside Clayton Lake in 1982. Five hundred prints laid down by eight different species embellish the site.

Not far from our destination we encountered a rancher and his son on horseback driving several dozen head of cattle toward us along a narrow, deeply gutted road. There was no room to go around the animals, so we stopped. The rancher, handsome and deeply tanned, galloped by, waving his hat. His son, a boy of no more than twelve or thirteen, stayed behind with the cattle. Shouting, scolding, darting left and right to round up the occasional mutineer, the young man kept his charges moving till they were past the car and we were able to continue on our way.

What skills that boy possessed, and what a legacy he carried. There aren't many like him, but God bless him and springtime and the great American West. I can't imagine a scene of greater purity or grace, or one that could have filled my heart with more joy.

Somewhere in the emptiness of Union County, about as far from anywhere, it seemed, as it was possible to go, we reached the landmark my host wanted me to see, a section of the long-abandoned Santa Fe Trail. Blakeley parked the car, and we began to walk. A stiff wind whipped at us over the plain. Above, a meadowlark hung suspended as it beat determinedly against the wind. With a scooping motion of his hand Blakeley indicated where the wagons had rolled, once deep ruts in the prairie but now only dim shadows in the flaxen grass and turpentine weed.

We followed the trail for a short distance, then stopped to enjoy the feel and the fragrance of the windswept plain. With a million acres in sight I had an easy time imagining a long train of wagons creeping toward me over the prairie, and hearing the high-pitched cry of the drivers and the crack of the whip recoiling off the hard sheen of the sky.

We watched for several minutes. Suddenly, from out of nowhere, five pronghorns bounded into view on the crest of a nearby rise. The wind screamed, and then as abruptly as the animals had appeared it fell silent, and a deathly stillness rose up in its wake.

I am not a hunter, and I am not a violent man. But the wind was provocative and the silence was deep. I cannot say with certainty that if I had had a gun I would not have used it.

THE VOICE
OF THE FLOWER

I saw a new heaven and a new earth.

Revelation 21:1

Georgia O'Keeffe's first extended visit to New Mexico was a mission of liberation. The year was 1929. O'Keeffe was forty-one. Throughout her life her dark face, rigid mouth, tightly pulled-back hair, and icy stare made her seem haughty and disapproving, like a pitiless nun about to pronounce sentence on a misbehaving student. (Her propensity to dress in black greatly heightened the effect.) But photographs taken during the months prior to O'Keeffe's sojourn in New Mexico show the drawn face and bewildered eyes of a woman who has turned her judgment on herself, and who can find no escape. She seems trapped in the frames of her pictures.

In a limited context she was a grand success. Edmund Wilson echoed the opinion of most critics when he called her "a woman painter comparable to [America's] best women poets and novelists." But she hated those qualifiers. Only Lewis Mumford could bring himself to tender the catholic praise she craved, calling her "the most original painter in America." And she hated the posturing, incestuous, overweening art world of New York. Success in a culture she increasingly understood to be poisonous to her nature had failed to produce what she needed most: an emancipation of spirit that would allow her to achieve the full flowering of her gift.

Her personal life, too, was deeply troubled. She was sick. None of her doctors could diagnose the problem, but one of them told her she was dying. As if that were not enough, her relationship with her husband, the photographer Alfred Stieglitz, was severely strained. O'Keeffe was strong-willed and persevering, but despite all of her efforts she had been unable to escape the huge shadow of Stieglitz, twenty-three years her senior, internationally famous, and her long-time patron and champion. On a western vacation with her sister Claudia twelve years earlier, O'Keeffe had passed through northern New Mexico and had instantly been charmed. Sensing that the region held the key to her liberation, she began negotiations with her childishly possessive husband for some time away.

Stieglitz fought her for weeks. At last, recognizing the possibly life-saving importance of his cooperation, he gave in. Late in April with her friend and fellow painter Beck Strand, O'Keeffe boarded a train in New York and embarked for the promised land.

She accomplished her mission almost at once. In New Mexico her health returned. She began painting with renewed strength and purpose. In the dreamy tone of her letters, in stories related by friends, one recognizes that sudden and perfect marrying of person and place, like Thoreau and Walden Pond, that changes a life, igniting the spirit and revealing a new and exhilarating direction. O'Keeffe and New Mexico were made for each other. The queerly attired artist who spoke with Amish plainness and sought through her work to reveal the essence of the natural world found in New Mexico's simplicity, directness, and unconventionality soul-satisfying reflections of herself. She began spending part of each year in the state. And though she didn't settle permanently in New Mexico until 1949, three years after Stieglitz's death, one senses that she never really left after that first emancipating summer. Here she is, writing to her friend Anita Pollitzer in 1929:

> The grain is ripe in the little fields along the Rio Grande valley, and as you drive along the country roads you see tall, wild sun flowers against the sky or against the mesa and pink sand hills and mountains the other side of the river—the people living in the little mud houses along the way.

In the evening I go up in the desert where you can see the world all around—far away. The hours I spend each evening watching the sun go down—and just enjoying it—and every day I go out and watch it again. I draw some and there is a little painting and so the days go by.

At Taos, O'Keeffe's headquarters during her four-month stay, she found a colony of artists, writers, dilettantes, and assorted human curiosities every bit as smothering as the one she had left behind in New York. She had little time for it. When she wasn't painting she was cutting loose, usually with her friend Beck. The two women gossiped, cussed, smoked cigarettes, threw off their clothes and baked in the sun. O'Keeffe decided that she needed to learn how to drive. After taking a few lessons she bought a new Model A Ford, then at the drop of a hat zoomed off into the wilds of northern New Mexico, sometimes on roads, sometimes not, with Beck and their new friend Tony Luhan, a Taos Indian.

O'Keeffe was a thoroughly unbuttoned driver. She pointed the car, she gunned the accelerator; Beck and Tony closed their eyes and prayed. Together the three friends dropped in on rodeos and Indian festivals, poked about in Anasazi ruins, explored mountains and deserts, built roaring campfires, drank bootleg whiskey, slept under the stars. (Only the muddy road to a remote village called Abiquiu stymied the intrepid driver. The defeat invested the town with an air of unattainability which would one day play a role in leading O'Keeffe to settle there permanently.) It is impossible to read about this jubilant summer of liberation and not be reminded of one's own coming-of-age, when that primal elation the world is capable of dishing out so generously is revealed for the first time and one learns that there is freedom to be had if one can only grasp the reins.

By August O'Keeffe had charted a new course for herself and was ready to return to New York, at least temporarily. Before leaving New Mexico she packed up a barrel of animal bones she had collected during her explorations of the high desert and shipped it east. Symbols of her newfound freedom, those bleached cattle skulls and sheep spines—now instantly recognizable images in the O'Keeffe iconography—became her definitive link with New Mexico. In New York they continued to nurture her; some became center-pieces in the powerful paintings she began to turn out. Critics did not understand the spirit of liberation embodied in O'Keeffe's bones and read them literally as symbols of decay and death, while surely they represented exactly the opposite. Decaying bones are found on or under the earth, yet O'Keeffe almost always depicted her skulls and pelvises floating above the land, as though they had been raised from the dead. That they retained their deathlike appearance in their metamorphosed state only affirmed that rebirth is a function of the soul, not the body, that freedom bestows on the emancipated the fever of youth, not the appearance. (O'Keeffe herself never looked young, even as a child.) Like the ancient rocks of New Mexico, like O'Keeffe herself, cattle skulls were aged and weathered but nevertheless vividly alive.

"To me they are strangely more living than the animals walking around," the artist wrote a decade later. "The bones seem to cut sharply to the center of something that is keenly alive on the desert tho' it is vast and empty and untouchable—and knows no kindness with all its beauty." Even trapped on the harsh desert floor, her bones achieved an exact, uncompromised freedom, which O'Keeffe knew could never be provided by an existence removed from the reality and truth of nature—and in her case, from the sight of it.

Two years later O'Keeffe's exploration of the bone motif led her to make one of the great statements on freedom in American art. Among the intelligentsia there was at that time much discussion of great American creations of one kind or another—novels, symphonies, and so on. Behind the talk was a genuine desire to extract from the American experience fundamental themes and modes of expression and to fuse them into a new national art.

But as the no-nonsense O'Keeffe was quick to see, the louder the visionaries boasted of Great American Art, the faster they hightailed it to Europe. Most of the big names in American letters and many of the small ones had already done time on the continent; those who hadn't were only waiting for the right moment.

O'Keeffe was an exception. She had little interest in the Old World. She didn't visit Europe until 1953, when she was sixty-five. One can almost see her standing on an East River wharf, shaking her head, tapping her toe, waving disgustedly as one more colleague sailed off in the wrong direction. O'Keeffe cut to the heart of the matter with customary directness: "One can not be an American by going about saying that one is an American. It is necessary to feel America, live America, love America, and then work."

Unlike many who had aspired to Great American Art, O'Keeffe actually knew her country, had seen it and tasted it and come to know its people: "I knew that our country was lush and rich. I had driven across the country many times. I was quite excited over our country and I knew that at that time almost any one of those great minds would have been living in Europe if it had been possible for them. They didn't even want to live in New York—how was the Great American Thing going to happen?"

Cow's Skull—Red, White and Blue was O'Keeffe's incisive answer to her own forcefully posed question. She created the work partly to poke fun at all the misguided souls straining to see their homeland from garrets in Paris and Rome.

But there was combativeness in her effort as well. O'Keeffe clearly intended to weigh in with her own candidate for the Great American Thing, but without fanfare and without ponderous theorizing. Here, she seemed to be saying—while you've been arguing, I've been painting.

No landscape, no New Mexico mountains or mesas repose beneath this cattle skull. Here, for once, it is all of America O'Keeffe means to portray. Suspended like a huge bird with powerful outreaching horns for wings, the deathly white, partially decomposed skull, exquisitely crafted, hovers over two fields of vertical red, white, and blue stripes. The design immediately calls to mind an American flag. Red stripes border the painting left and right; they are solid, protecting what lies between. Softer white and blue sections modeled like folds of cloth provide a supple underpinning for the skull. A dark, narrow band, the transformed support pole for the skull, runs up the center, separating the expanses of blue.

True to form, critics read the skull as a death motif, its suspension over the flag as a surrealistic symbol signifying everything from the downfall of America to Christ crucified. Freudians, who were rampant, saw in the tender folds of cloth, the vertical design, and the mysterious void in the center what they saw in practically everything O'Keeffe painted (and apparently the only thing they could imagine a woman was capable of painting): female genitalia, establishing beyond a doubt the plenary, tragic, repressed sexual feelings of the artist. (*"The labial sculpting surely an emblem of femaleness, the deep cavity a sign of deadened emotion, black and empty; and the cattle skull, the cattle skull . . . hmmm . . . well, perhaps . . . hmmm. . . ."*) Inasmuch as O'Keeffe famously had posed nude for Stieglitz's camera and cheerfully allowed the resulting photographs to be exhibited—revealing a woman strikingly un-self-conscious about her quite beautiful body and clearly at peace with her sexuality—she seems patently a less likely victim of repressed sexual feelings than the critics, none of whom had appeared nude in public.

O'Keeffe found the critics as misguided, and as silly, as the European sojourners. In her 1939 exhibition catalog she unburdened herself with this testy lecture: "Well—I made you take time to look at what I saw and when you took time to really notice my flower you hung all your own associations with flowers on my flower and you write about my flower as if I think and see what you think and see of the flower—and I don't."

Following this, one hesitates to plunge into the very dangerous waters of O'Keeffe interpretation. Nevertheless, with the sound of this irascible woman's irately tapping toe hammering in my ear, I'll bravely proclaim what I think of and see in her cow's skull. I think it represents the personal and artistic freedom she discovered in New Mexico; I see it as a powerful symbol of the possibility of freedom embodied in the American dream. O'Keeffe's skull is an unsightly thing, but that is because this eccentric, plain-faced woman knew that freedom is meaningless unless it extends to everyone—that the true measure of freedom in the United States is our willingness to grant it not simply to the beautiful and the comfortable but even to the most unsightly among us. The unsightly of countenance, behind whom a shadow of un-defined potentiality leads into an unknown but seemingly promising future, O'Keeffe protects with invincible red stripes and nurtures with soft white and blue. *Cow's Skull—Red, White and Blue* is a wonderful work that compellingly and masterfully celebrates the deepest meaning of freedom. For that reason the painting strikes me as undeniably great, and utterly American.

What O'Keeffe accomplished with a cattle skull she achieved time and again with the most routine scenes in O'Keeffe country, New Mexico, and in so doing she accomplished what is central to any artistic achievement: she transformed the ordinary into the fresh and new, granting us glimpses of things we have never seen before and thereby deepening our understanding of the world. Hers is the art of what William Blake called fourfold vision, a penetration of the surface of things into hidden realms beyond.

Somehow I forgot that when I prepared for my first visit to Abiquiu and Ghost Ranch, the two spots in north-central New Mexico where O'Keeffe kept homes and resided for the better part of fifty years. As though arming myself for a birding expedition with an Audubon field guide, I carefully packed copies of her paintings and a map, drawn by one of her disciples, that identified the locations of some of the artist's best-known works. Here is the famous Pedernal, there the Red and Yellow Cliffs, there the Road Past the View toward Española.

With map and paintings at my side I drove up the road connecting the two homesteads. It's a modern highway today, not the impassable quagmire that defeated O'Keeffe in 1929. Leaving Abiquiu, a somber, centuries-old Hispanic village of a few-score adobe homes, the road ascends a cliffside, then plunges straight into hot, barren country where the views are breathtaking and dire and where the splendor has a constantly sad and hopeless quality about it. Burnt rock, shattered rock: with each mile the landscape multiplies in ruination and hostility, revealing ever more clearly why desert lovers are the fiercest lovers of all. Even in the relatively benign high desert of New Mexico, a determined suitor requires a forgiving eye and a generous heart. To the north, towering garishly colored walls hem the route, their ravaged faces gashed by water and wind into deep, dark fissures. Early Spanish settlers peered into the hollows and heard the wind groaning and imagined *brujas* (witches) cooking up evil for a moonless night. At the base of each wall a massive tailing of broken rock, an echo of thunder and chaos, tumbles toward the road.

Everything seems to be coming apart. Even the level ground looks defective. One fears that the whole scene could collapse in a stiff wind. The only comfort, a small one, is the profusion of low-lying junipers deployed like the national guard over the countryside, as if to keep the peace.

It seems a vain hope. The land is big and harsh and unreasonable; it's beautiful only in the sense that doggedness is beautiful. Driving from Abiquiu to Ghost Ranch one has an easy time imagining witches and picturing bones rotting among the trees.

In a general way I could see that this was the land that Georgia O'Keeffe made famous. It had a look and a feel that vaguely reminded me of her paintings. I managed to pick out a few of her subjects, which had something like the shapes she recorded on canvas.

But the correspondences were loose at best. In some gross misunderstanding of the artist's function I had imagined that I would see in the countryside exactly what I saw in the paintings, and I saw nothing of the kind. The map was useless except as an aid for identifying the pedestrian landmarks with which O'Keeffe began her work. One might as well search for grapes in champagne! O'Keeffe was not a photographer preparing a field guide or a scientist explaining the molecular structure of limestone. What she produced was a transformed vision of what I saw on the road to Ghost Ranch. As she endeavored to make clear, no artist thinks and sees of the flower as she did. The Pedernal, the Red and Yellow Cliffs are not to be found in north-central New Mexico or anywhere else; they exist only in the artist's imagination. This explains William Turner's response to a viewer's remark that he had never seen a sunset like one Turner had painted: "But don't you wish that you had?" And again, Picasso's rejoinder to a complaint that a work of the artist entitled *Fish* didn't look like a fish: "Why should it? It's a painting."

As O'Keeffe reminds us of the power of the artist to cast the world in a new and unexpected light, so she illustrates by her own example the central importance of artistic freedom to the creation of that light. O'Keeffe found her voice only when she found her quiet place and was left alone to paint. That she needed to remove to one of the most remote spots in the United States in order to do so may have been because she was a woman painting at a time when women could not be free in the company of men, or it may simply have been a function of her own special needs. Whatever the explanation, she saw her opening and seized it. (Herewith I add a tribute to Stieglitz, who came to understand his wife's need for annual sojourns in the desert; in faraway New York he continued to champion her work until his death.) As a reminder to us all, I should like to see O'Keeffe's New Mexico homes declared national monuments and hung with two signs, one reading "Here Be Freedom and Vision!" the other, "Destroy Us and Die!" Along with Yellowstone and the Grand Canyon, these sites should be made required stops on every family's tour of the West. For here in the twilight of the twentieth century we stand in desperate need of artists who can discover and portray radiant and wondrous new worlds to inhabit our dreams and energize our actions. At the same time, failing to heed the critical example of Stieglitz, we are more reluctant than ever to grant them the freedom to do so.

Periodically some spoilsport conducts a survey foreordained to reveal the yawning gulf between America's undying love for the idea of freedom of expression and our willingness to actually grant it. Usually the survey begins with a warm, apple-pie question based on one of our cherished beliefs, like this from a 1992 poll by the Thomas Jefferson Center for the Protection of Free Expression: "Do you believe the government should be able to tell you what views you may or may not express?"

To that question ninety percent of the respondents shouted a resounding "No!" Then the crafty pollster burrows in, revealing just beneath the surface the bluenose, the timorous, the fastidious, the intolerant—and sometimes, deeper still, a glimpse of the totalitarian lurking in us all. The results of the Jefferson Center poll indicate that forty percent of us believe that the government has the right to deny First Amendment freedoms to artists. Forty-six percent of those questioned in a 1991 Research USA poll agreed that "Congress should ban the media from reporting on any national security issue without prior government approval." Half the respondents in a 1991 PEN Center USA West poll believe that books with "dangerous ideas" should be banned from school libraries.

Like most survey questions, those I have cited are dreadfully one-dimensional and do a poor job of examining the complexities and shadings of the issues they raise. Permitted to dig deeper, even an inveterate First Amendment advocate might find something to support in some of them.

But polls do at least one thing well, and that is to measure pure gut reaction. With that as a yardstick and with outright censorship of certain works of art and literature on the rise in the United States, it becomes distressingly clear that there is something about freedom of expression that troubles many Americans, something they find repellent and frightening. If that is so, what hope do we have of preserving what Georgia O'Keeffe found in a remote corner of the Southwest and glorified in a visionary portrait of a ravaged cow's skull and a grand old American flag?

(2)

It is the sky, said the artist John Marin: "It's a blank, empty wall . . . the most powerful emptiness I've ever known." It is the color, said the artist Marsden Hartley: New Mexico is "the only place in America where true color exists." It is the atmosphere, said the artist Julius Rolshoven: "I have traveled all over . . . in search of atmosphere, but nowhere else have I seen nature ever provide anything, even the conception, as it does in New Mexico." It is the grandeur, said the artist Frederic Remington: "This vast table-land west of the mountains is itself eight thousand feet in the air, yet viewed from there, the mountains scallop skyward, range after range—snow-capped—beautiful—overpowering." It is the remoteness, said the poet Amy Lowell: "In New Mexico you are almost as far away as in Australia." It is the peace and quiet, said the composer Ernest Bloch: in Santa Fe "they leave me alone so that I can work." It is the light, the altitude, the blending of cultures, the salutary climate.

For these and for a hundred other reasons, the impulse to create art is an honored tradition in New Mexico, tracing its roots back at least three thousand years to native peoples who sculpted tiny human figures of clay, sandstone, and wood, then decorated them with feathers and beads. Early in this millennium, artists began chipping their views onto a gallery of flat black rock faces on a tableland overlooking the Rio Grande. The medium proved to be unusually durable, and today the works, some fifteen thousand petroglyphs, can be seen where they were carved, on Albuquerque's West Mesa in the recently created Petroglyph National Monument.

Following the Spanish conquest, Hispanic artists in the north of present-day New Mexico became weavers and wood carvers; Indians produced exquisite blankets, baskets, jewelry, and pottery. Georgia O'Keeffe was not the state's first famous artist. The Cordova carver José Dolores López and the San Ildefonso potter María Martínez preceded her early in the twentieth century. The two produced magnificent works which today attest full acceptance into the mainstream art world: dramatically lit displays in fine museums, out-of-this-world selling prices.

Collectors searching for the latter but unable to find a López or a Martínez will have no trouble locating suitably inflated figures here, especially on Santa Fe's Canyon Road, the Fort Knox of New Mexico's art world, the Wall Street of things to hang on your wall. Somewhat carelessly, I now see, I once wandered into a Canyon Road gallery toting my son in a backpack. Jake was about a year old and had recently discovered the pleasures of flailing his arms insanely. In the middle of one room stood a narrow pedestal. On the pedestal teetered a piece of antique Indian pottery that the gallery owners, rather unwisely in my opinion, had chosen to leave totally unprotected from insanely flailing arms. The pot stood naked to the world and carried a price tag of $40,000. (I mean that literally: slapped on the side was one of those sticky yellow rectangles, the same ones they use at Wal-Mart, and it read $40,000.)

I wandered into the room, unaware that my life might be about to change forever. As we passed the pedestal, Jake reached out and took a poke at the pot. He missed. Horrified, I swung him in the opposite direction. He leaned out and took a poke at a $30,000 target. He missed again. (At one, my son had excellent taste in art but bad aim.) Whatever had brought me into the gallery in the first place having suddenly lost its allure, I took off tipsily for the front door, bobbing and weaving my way among the pots like a boxer trying to find his way to his corner after a bad round. I escaped unscathed, and solvent, fortified by new and important knowledge about art appreciation.

In the early part of the century Anglo artists from the East discovered Taos. An old Indian-Hispanic town of great beauty, earthiness, and charm, Taos possesses an electrifying spiritual quality for which Indians and Latinos have something of a cultural affinity but which many Anglos find so unfamiliar, and so thrilling, that they think they invented it. When they happen onto it they send out the word, and soon the place is sanctified by the official Anglo version of the electrifyingly spiritual, namely, boutiques and expensive real estate. In the case of Taos the transformation was slower than usual (it is in full swing today), thanks in large part to the influence of the legendary socialite Mabel Dodge.

Dodge wanted to put Taos on the map, but she had no desire to destroy the integrity of the town. She had spent a decade entertaining the likes of Gertrude Stein, Arthur Rubinstein, and André Gide at her villa in Florence. In 1912 she moved to 23 Fifth Avenue in New York City and soon was operating what the writer Lincoln Steffens called "the only successful salon I have ever seen in America."

It is a measure of the restlessness that plagued Dodge in New York that even with guests like Isadora Duncan, Emma Goldman, Walter Lippmann, John Reed, Margaret Sanger—and Alfred Stieglitz—enlivening her weekly soirees, she became increasingly afflicted with a faraway look in her eyes and a tendency to linger over the madeira. In 1917 she visited the fledgling art colony at Taos and succumbed on the spot. She built a home, divorced her third husband, married the Taos Indian Tony Luhan (who became Georgia O'Keeffe's friend and road companion in 1929), and set to work.

Mabel Dodge was not beautiful, but in other respects she shared some important traits with her adopted town. She was earthy and charming. She had nascent spiritual qualities. (An early New Ager who dabbled in the occult and consulted mediums, Dodge conjectured that *Taos* might be the plural of *Tao* and that this might prove a connection between the town and the religion.)

Unlike Taos, however, Dodge was rich and ambitious. Over the next several decades she undertook to transform this unsophisticated mountain village into a kind of summer camp in American arts and letters. It was a rare notable who didn't receive an invitation from her to visit New Mexico. She wrote, she phoned, she badgered, she promised keys to a rent-free cabin. And through the 1920s and 1930s a glittering array of creative artists traveled to Taos and Santa Fe to work and sparkle together. Dodge's biggest catch was D. H. Lawrence, but there were plenty of other museum-quality names who came directly or indirectly due to her influence—Willa Cather, Martha Graham, Ansel Adams, Edward Hopper, George Bellows, Carl Jung, Leopold Stokowski, Sinclair Lewis, Mary Austin, Aldous Huxley, Robinson Jeffers, Georgia O'Keeffe.

O'Keeffe was the last link with this luminous era, but the creative tradition in New Mexico remains as strong as ever. Probably it is now more authentically New Mexican than it was when Mabel Dodge ran the show. A 1992 *Newsweek* article complained that Albuquerque has "too many writers"; a few years earlier four of them made the *New York Times* best-seller list simultaneously. Santa Fe claims to sell more art than any other city in the United States save New York City and Los Angeles. The annual Indian market in Santa Fe (known affectionately to sellers as "the Indian markup") is the largest Native American crafts fair in the world. With some justification, though no proof, New Mexico claims to be home to more artists per capita than any other state.

What they produce is by and large safe, pleasant, wholesome work based on a proven catalog of themes endlessly repeated. The visitor to half a dozen Santa Fe, Albuquerque, or Taos galleries (there are hundreds) will see practically everything there is to see: peach-and-salmon sunsets shimmering on distant mesas; noble, weatherworn cowboys (many look quite miserable, as though they may be suffering from gunshot wounds); tall, well-fed, slightly spooky Indians who appear to possess important knowledge not generally available to Anglos; shameless O'Keeffe rip-offs; melancholy ponies; crumbling adobe walls. It is art that confirms rather than challenges, serving up lab-tested product in order to flatter potential buyers that they understand the world perfectly and that they can prove this by pulling out their checkbooks. Like the boilerplate Hollywood film, the formula novel, the corporate rock 'n' roll group, it is more antidepressant than art—soothing, stroking, and sedating the perceiver through the comforting repetition of agreeable images and themes.

The familiar beat, the passionate kiss rendered just so, the gruesome, well-lit murder, the pueblo at Taos: the power of the cliché is great, and so we reach for it again and again, like a superstition. It rules the marketplace, destroying the drive to create by eating away at the urge to risk, the strongest color on the artist's palette. Surrender to the cliché leads at once to the banal notion that the artist's job is to hold a mirror up to the world. That is how life is, says the novelist of her most recent tale of a glamorous man's sordid ascent to the boardroom, the film director of his latest ritual bloodletting: I'm simply reflecting the world. Never mind that that is precisely the excuse one might offer for defecating on a shiny floor; to reflect the world, and go no further, is to pardon it. Such a work by definition lacks irony, imagination, and dissent. It is the exact opposite of art, a loyal ratification of the status quo. Instead of a bold dream of a different world, it offers a timid view of our own.

In a land of timid artists, the king has nothing to fear. And in the United States—unlike countries where freedom of expression is nonexistent and where prison and even death may await the dissident—tanks and guns are not necessary to keep the peace. Here, the mere threat of censorship is enough to turn many of our artists into self-neutered aides-de-camp. The knowledge that subtlety, contradiction, complexity, or, worst of all, bad press is likely to sabotage the lofty goals of fame, fortune, and an appearance on *Oprah* is enough to keep most of the rest in line. (In 1997, the Authors Guild reported that some recording artists were softening their lyrics in order to break into the huge Wal-Mart market.) Thus arises the fat, happy lint-picking through the minutiae of everyday life, the obsessive self-analysis, the inoffensive recycling of safe, sanitized themes by many of our best-known writers, composers, and artists. Thus also arises the unwillingness of many to speak with passion through their work (and not merely at fund-raisers) to matters of social, economic, or political concern, the fear to identify and condemn evil, to celebrate virtue, to imagine beauty. Thus ultimately arises the pleasantness and orderliness of many of the galleries of Santa Fe, Albuquerque, and Taos.

But not all. New Mexico is home to a small but staunch band of independent painters, writers, filmmakers, and other creative artists who are any-thing but timid, who address the difficult issues of our time with passion and conviction. A few, such as writers John Nichols and Leslie Marmon Silko, have achieved widespread acclaim despite their heresies. The majority, however, have earned neither fame nor fortune for their trouble, though none I have talked to has mentioned either as a goal. They include a disproportionate number of Indians, Latinos, women, gays, lesbians, and others ill-qualified for the mainstream art world—people who because they express unconventional or unpopular points of view have more in common with Latin American poets and Asian playwrights than they have with the typical high-profile American artist or writer.

Native American artist and filmmaker Jean LeMarr told me that her work is driven by her desire to express the way that Indian people feel. She mentioned her film *Double Vision* and her etching *Seven from Hell,* both of which she created for the Columbus Quincentennial. The film is a documen-tary that presents Indians talking freely about Columbus's arrival in America and its aftermath. The etching derives from a tradition of LeMarr's Paiute–Pit River tribe. In the work, Columbus disembarks from a ship followed by a priest, a harlot, a pimp, a businessman, a murderer, a thief, and the devil. Each character is based on a recognizable figure—Andrew Jackson is the thief, General George Custer the murderer, John Wayne the pimp. Both works have angered many who have seen them. To LeMarr such anger betrays an un-cluttered, immutable view of the world: "Those people were closed to the Indian point of view. To consider a different way of seeing things was very difficult for them."

For some, seeing things a different way is so difficult that it becomes intolerable. Artist Frederico Vigil described for me a notorious incident in-volving his 19-by-7-foot fresco *Santa Madre Tierra—Gente Mesclada* (Holy Mother Earth—A Mixture of People). For several years the mural adorned a wall at St. John's College in Santa Fe. The work included many benign symbols of Latino, Indian, and Anglo cultures, but it was Vigil's graphic depiction of the world springing from a woman's womb that upset many who saw the fresco. St. John's president John Agresto called the mural "jejune, obscene, and obnoxious" and said he wanted it covered or removed from the campus. Early one morning in February 1990, a student smashed through a second-story window in the building where the work was housed, and destroyed it with a hammer.

Vigil was deeply shaken by the desecration. But, he told me, such an act could never cause him to change his view of the world or the manner in which he depicted it in his art.

(3)

Vigil's tenacity mirrored that of several other artists and writers with whom I spoke, none more so than the Santa Fe artist Judy Chicago. For more than three decades Chicago has treated risk as an obligation and conformity as a sin. Consistently choosing big, demanding, heretical themes (she hasn't a sunset or a melancholy pony to her name), she insists on being heard. Her use of female sexuality as a sign of woman's reclaimed identity and liberty has enraged some (mostly male) establishment critics but has not prevented her best-known work, *The Dinner Party,* from becoming one of the most discussed, viewed, loved, and despised American artworks of the postwar period. Like Picasso she regards free expression as a weapon that the artist chooses as deliberately as a painting technique. Art should not be free, Picasso maintained: "Art and liberty, like the fire of Prometheus, are things one must steal, to be used against the established order. Once art becomes official and open to everyone, then it becomes the new academicism."

No academic, Chicago has found freedom not by luxuriating in the inner circle but by pushing, testing, questioning, resisting from without. She is not content with official approval and does not seek it. Like Georgia O'Keeffe, she has wrenched freedom from a kind of desert, one Chicago might describe as a desert of truth, and thereby found a unique and compelling voice.

Judy Chicago and Georgia O'Keeffe share much in common. Both began visiting northern New Mexico in their early forties and moved to the state permanently after an extended courtship. Both have been denounced for the apparent sexual imagery in their work. Married but childless, brusque, opinionated, deadly serious about their work, both repudiate society's definition of how a woman should behave. Both are intolerant of worshippers and fools. (O'Keeffe's glower and sharp tongue sent many a flatterer away in disgrace. Chicago can be equally caustic. To an interviewer who betrayed a less-than-perfect understanding of the media employed in *The Dinner Party,* Chicago snapped: "Obviously you know nothing of needlework.")

Referring to the community of women artists, Chicago has honored O'Keeffe with the title "the mother of us all." In her autobiography *Through the Flower,* Chicago explains the reference and details her indebtedness to two other women, Virginia Woolf and Anaïs Nin. Chicago contends that her experience as a young artist enabled her to understand the tragedy of each of these women—Woolf's suicide, Nin's secret writing and anguish over publication, O'Keeffe's removal to New Mexico to live and work alone: "Before the women's movement, I felt that I, too, was faced with those same three choices: commit suicide, work in isolation, or accept the absence of recognition. Each one of these women had to live her life and do her work *without the affirmation of the society. . . .* The work of Woolf, Nin, and O'Keeffe, combined with my new knowledge of women's art, literature, and history, provided me with the impetus, the confidence, the nourishment, and the ideas to enrich my own form language so that it could allow me to truly be myself as a woman artist."

As an aside, when I met Chicago and suggested during our conversation that she may have been drawn to New Mexico because O'Keeffe was here, she practically leapt out of her chair at me. "I *didn't* want to be here because O'Keeffe was here!" she protested. "O'Keeffe had carved out her territory in New Mexico. I never imagined I'd be here!" When I responded that I was merely commenting on appearances, she shot back with as ironclad a formula for artistic integrity as I know of: "I *never* think about how what I do appears."

And both women created Great American Art. Like O'Keeffe's *Cow's Skull, The Dinner Party* incisively, movingly, and masterfully portrays the dream of freedom. Chicago's is a darker work, more about freedom denied than the O'Keeffe, but no less insistent on the primacy of the ideal and no less a celebration of it. *The Dinner Party* is huge—three banquet tables in the shape of an equilateral triangle, an ancient symbol of the feminine. Each table is set with thirteen places, deliberately invoking Leonardo da Vinci's *Last Supper.* Chicago's supper, however, which the artist characterizes as "a metaphor for women's domesticated and trivialized circumstances," is not for men. Instead it honors those who have traditionally set the table: forgotten women toiling in a male-dominated world. It is, says Chicago, "a shriek against injustice that has disallowed us having any pride in our history."

The elements that compose *The Dinner Party* are exquisite, extravagant works in themselves—hand-embroidered tapestry runners, linen napkins, flatware, goblets, painted-china plates. The 39 principal guests range through history from "the Primordial Goddess" to Georgia O'Keeffe. O'Keeffe's plate rises higher than the others, signifying her relatively more fully accomplished emancipation. The names of 999 additional "women of accomplishment" are inscribed on the hand-cast porcelain floor. Those of 400 volunteers who assisted Chicago in the creation of the work appear on a notice at the entrance to the exhibition room.

Such a brief description cannot do justice to a work that is so breathtakingly conceived, so beautifully and richly rendered that one feels stunned, physically assaulted by it. I saw *The Dinner Party* at its inaugural exhibition in San Francisco in 1979. I clearly recall the drama of the presentation—the huge room, the autumnal lighting, the lavish tables and their suggestion of enshrined royalty. A million people saw the work during fourteen exhibitions in six countries. In San Francisco, viewers filed past in an endless procession, solemnly remarking on the dazzling execution or the identity of the guests (Emily Dickinson, of course; but who is Trotula? Artemesia Gentileschi? Petronilla de Meath?), or shrinking from some perceived threat in the work, or denouncing the uppitiness of the artist. The room resonated in an undercurrent of voices. What remains strongest in my memory, nevertheless, are a sense of monstrous silence and my apprehension of the rage and heartbreak enclosed within that enormous triangle.

And of course those plates: massive as Crock-Pots, vivid as homegrown tomatoes, juicy as melons, earthy as sagebrush in morning dew, voluptuous as strawberries and brandy at midnight. With a design patterned after the life and work of the woman it commemorates, each plate is a spectacular china sculpture almost alarming in its audacity. A network of waves and scallops embellishes the design, suggesting a butterfly or a vagina, depending on whether the viewer is more entomologist or gynecologist. Admittedly the latter, I confess that I saw more sex than insects at Chicago's party.

But nothing sexy: one would need a ceramic fetish to be turned on by those plates. Too much time has been wasted praising or savaging them individually, when they must be viewed together to permit recognition of their importance. Collectively the notorious plates become a single evolving form. Through their diversity, the many components, each grounded in its own history but not bound by it, impart strength to the whole, which emerges as a perfect symbol of mutual struggle, resistance, and triumph. Like the black stripe in the O'Keeffe painting, the nebulous center of each plate is a wellspring of possibilities, the birthplace of an emancipating life force. As O'Keeffe found freedom in a remote landscape, Chicago found hers in the dark but empowering experience of women. Like O'Keeffe before her, she fashioned a powerful symbol for her discovery and incorporated it into a work of soaring imagination and originality.

Few artworks of the past several decades have stirred such controversy. There was no middle ground: people loved *The Dinner Party* or they loathed it. Many feminists loved it, naturally, but so did many apolitical men and women who simply enjoyed the grandeur of the work or the beauty of its execution or the engaging didacticism of the stories attached to the plates.

The toughness of the political message, however—Chicago's brash questioning of established values—was too much for some. It was bad enough that the artist elevated women to such prominence; that she did it so graphically, laying it out on a china platter, was unacceptable. Kinder critics dismissed the work as mere kitsch or pop sociology. Self-appointed guardians of white male purity sputtered in indignation. (Hilton Kramer called *The Dinner Party* "a grotesque embarrassment.") The morally righteous saw no butterflies and screamed "obscene." The work was exhibited for almost a decade. Then, in

1988, Chicago placed it in storage. Except for a limited engagement in 1996 at the Armand Hammer Museum of Art in Los Angeles, it has not been seen since.

Judy Chicago is patently a feminist but not the ball-crushing fire breather I had expected. On the contrary, in a gentle, rather old-fashioned manner, she took me—a miserable, flawed male—under her wing and nurtured me. Ten minutes before our agreed-upon meeting time, several miles from her home, my car died. Abruptly faced with the scary prospect of being tardy for an appointment with a woman who once smoked cigars and attended motorcycle races, I began to unravel. Not since the 1960s had I stood in a street cursing and waving my arms menacingly; a few decades later, minus only a protest sign, I did it again. A Good Samaritan in a Volvo comprehended my predicament and stopped. Together we rolled my moribund vehicle up an incline and into a safe parking spot. Then, with me perspiring profusely and babbling that I was late, perhaps dangerously so, for something terribly important, he drove me to Chicago's home. I arrived ten minutes late in a state of advanced trepidation.

The artist who for her ability to marshal hundreds of assistants for the achievement of a single goal has been called the Rubens of our time, who has inspired thousands with a dream of liberation from the thralls of history and disturbed the dreams of thousands more with images of giant vaginas, is a tiny, spirited woman who two centuries ago might have been a candidate for Fragonard's swing. (Today, self-assured, calmly authoritative, she might lead poor Fragonard out into the backyard by the nose, plunk him down on the swing, and order him to sit still while she painted *his* portrait.) Just past fifty but looking ten years younger, Chicago is a self-described fitness freak, an inveterate jogger (no picnic at Santa Fe's altitude of seven thousand feet), and, in tandem with her husband, the photographer Donald Woodman, a mountain biker of (here I am guessing) grim proficiency. Her hair is a magnificent and willful thicket the color of tree-ripened apricots. In fuchsia blouse and pants and purple-tinted glasses she greeted her tardy guest at the door.

I burst into the room like an encyclopedia salesman, threw up my arms, and began wailing, "My car! My goddamned car! What a piece . . . !" Chicago showed me to a chair and suggested firmly that I sit down at once. I'm sure she was thinking, "Another man and his *car!*" She was very kind to me. She said, "Why don't you relax for a few minutes. Can I get you something? Would you like a glass of wine? Red or white?"

As I sipped my wine I noticed that my hand was trembling. I fumbled in my briefcase for my tape recorder. Listening now to the first minute of conversation I hear my voice shaking. I hear Chicago in a soothing voice interviewing me: "How long have you lived in New Mexico? Where are you from originally? What do you . . . ?"

What I remember most about our time together is the pleasure and excitement of becoming reacquainted with art not as a reflection of the world but as an extension of the heart and soul, and with the artist not as soldier of fortune but as seeker after light. Chicago folded her feet beneath herself yoga-style and spoke with humor and passion about thirty years of risk and commitment to her artistic ideals. In our sorrowful gilded age when style sometimes passes for vision and integrity often is measured by the size of one's income, it was bracing to hear Chicago's timeless statement of purpose unsullied by qualifiers, uncleared ahead of time by a publicist.

"The artist's job is to tell the truth as he or she sees it," Chicago stated forthrightly. Before such a force the censor, the philistine, the community bluenose, the Congress of the United States, and the ordinary citizen careless with the riches of the First Amendment stand powerless. It serves as a reminder that the greatest danger to artists in the United States is not that they will be silenced but that they will fail to speak. Working alone, censors can throttle free expression only temporarily. Working in league with artists co-opted by the lures of wealth, success, and approval, they scarcely need to raise their fists.

In a modest way, New Mexico provides a hedge against such voluntary self-mutilation. "I need to have a tremendous amount of psychic space in order to work," Chicago told me. "Santa Fe has given me that—space and privacy and peace." She mentioned several cities to which she had considered relocating before moving to Santa Fe: "Los Angeles was like a paradise when I went to school there. Now it's an example of everything humans have done wrong. New York, too, is out of the question. Every year it looks worse to me. It's like watching the fabric of civilization come apart before one's very eyes. Artists who make it in New York have no choice but to insulate themselves from their surroundings."

Chicago recalled that Georgia O'Keeffe suffered a kind of silencing in New York and found freedom to speak only by escaping to New Mexico: "New Mexico allowed O'Keeffe the possibility of creating out of her own authentic voice. That's very difficult in the center of power because there you're bombarded by the mainstream perspective. The part of you that says 'That's not exactly how I feel' gets drowned out by the shouting of authorities telling you what's good." Chicago's move to Santa Fe produced results similar to O'Keeffe's. "Being in New Mexico, away from the center of power, has allowed me to stay connected to my voice."

Since *The Dinner Party*, Chicago's voice has been heard in several big and sometimes controversial multi-image works. The *Birth Project*, a collection of eighty needleworks designed by Chicago and executed by more than 150 needleworkers, graphically celebrates birth and creation, subjects central to the human experience but almost completely ignored by Western artists. *Powerplay* is a series of drawings, paintings, weavings, cast-paper pieces, and bronzes that present Chicago's view of male definitions of power. *The Holocaust Project* combines the artist's paintings with photographs by Donald Woodman and images designed by Chicago and turned out by a host of stained-glass and tapestry artisans. Taking as its premise that the Holocaust grew out of concepts of power and dominance still with us today, the work explores the significance of the Holocaust and illuminates parallels between its causes and contemporary conditions. Like *The Dinner Party*, these works please some people, infuriate others, and threaten others yet, but Chicago refuses to be stilled. Whether soaring in triumph or crashing in ignominy, she remains an indefatigable creator of the kind of art envisioned by novelist John Gardner. "Art should be a little less pompous and a lot more serious," Gardner remarked. "It should stop sniveling and go for answers or else shut up."

As an artist who routinely goes for answers, not all of them pretty, Chicago routinely encounters resistance to her work and collects her share of ungracious reviews. It was not until 1990, however, that she experienced outright repression.

"One of my goals in creating *The Dinner Party* was to see where we were historically as women," she explained. "If a woman worked at the same level of aspiration as men have worked traditionally, would the system support us? And at first the answer was yes. Everything was looking rosy. Five thousand people came to the opening. People were throwing flowers at me. All the early media coverage was positive.

"But that was in San Francisco. The art distribution system is controlled in the East. And what happened was that as *The Dinner Party* moved around the country and got closer and closer to the East, resistance began to grow. There were efforts to silence me." Several museums refused to show her work and highly critical reviews began to appear in the press. In the end, however, even in the dreaded East, *The Dinner Party* found admirers and enthusiastic support.

The result was what Chicago calls "a tremendous story of triumph—triumph over adversity, triumph over prejudice, triumph over resistance. When people all around the world organized to bring *The Dinner Party* to their countries, they demonstrated the power of art, the power of passion, the power that is generated when people work together for a larger purpose. Even in the face of resistance, *The Dinner Party* was seen. And it entered the art history books."

What it did not do was find a permanent home. A painting can hang on a wall, but *The Dinner Party*'s huge scale presented formidable financial and architectural problems that greatly hampered the search for a site where it could be exhibited permanently. Chicago fretted over the dilemma for several years.

Then in 1990 the predominantly African-American University of the District of Columbia (UDC) indicated that it would accept the work as the centerpiece in its new multicultural art center in downtown Washington. The center would feature artists of color, feminists, and others dedicated to the struggle for freedom and human equality. Chicago spoke of the vision that led to the creation of the center as "wonderful, positive, future-looking."

Convinced that she had found the right place for *The Dinner Party,* she donated the work to the university. In so doing, she embroiled herself in a controversy that revolved around some of the same issues that a year later defeated Anita Hill and which ultimately defeated *The Dinner Party.*

Before it could exhibit *The Dinner Party,* UDC needed to spend a considerable amount of money to accommodate the work and to ensure its safety. Congress funds the university. That public funding provided an opening for Chicago's opponents, who mounted a fierce attack. The Unification Church–owned *Washington Times* led the assault, running banner headlines about "obscene art," charging (inaccurately) that *The Dinner Party* had been banned by several art galleries, and grossly distorting the financial arrangements between Chicago and the university. The *Times* quoted an adult bookstore owner, who characterized *The Dinner Party* as "a dyke's-eye view of some of the tough broads of the past." Christian television chimed in, branding Chicago the Antichrist and repeating rumors that *The Dinner Party* had been crated up because it contained the devil. On Capitol Hill, opponents took over, against little opposition: Representative Robert Dornan inveighed against "this disgusting dinner table . . . ceramic 3-D pornography"; Representative Dana Rohrabacher called it "weird sexual art"; Representative Stan Parris pronounced it "clearly pornographic."

Amid this onslaught of self-righteousness, misinformation, and downright nonsense, the important issues of academic freedom, congressional oversight, censorship, and sexism never came up for debate. Acting on Representative Parris's amendment to punish UDC for "offensiveness to the sensitivities and moral values of our various related communities," the House struck the requisite funds from the UDC budget. Before the Senate acted, a student strike erupted at the university. Fearful of danger to her fragile creation and eager to support the strikers, who were asking for the same things *The Dinner Party* celebrates—freedom and empowerment—Chicago withdrew her gift to the university.

To the artist, this episode and Anita Hill's confrontation with Supreme Court nominee Clarence Thomas carry the same lesson. "We are at a point in history where we as women can now tell our truth but we can't enforce it. We don't have the institutional power to do so. That was the significance of Stieglitz to O'Keeffe: had she not had him to enforce her truth by introducing it into the system and then making certain it stayed there, she would have been just one more woman artist whistling in the wind. The fight over *The Dinner Party*, the fight over abortion, the fight over the Equal Rights Amendment, all began because of resistance to institutionalizing our gains and making them permanent parts of culture and history."

I asked Chicago to explain this resistance. What is there about feminism that should inspire the attacks on Anita Hill and the high-jacking of *The Dinner Party?* She answered unhesitatingly: fear of female power. "People misunderstand why women want to empower themselves. They filter it through inappropriate paradigms. For example, men see the world in terms of dominate or be dominated. Therefore, when a woman is powerful, people think that means she wants to dominate them. And nothing could be further from the truth."

When I spoke with Chicago she still had not found a home for *The Dinner Party.* Clearly she was distressed over this, for it raised the possibility that a work created in part to mourn a loss to history could itself suffer the same fate. Her best hope, she said, lay in strong public support not only for her work but for all art.

She recognizes this as a frail hope. Elitism in the serious art world has created a dangerous gulf between it and the general public, which neither understands nor enjoys most modern art and tends to regard it as an effete pastime for intellectuals and snobs. In such disinterest one glimpses the shadow of the inert citizenry that Justice Louis Brandeis warned against—"the greatest menace to freedom." Inertia at least partially explains the muted public outcry in recent years against attacks on Chicago, on the National Endowment for the Arts, on minority artists presenting unpopular alternative views of the world, and, in a chilling echo of the Nazi propaganda of the 1930s, on "degenerate art" by conservatives like Patrick Buchanan. Chicago is convinced that education offers the only hope of reversing what she sees as a distinct and alarming trend.

In the fall of 1992, characteristically unwilling to remain silent, she launched a series of civic forums designed to educate New Mexicans about the importance of art, not only to intellectuals and snobs but to everyone.

(4)

The first half of the 1850s was a brilliant period in American letters, one perhaps never surpassed in the grandeur of its vision or the richness of its achievement. In just six years we received five crowning works of American literature—Hawthorne's *Scarlet Letter* (1850), Melville's *Moby Dick* (1851), Stowe's *Uncle Tom's Cabin* (1852), Thoreau's *Walden* (1854), and Whitman's *Leaves of Grass* (1855). Behind these achievements lay a common understanding of the artist's purpose and the means for achieving it. Melville's Ishmael stated it loud and clear: "Give me a condor's quill! Give me Vesuvius' crater for an inkstand! . . . To produce a mighty book, you must choose a mighty theme."

It is advice now regarded as passé, a vestige of an unenlightened era when vision was not yet defined as an artist's ability to imagine whale-sized advances and when freedom of expression had yet to be understood as the grand freedom to express what the public wants. Here in the bright noontime of capitalism triumphant, we have risen above the notion of art as mirror of the soul. In obedience to our sage discovery that sales are the measure of humankind, we have recast art as commodity, like breath freshener, to be judged and rewarded according to its success in the marketplace. Vision is no longer a miraculous gift granted to a few gallant explorers to employ in their quests for new horizons. It is, in George Bush's immortal words, a "thing"—a tire pump. Today's public knows the selling price of the latest Van Gogh to be auctioned at Sotheby's but is acutely disinterested in the painting itself. One is as likely to read about a noted composer or writer in the financial or personality section of a newspaper as on the arts page. The masterworks of our time are corporate logos and advertising jingles, which trace their roots back not to *Walden* or *Leaves of Grass* but to the eighteenth-century English poet John Dyer's poem

The Fleece, a frisky celebration of the British woolen industry. (Of that sublime creation, Samuel Johnson growled, "The subject, Sir, cannot be made poetical." But everyone knows that Dr. Johnson was an old curmudgeon.)

Meanwhile, struggling writers, painters, and musicians are branded dilettantes (the Internal Revenue Service grants them five years to turn a profit or else be classified as hobbyists) and sternly advised by prudent friends to get a job—as if struggle were not exactly that. Public (and private) support for such indolence is widely seen as a variety of turpitude. Never mind that Mozart, Michelangelo, and most of the rest of the long-dead, foreign-born geniuses so beloved of the cultivated free-marketers who frame the debate all received and depended upon such support. Away with them! Let artists sink or swim according to the commercial merits of their products, as pantyhose magnates and mayonnaise kings do! (They don't, of course, but that is another story.)

No great and enduring volume can be written on the flea, Ishmael professed bravely. But these days it is *Forbes* and the *Wall Street Journal* we turn to for advice. And the advice is this: Fleas! By the dogful!

On a clear and serene Sunday morning in June I picked my way upward among shattered relics of the Cretaceous toward the base of an inviting vermilion cliff in north-central New Mexico. In the distance, Georgia O'Keeffe's adobe home stood out on the broken tableland like a neatly squared-off pottery sherd. Above in the hot burnished sky, a hawk of unknown lineage frittered away the morning, a Sunday flier with time on its great silent wings.

So compressed was the history of the slippery slope I was attempting to climb that each step took me not only higher but several thousand years forward in time. Every few minutes I moved into a new stratum dumped a few million years after the previous one. Each layer brought new shades and textures and mounting evidence of the truth of O'Keeffe's proud claim that "all the earth colors of the painter's palette are out there." An ochre slope leveled out among silver-green sagebrush, then ascended into white and gray limestone. A sidewalk of burnt-orange shales led into a dry wash of blue alkali, which dissolved in a crimson embankment, which disappeared beneath a stack of yellow bricks. In O'Keeffe country, the off-road rambler is explorer, historian, geologist, climber of rainbows.

O'Keeffe knew these badlands well. For half a century they were her backyard and her inspiration. In her paintings they look solid, but never use art for a hiking guide. Up close that smooth and firm-looking purple swath may turn out to be hundred-million-year-old siltstone with the integrity of a stale macaroon. When you're scrambling up a steep slope and the ground beneath your feet has the texture of Grape Nuts, it matters not that the incentive for your adventure hangs in the Philadelphia Museum of Art.

At the top of a huge curving hump that from below looked like a buried dinosaur I made a startling and spectacular discovery: a flesh-colored mono-lith about three feet in height with the shape, smoothness, and earnestness of a very large penis. Not one to shrink from duty, I studied the thing for several minutes, as though it were a sculpture. Perhaps it was. I had seen no evidence that anyone had preceded me into the amphitheater, but the phallus was so lifelike that I had difficulty imagining that someone hadn't had a hand in creating it.

I monitored my moral sentiments. Gazing at the monolith seemed to have left them unchanged. I was still firmly committed to peace, justice, and the American way; I still loved my wife; I had no desire to rush down the slope and commit a crazed homosexual act or rob a bank. There seemed to be no good reason to destroy the formation, yet I knew there were some who would do so. I wanted to ask them: What in God's name are you afraid of?

The composer Richard Strauss claimed that his orchestral skills were so prodigious he could write music that would make listeners taste lager beer. I have listened to much Strauss, always soberly. It turns out that he was an impossible braggart; the reformed alcoholic can imbibe him without fear. Heady though it may seem, Strauss's music, like all art, is only a model of the truth, a recipe for what is no doubt a very fine drink but in the end just that, a recipe. And no recipe can get you drunk.

It's a painting, Picasso reminded us. The principle applies to trash as well as to high art, and it explains why a film glorifying racism or a poem about the joy of severing human heads or a photograph of twenty registered nurses copulating with farm animals is no more dangerous than a visit with Strauss to a brewery. (I'm writing with adult perceivers in mind; children are a different matter altogether.) We cannot blame a murder on that violent film which the murderer watched just before committing the crime without explaining why a million other people watched the same film, then went home, fed their dogs, and chatted peaceably over their back fences with neighbors; and without dissecting the enormously complicated life of the murderer, laying out each piece of the puzzle and explaining why one piece should be blamed for the crime but not the others. Liberals have a hard time with this argument, though many are charmed by violent Elizabethan dramas, PBS murder mysteries, and Elmore Leonard shoot-'em-ups. That they take in these entertainments without fear for their own gentle souls suggests that their true concern may lie not with portrayals of violence per se but only those (rap lyrics, cop shows, blood-and-guts films) that the riffraff seem to enjoy. The lower classes apparently do not have reliable handles on their souls.

Similarly (conservatives have a hard time with this one), we cannot blame rape, incest, or disintegrating families on pornography without explaining why the thousand citizens who have sat on a hundred pornography commissions and viewed a million hours of films of seriously interpenetrating bodies have yet to commit a single sex crime or destroy a family. For all of their pretensions and illusions, the creators of what we choose for our recreational and intellectual amusements—and I'm speaking of the Faulkners and Mahlers as well as the trash merchants—contribute mere specks to the mass of knowledge and experience which we bring to bear when we formulate our actions. That is another way of saying that human beings are a lot more complicated than we give them credit for.

I happen to think that artists, writers, filmmakers, and others who choose in their work merely to reflect the world in all its misery ought to set their sights higher, not because I believe they're causing more murder and mayhem—they're not—but because life is short and the gift of creativity is precious, and they could use their gifts just as easily to search for the light that the world desperately needs as to plumb the darkness they're bringing it. The search may not be fashionable, but it is certainly venerable, as the British composer Sir Michael Tippett reminded us in a television address a few years ago. Tippett's words remain for me the single most eloquent statement of the artist's purpose that I know of:

> Deep within me, I know that part of the artist's job is to renew our sense of the comely and the beautiful. To create a dream. . . . I have been writing music for forty years. During those years there have been huge and world-shattering events in which I have inevitably been caught up. Whether society has felt music valuable or needful I have gone on writing because I must. And I know that my true function within a society that embraces all of us is to continue an age-old tradition . . . to create images from the depths of the imagination and to give them form. . . . Images of the past, shapes of the future. Images of vigor for a decadent period, images of calm for one too violent. Images of reconciliation for worlds torn by division. And in an age of mediocrity and shattered dreams, images of bounding, generous, exuberant beauty.

The search for images of beauty is, of course, a search for truth. And the mind that demands an orderly world devoid of subtlety or contradiction—what Jacobo Timmerman called "the totalitarian mind"—requires beauty and truth to be fixed and immutable. Contrast this with Judy Chicago's contention that her job as an artist is to tell the truth as she sees it, a sentiment repeated to me in relation to their own work by both Jean LeMarr and Frederico Vigil. None of these artists and none of the others with whom I spoke claimed to have a monopoly on the truth. All were satisfied to debate their ideas openly through public exhibition and consideration of their work, then to let the chips fall where they may. Their willing admission that they may not have all the answers should cheer the intolerant, though the readiness of these artists to duke it out in the marketplace of ideas may not. Lacking Thomas Jefferson's confidence that the path to truth lies in free argument and debate, fearful that their own ideas may not stand up under such scrutiny, the closed-minded reflexively take up their blue pencils and their hammers and with these tools of domination attempt to silence the disobedient.

It doesn't work, of course. Those frightened souls ought to stop fretting about artists who refuse to toe the line and should instead begin to worry about why in a nation founded on the sublime principle of freedom, so few freely express what is in their hearts, and so many find something admirably American about that. Observed Alexis de Tocqueville: "I know no country in which, speaking generally, there is less independence of mind and true freedom of expression than in America." Rather than silence or compliance, we need musicians, dancers, actors, artists, and writers screaming a thousand different visions of the world. And then we need to trust that the American people are intelligent and mature enough to make up their own minds about which visions they will follow into the future. It seems to me that if we can't do that we might as well get out of the freedom business altogether.

The slope eased, and I moved into the shadow of the wall which a few hours earlier I had spotted from the highway far below and had set out to reach. Several hundred feet high and perhaps a quarter mile wide, the immense buttress formed the high end of the ramshackle ascending alleyway where I had spent most of the morning. Craning my neck, I prowled the base of the wall in search of a crack or a gully I might follow higher still, but without success. My upward travels for the morning were over.

After the cheery and variegated attractions of the climb, the monochromatic end of the road—an enormous recess done up in relentless Mercurochrome red—came as a disappointment. It was as though I had stepped off a spaceship in the midst of the Martian wilds. The towering wall, shattered boulders strewn about like bodies after an explosion, the earth itself, a deep layer of sandstone dust: all of it was stained a thick, eerie red. It smelled musty and looked beaten and felt as dead as a graveyard. I was sure that one of those boulders came screaming down from the top of the wall once every hundred years or so, and I had a vague fear that the next visitor might be due any minute.

A bit dejected, I poked about in the cool shadow of the wall in search of a place to rest. Quite unexpectedly I came across a single plant, a penstemon, flourishing in those otherwise bleak surroundings. No more than the span of a hand in height, the plant had several stems, each topped by a cluster of bright purple flowers.

I felt as though I had run into an old friend on a street corner in Rangoon. Elated, I plopped down beside the penstemon and stretched out my legs. With a sigh I unhitched my gaze and allowed it to tumble down the slope and out over the countryside.

The view was uninspiring. A dreary haze clouded the lowlands. O'Keeffe's home was no longer visible. The distant hills looked dry and dingy. The earth shimmered in a blaze of sunlight. I felt the hot air and the smothering sense of the desert rising up to meet me.

I turned and glanced down at the penstemon. It looked exquisite. Its survival in that hellish spot seemed utterly miraculous. Yet there it stood, strong and resilient, dug in against pestilence, fire, and flood, thumbing its nose at a sky that occasionally rained brimstone, painting the blood-red earth with beauty and with life.

I touched a stem and slipped my hand under the delicate flowers. Cradled in my fingers the tiny blossoms looked grand and indomitable. A penstemon is not the frail creation it may seem to be. Given half a chance, it could overspread the world.

RIVER OF
WINGS

If there is magic on this planet, it is contained in water.

Loren Eiseley, "The Flow of the River"

J ake says, "We go to dinosaur museum." He nods his head to confirm the decision. Then, taking my hand, he leads me to the front door.

My son has a bewitching smile, killer-blue eyes, brontosauran charm, and most of all, a level of determination in matters Jurassic that are hard to resist. But this morning I have made my mind up to prevail. "Let's go to the river. Let's go see the ducks."

A brief impasse ensues. Ultimately I win out. I strap him into his car seat, check to see that the buckle is secure, and off we go.

About us a languid June morning unfolds in Albuquerque. The air is heavy and hot, the sky late for work, a sleepy-eyed, slipshod blue. Crossing town I check the buckle again, then ask a question much on my mind lately: Do I watch over him too closely? I'm always one step ahead of him, always saving him from disasters that might teach him something useful about the world. But where do I draw the line between parental responsibility and overprotection? He's a little boy. He doesn't entirely get it about scalding water and broken glass. Of course I overprotect! Plus he's my only child. That counts for a lot.

I look at him in the rearview mirror, taking in the world with such gusto and such ease. Sometimes he sings to himself. Racking my brain for the motivation for these performances I usually come up short. Maybe he's trying to teach me something useful about the world. He catches my eye in the mirror, and that makes him laugh—just the sight of an eye. He laughs as his grandfather did, full-tilt, all the way from his toes. The joy of it, the purity, makes me laugh too. Suddenly a warm wave envelopes me and fills my heart, and I feel the unfathomable waters that join us and the current that carries us on.

Waiting at a traffic light on West Central Avenue I notice a prickling in the soles of my shoes. I realize that the floor of the car has begun to vibrate rhythmically beneath my feet. Quickly the disturbance swells into something raw and menacing, like the sound of a bass drum pounding inches from my face.

Whomp! Whomp! Whomp! Whomp!

The car recoils with every punch. It takes me only a moment to remember. Turning, I see beside me a kid in a very bad car, a kid with an attitude, a cute girl about sixteen, and a sound system from hell.

My first thought is: *Is he the one . . . ?*

He rides low in his seat. He is vain, imperious—a sultan nibbling grapes. He does not turn to acknowledge the world, ever. He directs a cold stare across the void into the soul of the car ahead.

He is white or brown or black. He may be bareheaded or he may sport a ball cap, sometimes reversed and pulled down to the collar in back to showcase his forehead. Often he wears a mustache, a downy, pathetic thing so clumsily attached it appears it might not survive the day. He smokes. He glares. He jabs his finger at the windshield. He says "fuck."

The girl is less studied, breezier. Her eye shadow is a disaster. Her scent (one guesses) is towering. Her hormones are deafening. She laughs, displaying her teeth. She tosses her head. She will turn to acknowledge an event or to be recognized. Only when she remembers her power (recently discovered and still in the testing stage) and through some adorable jingle-jangle of her body attempts to wield it does she appear as self-conscious as the boy. She is ready to play, the season of passion being short. Soon she will be fat with babies, and then merely fat. Sometimes at her television set she will remember these days as the best.

They do not talk, because not even the voice of God could be heard above the din. They communicate viscerally, in minute adjustments in attitude, in carefully staged tableaus. They live like this, above the volcano—or he does, for sometimes he replaces her with two or three boys much like himself. He is no more troubled by the thunder in his car than you are by the ticking in your chest. His vehicle is part of his body, a newly sprouted extension of his reproductive system. He strokes it and waggles it at girls. He polishes it to a blinding sheen. He does not drive at an excessive rate of speed; rather, he operates his car slowly and tenderly, as if to demonstrate his understanding of women. He changes tapes with the air of a man loosening the buttons on a blouse. He moves his hands on the steering wheel as though he were caressing a silk slip.

He grew up poor and forlorn of hope in a society that prized wealth and station above all else, and that venerated products, and that spoke the language and dreamed the dreams of men who own oil companies. Life is sales, was the motto, and sales are profits, and profits are power, and power is freedom, notably the freedom to purchase products. By the time he entered the seventh or eighth grade he had been branded a misfit, though in fact he was supremely fit, having correctly deduced what some of his classmates would labor to high school and beyond to grasp: that however much he might aspire to own an oil company and however diligently he might work toward that end, he would come up short. Far short. So when he dropped out of school it was not tragic, as many claimed, but prudent.

He found other boys who had fathomed the rules and who had devised an alternative plan. He allowed himself to be beaten up by them to demonstrate that he understood the order of things. He committed petty crimes to prove his enterprise. The strategy seemed to work. Slowly he was accepted into the organization. He found security and camaraderie. He acquired modest profits. He bought a car and a ruthless sound system. Cute girls began to show up out of the blue. They rode around with him and drank whiskey with him and went to bed with him. It was possible for him to imagine that he was on some sort of a career path.

He bought a gun. It was a ridiculous thing, practically homemade. It sprayed bullets like rats flying out of a culvert. He acted crazy with it. He lay on his bed playing with it. He stuck the barrel into his mouth and felt his spine go cold. He staged mock shootings with the gun and practiced cradling it softly in his fingers, like a baby bird. In his final test he fired it randomly at a group of kids as he flew by in his car.

He missed, but that wasn't the point, not that time. He passed. He was ranked into the gang. Now he could beat up the guys who hung around the edges. Now he could commit more meaningful crimes. Mostly that meant dealing drugs out of motel rooms on West Central. He got a finer gun, something magnificent. It fired his dreams. He lived in constant fear for his life, a feeling that was exquisite. Fearing for his life made it seem precious, a perception he had never had before.

Before long he realized to his amazement and satisfaction that he had some of the things that owners of oil companies have—a car, guns, women, cash, a little turf. But there was one thing they had that he did not, that he would never have, and that was respect. Not having respect, not having even a prayer of acquiring respect enraged him. One Saturday afternoon he drank beer and watched a ball game. He ate dinner with his family but, embarrassed by their unimportance, said nothing. He slipped out soon afterward. His mother looked at his father and felt anguish that was as deep and black as the ocean. His father felt as though his heart had been ripped from his chest. They held each other and prayed.

It was June 13, 1992. He picked up three other boys, and they cruised Central Avenue. They were pissed. They drank beer and fooled with their pieces and cranked up the sound. Beneath them Central Avenue shook like an earthquake. Shortly after midnight they drove to the top of West Central, out past the seedy motels and the gasping neon signs, to the high point where the street levels off and where during the day you can look back down the hill at the ribbons of cottonwoods lacing the river, and where you can look off in the other direction and see flat-out like a hundred miles an hour all the way to L.A. Where the Sky Court Motel used to stand, by a broken-down, kicked-out sign advertising "Cars For America," they turned right and moved slowly and tenderly down Estancia Street, past the long wall mural with the red convertible and the white dove and the blue sky and the Blessed Virgin and the actor Edward James Olmos and the educator Dolores Gonzalez and the pacifist

Martin Luther King. And the words *Paz* and *Unidad*. The sound crashed in the car and the beer ignited and the rage boiled over. In the parking lot beside the apartment building they saw the kids they had been looking for.

He stood on the accelerator. They went flying by. Whomp! Whomp! Whomp! Whomp! they poured fourteen white-hot, soul-satisfying, respect-building shots into the parking lot. They didn't look back. They took the corner on two wheels, screamed down Avalon, careened onto Coors or Bergquist or Central, and vanished into the night.

No one knows who they are. No arrests were made. They will never be caught—not for this grievous offense, though they will die young some other Saturday night or go to prison for something else or grow old in crowning bitterness, emptiness, and despair. But for this, no. So I check the buckle on my son's car seat and I look at the kid in the low-slung car, and I wonder if he is the one.

In the parking lot Tyrone Carter went down. Benny Esquivel went down. Tyrone was lucky—his wound was superficial and he recovered quickly. Benny was not lucky. A bullet slammed into his neck and shattered his spinal cord. He was rushed unconscious to University of New Mexico Hospital and awoke the next morning a quadriplegic. For the rest of his life he will breathe with a respirator and urinate with a catheter and eat food from a spoon dancing in someone else's fingers. Benny Esquivel was fourteen.

We park near the river, and I lean back in my seat and gaze out at the cottonwoods and think about these crimes—the crime committed against Tyrone Carter and Benny Esquivel, the crime of attempted murder; and the crime committed against the boys who pulled the triggers, the crime of infanticide. And I force myself to remember the wonder and beauty of the boy at the traffic light, the boy who wanted so much for me to see him.

I am a man whose first impulse at the sign of trouble is to head for the hills, and whose coping machinery falls into disrepair if I go more than a week or ten days without a good suck of mountain air. Like many before me, I prescribe a strong dose of nature when the body is ailing or the soul is dismayed. John Muir assured us that in the mountains cares will fall off like autumn leaves. Thoreau found practically everything worth seeking in wild nature—hope, health, art, spirit, the preservation of the world. Gary Snyder includes on his list freedom, expansion, release, and the opportunity to be crazy for a while. Prisoners take solace from glimpses of sky, and all sorts of troubled souls—schizophrenics, drug addicts, juvenile delinquents—appear to benefit from visits to wilderness. No one is immune. Said Ronald Reagan of his 688-acre California ranch, "Everyone has his own Shangri-La, his own way of getting away, and this is ours." In this we were to understand the truth: the Great Developer was not the scourge of the earth after all, but a simple tree hugger!

If nature is good medicine, then the residents of Albuquerque must be among the healthiest urban dwellers on the planet, for few metropolitan areas enjoy more splendid natural settings. The valley in which the city rests is huge: a vast, sweeping, slightly concave dish ideally designed for collecting light, width, and space. These it distributes to valley residents like electric power. Because the three tend to be disorienting, they infect many Albuquerqueans with a slightly queasy feeling, a concern that their city may be floating. From anywhere in town one looks out as though from the deck of a ship, and gazes a dizzying distance, and grows a little lightheaded at the volume of the surroundings. Clouds drift by like rowboats. The sun and moon cruise through, closer and bigger than they are in other places. They pop up and down reliably and move smartly, rekindling one's appreciation for the software that keeps them on track.

To the east tower the Sandia Mountains, a range of great ruggedness and beauty. The mile-high west face of North Sandia Peak teeters over homes in Albuquerque's Northeast Heights broadcasting the latest bulletins from the high country. Rocks! Trees! Blizzards! It's like a Times Square news marquee but smarter. That face provides Albuquerque with one of the most magnificent urban views that I know. Snow-white in winter, rocky-gray or ponderosa-green in other seasons, dependably fuchsia at sunset, it is beloved throughout the city, a proud emblem on the municipal coat-of-arms.

To the west only a cluster of miniature and long-extinct volcanoes interrupts what is otherwise a horizon so straight it might have been ripped from the sky along a ruled line. The combination of high mountains on one side and low horizon on the other endows the city with an eccentric tilt. The sun rises above the shoulders but sets at waist level: in one direction wild mountains, in the other endless horizon. The West is thus perfectly encapsulated in the valley of Albuquerque. The immediacy and grandeur of these surroundings are striking, and rare for a major metropolitan area.

I have saved for last Albuquerque's best-known work of nature because, from the city's point of view, it differs from the others in important and, as I see it, perplexing ways. Daily, thousands of residents traveling east or west across one of the city's bridges glance out and note what is otherwise an almost completely overlooked fact about their city: a river runs through it. Not just any river, mind you, but the Rio Grande, the great one. Two thousand miles in length, the continent's second-longest river, and legendary in beauty, wisdom, and charm, the Rio Grande is in most parts of New Mexico spoken of in hushed tones and accorded the deference due a respected elder. In Albuquerque, so far as I can tell, it plays almost no role in the conscious life of the city. The river so generous that it irrigates more crops than any other save the Ganges, so rich in lore that it provided Paul Horgan with the material for a Pulitzer Prize–winning history, so diverse that it exhibits between its endpoints every mood from hysterical (one of America's first officially designated wild rivers) to dead calm (sometimes it dries up) is, in Albuquerque, the River of No Respect. Search for a spot where you can enjoy a panoramic view of the waters, and you will likely fail. Seek a broad esplanade where you can picnic with your family or take in a concert or fly a kite, and you will fail. The soft and sensuous river is everywhere corseted brutally, locked up in jetty jacks, forests of tall trees, and tangled undergrowth that are practically impenetrable. To get your hands on this beauty you'll have to do some powerful unzipping.

Here and there it is possible to break through to a clearing with space for three or four. To head north or south from there one quickly needs a boat. In Albuquerque the Rio Grande flows unheralded between its heavily guarded banks, a subject of civic interest only when it waxes in some new source of pollution (in 1993 the Rio Grande was designated "America's Most Endangered River") or when a new bridge is proposed ("Bridge Over the River: Why?" pleaded a sign at the proposed site of the Montaño Bridge, a bridge constructed in 1996 after years of debate and against bitter opposition). Otherwise, Albuquerque is a dry town.

This is plain tragic, and something ought to be done about it. More than bridges, more even than pollution controls, Albuquerque needs to get to know its river. The city needs wide views and river parks where its citizens can enjoy wiener roasts and fireworks displays. Upriver dams have effectively ended the threat of floods, so the gruesome jetty jacks are no longer needed. Get 'em out of there! A new long-range plan by the city will take much-needed steps to preserve the plant and animal life along the river's edge. But the plan says little about the river itself and nothing about its capacity to stir the imagination and lift the heart. "There is something in the scenery of a broad river equivalent to culture and civilization," Thoreau confided to his journal:

> Its channel conducts our thoughts as well as bodies to classic and famous ports, and allies us to all that is fair and great. I like to remember that at the end of half a day's walk I can stand on the bank of the Merrimack. It is just wide enough to interrupt the land and lead my eye and thoughts down its channel to the sea. A river is superior to a lake in its liberating influence. It has motion and indefinite length. A river touching the back of a town is like a wing, it may be unused as yet, but ready to waft it over the world. With its rapid current it is a slightly fluttering wing. River towns are winged towns.

To those who struggle daily with the onerous problems facing the city, my faith that Albuquerque's salvation may lie to some small degree in the waters of its river may seem naive. Perhaps. But these are desperate times, and they demand desperate measures. Among America's cities Albuquerque is one of the best—a progressive community blessed with a beautiful setting, marvelous weather, a healthy business climate, quiet, tree-lined neighborhoods, good schools, great museums, an outstanding university, and a rich cultural life. Its grand old downtown area is fighting back, reclaiming the action from the hideous malls. The city has a splendid convention center, a fine symphony orchestra, great music, sports, and entertainment, and America's handsomest airport. For good reason Albuquerque is regularly named to lists of best places to live and work.

It is also a city which, like all others, is fighting a deadly battle against crime, poverty, unemployment, a deteriorating educational system—the whole contemporary urban nightmare. For many young people it is a cruel place to grow up. According to Manny Vildasol, program coordinator for the Gang Intervention Program at the Albuquerque Juvenile Probation Parole Office, "Albuquerque is a powder keg waiting to blow up." During 1992 the number of known gang members in the city increased from five thousand to sixty-five hundred, the number of gangs from seventy to one hundred. Drive-by shootings are routine. Vildasol paints a depressing picture of a quarter-century of neglect and irresponsibility by social agencies consolidating their power at the expense of communities, treating symptoms rather than under-lying causes, and getting fat in the process.

"Our problem is very, very big," he told me. "We've relinquished our responsibilities to the communities and to the young people. We've taken power away from the people rather than investing them with it. As a result we have ignorance, and ignorance keeps people enslaved. We've got to return power to the communities at the street level, get them to start mentoring themselves instead of doing it for them.

"People from the media, the government, the agencies have to be held accountable for their actions. And instead of hit-or-miss, we've got to begin affecting the child's life on a daily basis. You can't see a kid once a month and expect it to make a difference."

I mentioned my interest in the Rio Grande. Vildasol turned the river into a metaphor for everything that has happened to our cities during the past generation. "In the old days the Rio Grande was pure. You could drink the water. But then it became polluted. Families began to break apart. Our educa-tion system failed. Unemployment grew. People lost hope. The force became too great. The river flooded its banks and broke through in little creeks into the nearby neighborhoods, into the South Valley and along South Broadway.

"And that was where we had our first gangs. Most people think they're still confined to those areas. But today the whole city is flooded. You've got kids all over town involved, up in the Northeast Heights, out in Rio Rancho, everywhere. The pollution has spread across the entire city."

Indeed, it's a rare street where one feels entirely safe walking after dark. The population swells. Competition for jobs and decent housing intensifies. Cultures clash. The value of becoming rich and acquiring products proves unequal to the challenge of lifting the city's sights—and the nation's. Rather the opposite occurs: it poisons the spirit. Families disintegrate, education collapses, hatred intensifies. Suddenly ten-year-olds are carrying guns. This strikes me as an entirely understandable response to the bitterness and disillusionment young people must feel when they come face-to-face with the fact that we have failed to provide them with meaningful goals and not only the hope but the means for reaching them. The sky-shattering potential of these wondrous creatures evanesces; to paraphrase Antoine de Saint-Exupéry's poignant words, the clay of which they are made hardens. And they are lost. Nearby the river flows softly past the cottonwoods, but we have hidden its beauty from them.

Jake and I thrash through a thicket to the water's edge. It is June, and the river is lush, full-throated. A seasonal backwater pools beside us, a humble sanctuary for homeless water bugs and dragonflies. Pale grasses born to the water's edge wade ankle-deep in the newly formed shallows. They look slightly forlorn at the change in plans. Ebony swallows—slick-coated, delta-winged—skitter past, scant inches above the water. Overhead a squad of mallards cruises by, the essence of cool. Dark brooding cottonwoods, lavender-tasseled tamarisks, the odor of damp earth: it could be a quiet day in the country, but we're just a pebble's toss from the Central Avenue bridge, laboring under six lanes of morning traffic. If I stop and think, I'm aware at once of the commotion, so I do my best not to stop and think. To the degree that I succeed, the world beyond this place remains as invisible as this place is to the world.

Before us, stippled in dark green and gold, strumming along like Spanish guitars is El Grande himself—not exactly wider than a mile but a helluva thing to see. There is a spot at Niagara Falls where it is possible to stand at the very brink and feel the water in your face and the thunder beneath your feet and stare straight down into the horrifying abyss. You want to jump. Here at the river's edge lurks a similar compulsion. There is no thunder or plunge, of course, but it's not those that tempt you at Niagara Falls; it's the fever, the sense of two hearts beating as one. The flow of the river is mesmerizing, inexorable, a great army on the march. You want to join. Somewhere John Muir writes of standing at the lip of a falls—it must have been in Yosemite—and imagining himself a sunlit drop of water leaping pell-mell into the void.

Well, what a fine thing that would be! I'm not much of a swimmer, but this river, this surge. . . .

In honor of Muir, Jake and I embark on a fantasy vacation of our own. Jake, you're a snowflake. (He pretends to understand.) You fall in Colorado, in the San Juans. (Falling he knows.) One afternoon you melt. (We try. I'd give anything to know what that feels like.) You slip into a stream. (Hey, it's like climbing into a bathtub.)

Okay—kiss your mom goodbye. (SMACK!)

We leap pell-mell into the void. Figuratively speaking, of course. From Colorado it's about a week to Albuquerque, one fun gonzo slam-dunking computers-are-down week barreling through canyons in northern New Mexico. Then bottom out near Santa Fe, sober up in Cochiti Reservoir, and roll into Albuquerque with a sly wink and a chest full of contrived dignity.

We gaze downstream while I check my mental map. I call out stops like a conductor, which in a way I am. *Socorro next! El Paso! All out for Big Bend! Laredo! Get ready, folks, Brownsville next, then hold on to your hats. . . .*

Gulllfff of Mexxxicoooo!

I don't stop to explain the gulf. Who could explain the gulf? We just keep on rollin'—Tampico, Havana, Santo Domingo, Dakar, Cape Town, Karachi, Jakarta, Singapore.

I remember a long-ago family vacation and a balmy summer evening in Halifax, Nova Scotia. My father took us to the train station, as he sometimes did when we found ourselves in new and exciting places. We watched passengers board the Canadian National Railroad at the beginning of the long journey to Vancouver. I'll never forget the look in my father's eyes when the whistle blew and the cars lurched forward and the adventure began. He said he wanted to do that someday, take the train across Canada. It was a dream he never fulfilled—not a tragic loss but a regrettable one. He had many dreams; some he fulfilled, some he pursued to the end. He died with the grace of a river.

Jake is a thrower of rocks. While the river and I babble on, he raises the level of the water. He's only three; does he understand a word of this? He has a hell-bent style of pitching that reminds me of Giants great Juan Marichal. He throws with a kind of moral fervor. His delivery is so thorough and so selfless it nearly chucks him into the river. He chooses his weapon, he aims, he rushes forward, he cocks his arm, he throws, he stumbles—

I lunge, stopping him inches from the water. Through these heart-breakingly short and swift years I've kept a tight rein on his flesh and bones. But I've tried, too, to unshackle his eyes and ears and maybe even his heart once in a while. We've climbed mountains together, with him perched like lunch at the top of my pack. We've picked apples and fed them to neighborly horses. We've visited the dinosaur museum, often. We've listened to Thelonious Monk, incessantly. That's like falling into a river.

I tell him about the raft his grandfather and grandmother built for his dad. It was the summer of 1956. I was thirteen. The raft was a long green Buick with a grill the size of a xylophone. From Pennsylvania we floated west and west and west, like Wordsworth in his borrowed rowboat, our eyes trained on the horizon's utmost boundary. Far above was nothing but stars and the sky.

I was never the same again. I knew then that one day I would go west and never return. On the night of July 24 we put ashore at the Sky Court Motel in Albuquerque, New Mexico. I know the date because following our return home we put together a souvenir scrapbook of the trip. I still have it. Pasted on the page for July 24 is a postcard of the Sky Court Motel. The card is a soothing 1950s period piece, a head-on view of the motel done up in washed-out, hand-tinted pastels. The scene has a faraway, dreamy quality about it. It appears to have been rendered by someone who loved the place.

Towering over the motel is an elaborate sign with a painting that depicts a range of brown and craggy New Mexico mountains. Above, tall yellow letters on blue sky announce the end of the journey: "This is it! The Sky Court!" The rest of the sign is given over to vital information about the motel.

It is air-conditioned. It boasts twenty modern units. The rates are reasonable. Inspection is invited. Important for the late-arriving traveler, there is a vacancy, always and forever.

Beneath the sign stands the office, a one-story cube of white brick. Paved lanes on either side lead back to the rooms, which appear to be separate units—neat, private homes, standard for 1950s motels. Each tiny house comes equipped with an awning and a pocket-sized lawn, complete with shrubs, trees, and lawn furniture. At the end of the lanes stands a forest of cottonwoods and evergreens. The sky is a quiet gathering of breathy clouds, white at the top, running to peach where they drift in among the trees.

It is a very peaceful scene. No cars or people are visible. The Sky Court seems hewn from the landscape, like a clearing in the woods. It looks like a place where you could get a good night's sleep.

I lived in New Mexico for six years before I got around to paying my respects to the memory of the Sky Court. One afternoon I went looking for the place. I drove across the Central Avenue bridge and up the hill on old U.S. Route 66. I don't remember what the neighborhood was like in 1956. Today it's an ugly and depressing hodgepodge of fast-food joints, secondhand stores, and dilapidated motels. Iron bars seal the windows of many of the establishments.

Where the street levels off at the top of the hill I found the lot that corresponded to the address on the postcard. It's a weed patch now. The towering sign, the office, the little landscaped houses, the trees are all gone. The peach-colored clouds are gone. There is still a vacancy at the Sky Court, but it has taken over the entire motel. All that stands in the lot today is a derelict sign advertising "Cars For America."

Amid the weeds and broken glass I made out the foundations of a few of the old rooms. Standing in the doorway of one of those forlorn spots I gazed into the interior and pictured myself a boy of thirteen sleeping blissfully at my feet. Suddenly I felt a terrible ache in my gut, for me and for my parents, for all those distant hand-tinted years. Most of all for a good night's sleep.

I crossed Central and drove down Estancia, past the mural with Edward James Olmos and the white dove and the words *Paz* and *Unidad*. I stopped at the parking lot where the kids shot Benny Esquivel. He grew up in this neighborhood. He used to play on two good legs in the empty lot where I slept well the night of July 24, 1956. I thought about him in his wheelchair, and I thought about his parents. And then I didn't know what to think.

Jake and I wander under the bridge. In a shallow pool that has split off from the river a huge carp thrashes about in terror. Back and forth across the water it beats, half its body exposed above the surface.

We watch and then turn away. The underside of the bridge is a series of lateral tunnels leading across the river. Each succeeding tunnel leads deeper into the water. But the first few are dry, and we are able to enter them to see what they hold.

Inside we find literature. Kids have discovered the river after all. The walls are thick with graffiti: tall, bold, indomitable outcries that undergird the bridge with a strength and a vitality it could never have known before. The colors are brash and exciting, the designs fantastic, the energy soaring. Pushing and shoving for wall space, one word flows into the next, revising and updating the manuscript, shaping it into ever more eloquent sentences, paragraphs, and chapters. In a hundred pages of this epic tale I manage to find two words that I can read: AEROSOL GODZ. But the meaning of the text is unmistakable. This is a work about passion, the passion of kids mad to live, mad to talk, mad to be saved—in Kerouac's words, "desirous of everything at the same time, the ones who never yawn or say a commonplace thing, but burn, burn, burn like fabulous yellow roman candles exploding like spiders across the sky."

The tunnels slip one by one into the river. The farther we go the grander the narrative gracing the wall. When we can go no farther I gaze into the next tunnel and then the one beyond, past the deathless sagas of Odysseus, Jason, Gulliver, and Huckleberry Finn, to stories only now being written. Somewhere out there at the edge of daring, an aerosol god clings to a wall, composing a tale that will change the world.

I take my kid and hug him. I show him the great current, the power and majesty of it, the way it is possible to move with it instead of struggling against it, in order to absorb its strength. Suddenly I see where it could end and what the river could do to stop the terrible crimes. And I know that I could bring these wonders to pass simply by speaking to my son.

Here is what I could say:

We don't know what to do. We're helpless in this. Get out while there's still time. We can no longer go, because we are old and afraid and because we have lost our vision and our will.

But for you there's a way. Take the others. Take Benny and Tyrone. Take them all, the millions, our darlings, the boys and girls with their toy guns, their little cars, their beautiful smiles. Laugh, sing songs, build boats, push off into the swift and confident stream. They will follow you, I promise. Go now, you know the way. We will think of you and dream of you on your grand voyage—south and south and south, past the wide fields, the shining mountains, the ravaged cities. South to the infinite sea.

DESERT GENESIS

All the past we leave behind,
We debouch upon a newer mightier world, varied world,
Fresh and strong the world we seize.

—Walt Whitman, *"Pioneers! O Pioneers!"*

(1)

The pursuit of the elusive American is probably a hopeless quest, one best left to incurable romantics and fools; a hunt for Bigfoot is as likely to bag its prey. An esteemed social scientist sums up a lifetime of research by announcing that Americans are a mobile people. Somehow he factors out of his hard-won equations the millions who die within shouting range of their childhood homes. A historian professes that we are generous and gregarious, a heartwarming compliment which, however much we may want to believe it, overlooks countless survivalists hiding out in the mountains of Idaho, misers in Kentucky and Rhode Island, Social Darwinists in Ohio. Frederick Jackson Turner characterized us as practical and versatile; as a man who cannot hang a picture without putting out someone's eye, I offer myself as a dangerous counterexample. Tocqueville tramped deeper into this thicket than anyone else and compiled the longest list of adjectives: natural, frank, open, insensitive, ambitious, and a hundred others. Each rings true of some of us, false (glaringly so) of others. "The city street is crowded," observes Richard Rodriguez, "and we are each preoccupied with finding our own way home."

Surely any endeavor to describe the essential American is doomed from the start. Like a mammalogist going after musk ox, any such effort must assume that we are a distinct and identifiable species and that a skilled observer, given sufficient patience and a powerful enough set of binoculars, can successfully deduce our mating habits and migration patterns.

Walt Whitman, our preeminent field biologist, disposed of that theory in a few words: "Each of us sings what belongs to him or her and to no one else." Whitman's discovery compelled him to create a new poetic form, one that catalogued not only the adjectives but the people themselves—the Yankee girl, the paving man, the canal boy, the conductor. He has often been rebuked for his invention (it occasionally soars to the heights of a census report). But no other form could encompass America.

Whitman discovered us in midsong, caught up in the tumult of our counterpoint. Suppose we return to the downbeat, to that startling moment when the Yankee girl and the paving man broke into song. I am thinking of the instant when the two first beheld the promise of America and marveled at its length and breadth and essence. Perhaps it is moments of stark beginning like those which define us as Americans. If so, then perhaps we should search for our distinguishing characteristics not in the content of our characters but in the commonality of our birth experiences. Not long ago I met a man who provides an apt illustration of my point. Jorge León is a native Guatemalan. In 1986 he entered this country illegally by way of Mexico's Sonoran Desert. Today, having overcome a series of enormous obstacles, he is a legal resident of the United States who lives with his family in Albuquerque. León is a very different man than I, and I'm confident that Alexis de Tocqueville would have had a hard time finding an adjective that characterizes both of us with any degree of accuracy. Yet we are both Americans. What does that mean?

As I tried to imagine León's long and difficult trek across the desert on his journey to America, I found myself thinking about two other journeys— neither of which I ventured upon but both of which I can picture so clearly and feel so deeply that they resonate with the quality of memory. One was an ocean voyage that carried my mother's ancestors from England to Massachusetts in 1628. The other brought my father's parents from Scotland to New York City a century ago. I have no hard facts and can recall no family traditions relating to either journey. And yet I can picture the details of each voyage and imagine the excitement of the moment of arrival and, most of all, sense the apprehension that my ancestors must have felt at the inscrutable prospect opening before their eyes. Perhaps that is because it is a prospect which has opened before my eyes as well.

I wonder if all of us—Indians, immigrants, descendants of immigrants—might not share such a memory of disembarking in America. For Jorge León and some twenty million others, the memory recalls an actual moment of arrival; to the rest of us, a telling recollection has been passed from those who were there. Dusty and true, it resides in the collective American consciousness like the steps of an ancestral dance. It provides us with the one thing that unites us as a people—an image of pure potentiality, a picture of a land dependent for its shape and sustenance not on the hand of God (though in times of trouble we often fall back upon that comforting delusion) but on our own weak and untried hands.

The more I thought about my ancestors' journeys, the more I wanted to see one of the landscapes that inspires these cultural memories of daybreak in America. So it was that one early-winter morning I headed south for the desert where Jorge León first beheld the empty canvas of America spread out before him.

Antelope Wells, New Mexico, may be the loneliest border station in the United States. Forgotten, forlorn of fuss and nearly of purpose, it clings like a clod of mud to the underside of the boot heel that presses down into the Mexican states of Chihuahua and Sonora from the southwest corner of New Mexico. Most crossing points along the southern frontier are narrow zones of civility dug in somewhat precariously between two kick-ass border towns. Antelope Wells is an exception. Here there is no town at all, not even a sleazy cantina where you can drop in for a beer and nachos. It's thirty miles to the nearest settlement in Mexico, forty to the closest in New Mexico, a place called Hachita that is for all practical purposes a ghost town. Both Mexico and the United States maintain the barest of checkpoints at Antelope Wells. A trailer, a gate, a few unremarkable buildings—and beyond, in all directions, skinflint desert, low-lying and chaste, a useful reminder of the earth's ability to meet its expenses whatever the cost.

The continental divide slices through a few miles to the west, separating the Chihuahuan Desert from the Sonoran. The Chihuahuan Desert, of which Antelope Wells is a part, is higher and cooler than the better known Sonoran Desert, whose saguaro cacti are familiar to all visitors to southern Arizona. At an average elevation of under six hundred feet, the Sonoran is the hottest North American desert; many aficionados believe it is also the most beautiful.

To the nighttime immigrant, such distinctions are no doubt academic. The Chihuahuan and Sonoran Deserts are both big, wild, dangerous, and notably deficient in the amenities we commonly associate with the good life.

On average, five vehicles a day pass through the checkpoint at Antelope Wells. Most are connected with the cattle ranching that takes place on both sides of the border. Driving in I wondered how Herefords and Angus could prosper in a land that seemed expressly designed for lizards and scorpions. A brief reconnaissance at the border answered my question. Rolling east among the native plants was a sparse cover of khaki-colored grass. Perhaps a mile away stood an assortment of apparently contented cows, creating an odd desert pastoral. Nearby ran a dark band of mesquite, which I knew that cattle have learned to browse.

As if to answer a second question, regarding the origin of the name Antelope Wells, a herd of a dozen or so pronghorn antelope bounded into view and lowered their heads to graze near the cattle. Not far from the animals stood an old tin-blade windmill, spinning and clattering as it sucked water from deep in the ground into a shallow but no doubt sorely appreciated stock pond.

Like the border station, the road to Antelope Wells is two or three grades below standard issue. It's gravel the final ten miles to the checkpoint. Deserts don't deal with water well, and when the road is wet it's a muddy hell. To avoid getting bogged down in the muck, which forms at the first sign of moisture, customs agents come in on four-wheel-drive vehicles every day of the year. A light rain was falling on the November morning I drove south from Hachita, an anomalous start to a day in the desert. In the distance a curtain of mist drifted back and forth over the face of the Animas Mountains. The air was heavy and cold, the landscape huge, the road as empty as Saudi Arabia.

Beyond my windshield the desert looked strange and wonderful. I punched some John Coltrane into the tape machine, cranked up the volume, rolled down the windows, and jerked the car onto the left side of the road. Every minute or two I hit a sloppy spot, launching the back tires into a frantic spin, the rear of the car into a wicked bump-and-grind. With an urgent sax honking instructions beside me, I gripped the wheel and finessed the pedals, putting to work the driving skills I had perfected as a kid driving the icy winter roads of northwestern Pennsylvania.

I was on my way to a place where I could see America come up with the sun. I planned to explore the boot heel that day, rise early the next morning, and greet the dawn on an appropriate lick of sand somewhere near the border.

Hearing Jorge León's tale of the dire conditions in Guatemala that had set him on his long journey to the United States reminded me once again how easily we Americans overlook the greatness and uniqueness of our country. We are good at bragging about its virtues and ideals, but in our forgetfulness we often practice them sloppily, back wheels spinning in the mud. Sometimes we get bogged down completely and revert reflexively to outmoded ways of thinking and behaving. We forget that much of the world is only too familiar with those modes and is waiting, with less and less patience, for us to lead the way in new and different directions. I wanted to set my compass by those directions, and I was confident that a quiet spot in the desert at sunrise would be a good place to do so. Coltrane, cold rain, fishtailing giddily in the mire—it was all part of the search.

The gap between what we say and what we do reminds me of a bus ride I once took on Mexico's Yucatan Peninsula. I had a choice between a broken-down school bus and a sleek modern vehicle with the proud words *de aire accondicionado* emblazoned on the side. It was May and the temperature was 115 degrees. I took the air-conditioned bus.

Minutes after leaving the station I regretted my decision. The cooling system was out of order. The temperature in the bus quickly shot up to an infernal level. The air thickened with the mingled odors of oppression and moist passengers. With an all-day ride ahead of me I began to panic. I tried to open my window but discovered that it, like all the others in the vehicle, was permanently sealed. Squirming and sweating I solicited the help of the man seated beside me. "What can we do?" I asked. "I'm dying."

He glanced at me as though I were crazy. "It's an air-conditioned bus!" he barked.

I shoved past him and went forward to talk to the driver. "This is hell," I said. "I can't even open my window."

"Of course not," he said, not even looking at me. "It's an air-conditioned bus." He pointed to a notice over the windshield which confirmed that I was indeed traveling by air-conditioned bus. Then he shook his finger and motioned for me to sit down. It was obvious he had me pegged as a troublemaker.

The cool air never came on that day. I passed the miles sweltering and fuming, newly acquainted with the gulf that occasionally opens between seductive fantasy and agonizing truth.

"To arrive where you are, to get from where you are not, you must go by a way wherein there is no ecstasy." So advised our canniest travel agent, T. S. Eliot, who apparently knew something about illegal border crossings. It was by walking across the desert somewhere west of Antelope Wells that Jorge León got to where he is from where he is not. It's a popular area for midnight immigration, but only for the hearty. Because the region is so wild the U.S. Border Patrol wastes few of its resources there. In two days of snooping around the boot heel I came across not a single patrol vehicle. The customs agent at Antelope Wells told me that plenty of immigrants attempt the passage. "They'll walk across anything," he sniffed, curiously unmoved by what I took to be remarkable tenacity and courage. He added that since the likelihood of interdiction is small, most of those who prepare well for the rigors of the journey probably complete it.

Forbidding though the region may be, it boasts a colorful if abbreviated human history. Caves on some of the mountainsides contain evidence of early human habitation and mining of turquoise deposits. During the mid nineteenth century, Apaches led by Cochise and Mangas Colorado hid out in the Animas and other mountains near the divide. From there they led raids on wagon trains and white settlements in southern Arizona and New Mexico. Prospectors came in and, in their unfathomable way, turned up deposits of gold, silver, copper, and other minerals, much of it poor in quality. Since then, mines have operated intermittently in the vicinity, usually without much success.

The region's most celebrated event took place on the morning of March 9, 1916, when Pancho Villa and a thousand Mexican revolutionaries crossed the border sixty miles northeast of Antelope Wells and attacked Columbus, New Mexico, a settlement of five hundred residents. Though he was cut off immediately and pursued back into Mexico by General John Pershing and five thousand U.S. troops, Villa gained the distinction of becoming the only man to lead a foreign army in an attack of the United States mainland since the War of 1812.

Exploring the boot heel, driving the desert roads that wamble over the landscape like crazed prospectors, I had a hard time imagining a party of immigrants moving over that wild expanse. It wasn't simply the physical obstacles of such a journey that impressed me, though those were clearly huge. As time passed and I grew more accustomed to the surroundings, I began to be disturbed by something more fundamental: a sense of bare, pitiless earth, of nature stripped to the bone and waiting to lash out. Obviously alone and in no danger, I sensed a nagging presence wherever I went. Partly the feeling must have resulted from stories I had heard about *coyotes,* those occasionally treacherous entrepreneurs who guide undocumented immigrants across the border.

But at a deeper level something primitive was at work—the demon who freezes the blood when the stairs creak at midnight. In the yawning spaces around Antelope Wells, I wasn't sure that the door was locked.

I'm a newcomer to deserts. I'm still uncertain of their habits and their expectations. Mountains I know well and enjoy even on their worst behavior. To me they are the most soothing and welcoming of earth's offspring.

There is nothing soothing or welcoming about a desert. A desert is brash and uncompromising, a demanding host with little patience for smooth talk, subtlety, or illusion. Somewhere near Hatchet Peak, pestered by curiosity over the nature of the terrain and itching to come to grips with my fears, I exercised my God-given American right to slam on the brakes and leave my car rocking on its springs beside the road. I hopped out and took off on foot across the desert floor.

The rain had lifted; the sky was clad in gray stucco from horizon to horizon. Beneath my feet the dark earth yielded with the consistency of a warm Hershey bar. I had no worries that I would lose my way or my car: each step that I took left a shoe-shaped calling card in the goo. Besides, I could see for twenty miles in every direction but northeast, where the pasteboard-gray form of Hatchet Peak leaned against the sky like an abandoned sandwich board.

My walk was short but exhilarating. Though the terrain was everywhere decked out in flamboyant desert plants, they were spaced widely enough that I could weave my way easily through the maze. Given the desert's predilection for straight talk, I had no difficulty figuring out the master plan, which as I see it is to figure out as many ways as possible to deploy thorns.

But beneath that prosaic rubric there is room for endless variety and charm: tall spindly cholla and ocotillo, thin mouse-eared prickly pear, fat barrels, sleek swords, teetering vases, goofy spheres, hairy jawbones, fuzzy giraffes, bearded vultures. Up close, colors are equally varied. At a distance they blend into an even, practical shade of green. On the morning I visited, that persistent hue, luminescent from the rain and pale from the late season, seemed to float on the desert floor like an overgrown lily pad. Here and there a patch of color flaunted impudently. Me! Me! (Vulture bud, platinum blonde.) Me! Me! (Jawbone tumor, Ferrari red.) Each plant revealed its true character with utter candor.

The yucca is a thick handful of up-pointing, finger-slim leaves, each tipped by a long, wicked thorn. Through adolescence the plant contains itself, barely, growing randier by the day. At the appointed moment it sends a slender shoot ten feet straight into the air, tops it with a brassy crown of white, bell-shaped flowers, and enters its glory as a brazen pin-up queen.

The glory is short-lived. Before long the flower fades and the plant begins to resemble a mess of corroded plumbing. The ever more haggard and unsightly yucca deteriorates month by month, its tired stalk leaning farther and farther from the vertical but unable to fall. I traversed whole acres of these defeated beauties. Their bones creaked, their heavy crowns drooped like tired heads in the hallway of a nursing home.

Back at my car I took a last look over the landscape. Not twenty yards away a slight movement caught my eye. Suddenly a very fat, very black javelina—a kind of wild hog—stepped onto the road. The creature regarded me with interest, as though I might be something good to eat. Raising its snout it examined the air for signs of nutrition emanating from my direction. Then it snorted insultingly: unpalatable! Showing no further interest, the animal waddled across the road and disappeared into the brush.

There is only one great thing, the Eskimo sings: to live to see in huts and on journeys the great day that dawns and the light that fills the world.

In the last embrace of darkness that preceded the dawn I staked out a patch of ground perhaps a quarter of a mile north of the Mexican border and turned my eyes to the sky. Above the eastern horizon, Jupiter poised brilliant and laser-sharp, trailblazer for the sun. The sky sighed and parted, and the first rays of light streamed in like a hail of sparrows. The eyes of the Animas blinked open in bronze. With majestic languor, creaking with age, the shadow-pocked desert unfurled over the planet toward the benighted west. Tawny and gnarled, it reminded me of a great parchment, a document written in the language of women and men. I had always thought it would be mountains, but perhaps it was deserts where I would grasp at last that essential truth, that humanness and nature are one.

I shivered and poked my hands into the pockets of my jacket. A desert hawk sailed by and snarled. The raw light seemed lazy and dense, uncertain of where to tether for the day. Mingled odors of salt and the sea rose from the desert floor. I felt suddenly that I was standing on the bow of a ship, waiting to disembark in the unknown country that beckoned to the north, beyond the veil of the desert dawn.

Slowly and uncertainly I turned to face that direction. I couldn't be sure, but I guessed that the expanse before me might be a place of beauty and opportunity and contentment. Somehow it seemed like a country where a weary traveler could find a home and a good life, a land where a person could be free.

(2)

Jorge León lives a block from the Santa Fe Railroad tracks in a dusty, hardscrabble neighborhood of Albuquerque that is home to many of the city's warehouses and auto body shops. León and his wife, Lupe, their three children, and Lupe's sister, Maria, share a small apartment in a two-story building that appears to have been pounded together from warped plywood and rapidly uttered prayers. One evening León greeted me at the top of the stairway that mounts one side of the building. With me was Peter Simonson of the Albuquerque Border City Project, a nonprofit organization that works to ensure the civil and legal rights of recently arrived immigrants. Simonson speaks fluent Spanish, as I do not, and he had agreed to join me to help me piece together the Leóns' story.

The apartment reminded me of rooms in brownstones on New York's hellish Lower East Side, where I hung out with friends during the late 1960s and where I lived, briefly, in 1968. There were several sizable rooms with high ceilings and badly worn wood floors. León led us into the living room, where he introduced us to his wife and sister-in-law. A bare bulb hanging from the ceiling suffused the room in flaxen light. The walls were paneled in fake pine and hung with a spirited display of calendars and thrift-store art, much of it arranged at whimsical angles. (Whether this was deliberate or a tribute to the building's inclination I couldn't be sure.) An assortment of dilapidated sofas, chairs, and tables crowded the room. Each piece of furniture was strewn with blankets and clothes, leading me to guess that the room served as a combination of living room, bedroom, and closet for some of the apartment's six inhabitants.

Jorge and Lupe León have dark features and straight, coal-black hair. Jorge is burly; Lupe delicate, almost gaunt. He wore a red-and-blue checkered shirt; she a pink sweater so bulky and bright she seemed lost within it. She was pregnant with the couple's fourth child.

Lupe served fruit juice and crackers. Then she joined her husband and Maria on a sofa across from Peter and me. Now and then a child walked or crawled into the room or climbed into Lupe's or Maria's arms. Sometimes the conversation was interrupted by the clatter of freight cars passing not far from the front door, or by the sound of a train whistle crying in the night.

Jorge León grew up in Chichuamel, a village of five hundred residents in the mountains of Guatemala not far from the Mexican border. He is of Mayan descent. His native languages are Kanjobal, the regional tongue, and Chu, a local dialect. Unlike many people of his region, he also speaks Spanish. His parents were subsistence farmers who eked out a living growing corn, beans, potatoes, and a few other staples.

"It was a tough life," León told me. "If you didn't harvest you didn't eat. I started working alongside my parents when I was very young. The year I was twelve we needed money badly, so I started crossing the border into Mexico to pick coffee around the city of San Cristóbal de las Casas."

Growing up close to the land, León learned that there is a natural order to things, a pattern of events that recurs year after year. He did not learn until much later that the natural order in Guatemala is not the same as it is in other countries. In an effort to explain the difference, Guatemalans sometimes invoke the Mayan myth of the thorny flower. This fragment of native lore will ring true for anyone who has contemplated the yucca plant of the American West. The myth teaches that the universe, like the thorny flower, has two aspects: the first is beauty; the second, suffering.

The color of the mountainsides surrounding Chichuamel is of the deepest green. The vegetation is thick, the odor rich, the earth passionate and life-giving.

During León's youth, communist guerrillas ranged through these sublime surroundings, working to secure food, jobs, and political power for the poor. "The guerrillas tried to help the people. But too bad if you were against them," he said. Sometimes the bodies of villagers who refused to cooperate with the guerrillas were discovered in ravines or irrigation ditches, riddled with bullets.

In an effort to stamp out the insurgents as well as to consolidate its own position, the Guatemalan government instituted terror as an instrument of political policy. Thus it became the natural order of things for representatives of León's government each year to remove the eyes, ears, tongues, fingernails, nipples, and genitals of several thousand Guatemalans—few of them guerrillas—and then to shoot them, crucify them, bury them alive, or throw them from helicopters into active volcanoes. Each year thousands of women were raped by soldiers, and thousands of children were orphaned, and thousands of Guatemalans disappeared without a trace.

In its natural state the land around Chichuamel was fertile. But for León's family and other villagers, finding land in its natural state became harder and harder to do. Government troops stripped the forests, spread toxic chemicals on the fields, and poisoned water supplies, often for no other purpose than to increase the people's misery. To find arable land, farmers were forced to climb higher and higher on the mountainsides. Some had to tie themselves to trees while they plowed, to avoid falling off their fields.

Each year in the natural order of things some fifty thousand Guatemalan peasants were dispossessed of their land. The land was turned over to the two percent of the Guatemalan citizenry who are rich and who live by U.S. chief justice John Jay's motto that the people who own a country ought to govern it. The Guatemalan two percent owned seventy percent of the land and more of it every year. They owned the military, the police, the judiciary, and most of the public officials. When they were not busy running the country, the two percent attended symphonies and garden parties. In the natural order of things, guests at Guatemalan garden parties often included U.S. government officials and representatives of American corporations, which have established more branches in Guatemala than in any other Central American country.

In the pattern of events each year (the years of the Carter administration were the exception), the U.S. State Department discovered remarkable progress in human rights in Guatemala. The president of the United States praised a new Guatemalan dictator, who the president said was a vast improvement over the last dictator, whom the president had praised the year before. The U.S. Congress increased aid to the Guatemalan military so that it could purchase helicopters to ferry its people to the country's volcanoes. The Pentagon trained Guatemalan army officers at the School of the Americas in Fort Benning, Georgia, and dispatched advisers to Guatemala to teach methods of counterinsurgency warfare to teenage boys. The oligarchy grew more voracious, the guerrillas fought more tenaciously, violence begat violence, and bloodlust engendered enemies even thirstier than itself.

"He is damned always to do that which is most repugnant to him," Arthur Koestler wrote in *Darkness at Noon.* "To become a slaughterer, in order to abolish slaughtering, to sacrifice lambs so that no more lambs may be slaughtered, to whip people with knouts so that they may learn not to let themselves be whipped, to strip himself of every scruple in the name of higher scrupulousness, and to challenge the hatred of mankind because of his love for it—an abstract and geometric love."

Each attempt to balance the equation led to a new imbalance. The mathematicians in Washington and Guatemala embraced a linear algebra of evil, which posits that opposition to insanity places one automatically in the camp of the sane.

But the algebra of evil is not linear, it is circular, and it leaves no place for sanity. One cannot stand anywhere on the circle and not be part of it. In Guatemala the circle spun faster and faster, gathering more and more people into its circumference. Bewitched by the cool logic of action and reaction, the mathematicians failed to see that the only hope for sanity lay in standing completely apart from the circle and crying "Stop!"

One night in 1981, long after the hour at which most residents of Chichuamel had retired, government troops entered the town. Choosing dwellings at random, soldiers broke down the doors, stormed into the houses, and murdered families in their beds. Thirty-five people were killed that night: one of every fourteen townspeople. Seven of the dead were children.

Three years passed. One day soldiers returned to Chichuamel. With them was a recently captured guerrilla whom they had tortured. The troops lined up the town's citizens in the village square. An officer ordered the guerrilla to point out anyone who had aided him and his comrades with food or supplies.

The guerrilla walked along the line. One by one he picked out five men of Chichuamel. Each was brought forward by the soldiers. Then, in full view of his family and fellow townsfolk, he was decapitated with a bayonet.

León was impressed into the Guatemalan army. "I didn't want to join," he said. "But I had no choice—they killed the ones who refused to go. They gave us guns and a little bit of training, and then they took us to a camp in the southern part of the country near the El Salvador border. Pretty soon everybody was talking about war with El Salvador. I didn't believe in what the government was doing. One day it was war with El Salvador, the next day it was war against our own people. It was wrong."

León began making secret inquiries among his fellow soldiers. He discovered that many of them were as frightened as he, and as uncommitted to the government's cause. With four others he began making secret plans to desert. One night, knowing that a firing squad awaited them should they fail, the five men disappeared into the countryside.

León made his way across Guatemala. A fugitive not from justice, he believed, but from injustice, he feared constantly for his life. His destination was the highlands of southern Mexico. Slowly he was perfecting a fine and rare ability, one he had first practiced as a twelve-year-old coffee picker: the ability of foxes, the ability to disrespect and overcome borders at will. Such dexterity is one mark of a free person, and León is surely that—a free person, a person of conscience, and, like all such persons, a refugee.

He was not the only Guatemalan seeking asylum in Mexico. León's fellow countrymen by the thousands were streaming into Mexico to escape the violence of their homeland. To reach a safe haven, some of these people spent weeks in the mountains without adequate food, clothing, or medicine. Many died en route. The Mexican government transformed the city of San Cristóbal into a refugee center and attempted to provide food, shelter, and work for the dispossessed Guatemalans.

By coincidence, León arrived in San Cristóbal as a refugee at almost the same moment I arrived there as a skylarking tourist. I should say as a very hot skylarking tourist, for it was San Cristóbal to which I was headed on my grossly misadvertised air-conditioned bus ride. The former capital of the state of Chiapas, the city is today best known as the site of the peasant uprising of January 1994; it remains a center of popular resistance to the Mexican government and oligarchy.

Chiapas shares important geographical, historical, and cultural ties with Guatemala. It is beautiful, haunting terrain. It is big and high and open, encircled by magnificent vistas. It broods in the dreamy scent of mesquite and ironwood fires that burn continually in the fields. On the mountainsides, clusters of white-shirted workers hang frozen to the slopes like patches of snow.

The contrast with the Yucatan, where I had spent several weeks exploring Mayan ruins, could not be more striking. The Yucatan is low-down jungle—old, hot, oppressive. It's for sweltering and ruminating on the past. San Cristóbal de las Casas is a paradise in the clouds—young, cool, robust. It's for breathing deeply, making plans, and overdosing on Mexican pastries.

I stayed for a week. Most days I visited an Indian market in town or in one of the surrounding villages. What a life force those markets possess! Rocking, jammed with frenzied shoppers, the aisles threaten to burst from a deluge of energy and vitality. The air echoes in the quick, chittering sounds of a dozen throaty languages. Merchandise is inspected, bargains struck with the smoothness of ritual. No less than buying and selling, it is the necessity for human interaction, for give and take, that brings these people to the market.

Looking about, I recognized faces from portraits I had seen carved on Mayan temples; only the deep brown and luster of the eyes were new to me. The men dress plainly, many in white shirts and dark trousers. The women are pure razzle-dazzle; they primp, they glitter, they glide like swans. Each blouse and shirt is unique, a daring pastiche of rollicking textures and hues, one joined to the next with breathtaking aplomb. The regional costume bespeaks a primal understanding of the creative power of mingled differences. It's pure jazz, reminiscent of pianist Bill Evans's observation that group improvisation fulfills the human need for sympathy from all members to bend for the common result.

Wandering rows of baskets, stacked fruit, and hand-woven serapes, I sometimes attempted sheepishly to bargain over a purchase. Always the results were disastrous. Mostly I studied faces till someone looked up and caught my eye; both of us would quickly turn away in embarrassment and in fear. More than anything, I wanted to see into the lives of those people, to glimpse the textures and hues of their daily routines and their dreams. If I could have bargained for those I would gladly have parted with my last peso. Since meeting Jorge León I've often wondered if I may have passed him once in a market in San Cristóbal—if I may have brought home my souvenir at last.

León resided near San Cristóbal and there found regular employment as a field worker. But before long a new kind of violence asserted itself.

"The Mexicans started to hate the Guatemalans," he told me. "There were too many of us. They said we took work away from them. The plantation owners began cutting our wages. Life became very difficult. Often there were no jobs and you might not eat. Even when there was work, the wages were so low it was hard to get by."

Inevitably the fox began thinking of moving on again, this time to the United States. Dreams of justice, freedom, and equality played only a minor role in his decision to seek a new home; what León knew about the United States he had learned not from stories about George Washington and Abraham Lincoln but from insignias on rifles and tanks, from newspaper photographs of American ambassadors and business leaders grinning at butchers. In Guatemala the United States convinced not by arguments, similes, or rhymes, as Whitman so deftly noted, but by its presence. When León departed San Cristóbal and set out for northern Mexico, he was searching not for the cradle of democracy or the light of the world but merely for a job and a good place to hide. When he traversed the desert and entered the United States on a moonless night in 1986, he did not stop to kiss the earth.

The new arrival moved from one town to the next, following the crops: picking chiles, eggplants, cucumbers, and tomatoes across the southern frontier. In Florida he met and married Lupe Ramirez, who hailed from a village near his own in Guatemala. The two worked the fields together and began to raise a family. One day with Lupe's sister, Maria, they entered the federal courthouse in Miami and asked for political asylum.

"We told them we were from Guatemala," Lupe said. "They acted surprised. They said Guatemala was a democratic country. You couldn't be a refugee from Guatemala since there was nothing there you needed to take refuge from." Political asylum, it turned out, was a blessing reserved primarily for refugees from countries that were enemies of the United States. "They didn't give us much hope," Lupe said. "But they gave us a hearing and working papers we could use till our case came up for review."

The hearing was not to be held for several months. The three could at last work legally; ironically, they could not find employment. An old pattern had reemerged. Like southern Mexico not long before, southern Florida was jammed with immigrants. Work was scarce, pay low. As competition for jobs intensified, prejudice against new arrivals mounted.

The Guatemalans decided to go elsewhere. They gathered up the Leóns' two children, piled into a beat-up van, and headed west. Somewhere they picked up four of their countrymen just arrived in the United States via the desert.

There were nine in the van. The vehicle fairly screamed. Somehow they made it as far as Las Cruces, New Mexico. There they were stopped by the police. Jorge, Lupe, and Maria were arrested for transporting undocumented immigrants—the four hitchhikers—and were turned over to immigration authorities.

Writing of an illness that afflicted him during his middle years, John Donne compared himself to a map that his physicians went over like cosmographers. If we are maps, then the manner of mental border we erect reveals much about our willingness to entertain what is foreign. We can have open borders allowing easy passage in both directions, or we can remain forever imprisoned behind barbed wire and cement.

At the port of entry into the United States in Columbus, New Mexico, I met a customs agent whose borders were as porous as gossamer. He was a career bureaucrat with twenty years in the Immigration and Naturalization

Service (INS) and all the perks to which he was entitled—a cramped, poorly lit office, shiny yellow-green walls, a desk piled high with communiqués from Washington, stale coffee for his guests. He should have been a slave to fiat and fine print, but he was not. What went wrong?

One of the attractions of Palomas, Columbus's sister town just across the border, is liberated pharmacies. Many drugs that are illegal or tightly controlled in the United States are as common as aspirin in Palomas. In recent years one of the town's principal drawing cards has been AZT, a drug that has proven to be of considerable benefit to some AIDS sufferers. Because AZT may not be brought into the United States, it is one of the customs agent's melancholy duties to confiscate the drug from pale young men and women returning to the United States from the sinful side of the border.

I was an unannounced caller. The agent had kindly taken a few minutes off from his work to tell me about the customs business. Across from his desk a spotless window looked out on a line of cars moving slowly north. At first, he said, he hadn't understood. He had his orders. He seized it all.

But the gathering stream, the ravaged faces, the desperate eyes. . . . He knew the moment the guilty ones lowered their windows, the way they smiled and cleared their throats. With those people he took extra time. That was his cover. He turned their cars inside out. Always he found what he was looking for, foolishly taped under a seat or squirrelled away in a corner of a suitcase. When he found it he pretended not to see it. Then he smiled back at them and cleared his throat and sent them on their way. He told the story with a certain amount of pride. He was a refugee—a free man.

Some are not free. Some sequester themselves behind borders as unscalable as the once-impenetrable Berlin Wall. Peering across their own brutally constructed line at the Guatemalans, INS agents did not see dignified people with a right to be treated decently and fairly; they saw small, poor, unrefined, dark-skinned foreigners who did not speak English, and they deemed those inconveniences beneath dignity. Agents confiscated Jorge's, Lupe's, and Maria's working papers, pronounced them worthless, and destroyed them. They separated Jorge from his family and led him away. Then they placed Lupe, Maria, and the children aboard a plane and flew them to a detention center in Nevada. There the women were told that they were going to be deported to Guatemala.

Lupe was pregnant with the couple's third child. Her frantic inquiries concerning her husband's whereabouts were rebuffed. Six hundred miles away in a cell in New Mexico's Valencia County jail, Jorge was denied all news of his family's fate. He assumed they had been deported and began to despair of ever seeing them again.

(3)

Long after arriving in this land, we bewildered immigrants still gaze back fondly on a cherished past. Reborn here, we are not yet alive to the knowledge that the United States is fundamentally different from the places we left behind. We remain tied to our old tribal habits, those carefully drawn sets of cultural borders that define and placate the world for us—ways of courting, feasting, understanding the tides. Those sovereign borders cannot be overrun, as the Chinese in Tibet, the Europeans in native America, and the oligarchy in Guatemala have discovered: pluck off the arms and legs of a hundred generations of a people and they will still laugh in your face and drive you crazy with their music. Culture, like matter and energy, cannot be destroyed. It can be transformed, but only through the slow and unpredictable workings of time.

In wide America, in this sprawling map of dizzily drawn borders, we find no common culture, nor should we expect to. Time has been at work, dilatorily, for a few hundred years in this nation, not even long enough for us to agree on a speed limit, let alone a culture. What passes for common culture today consists of that which is dear to no one—media circuses, presidential campaigns, the annual hush leading up to the announcement of *Forbes*'s 400 richest Americans—rather than that which is dear to all. The latter will come. But given the riotous dissimilarities of the ingredients with which we began, we shouldn't expect to see it in our lifetimes or in many lifetimes to come. While we are around, the Irish will still grow misty-eyed on Saint Patrick's day and move their feet to ancient but still familiar rhythms. So, in our own ways, will we all.

Meanwhile, we grow impatient. The storied melting pot has barely begun to simmer, and already we have cast it aside in favor of a salad bowl and other easy-to-prepare metaphors, all in a desperate effort to describe our manner of coming together. Conditioned to expect a tribe we demand a fully formed, perfectly seasoned American—at once! Impatience ignites our culture wars, which stem from the crotchety notion that we must agree on a language, a view of history, a shelf of reading matter, and explanations for eclipses and opposable thumbs. Impatience drives our compulsive discussions about assimilation. Assimilation is enforced melting. Let the Indians assimilate; that will solve their problems. What's wrong with the Puerto Ricans? Why won't they assimilate? And those strange ducks over there—who are they? They copulate vertically, they write in palindromes, they worship cobalt. Let's assimilate them!

Assimilate them to what? To my way, of course. Read my books, worship my god, move your foot *this* way, you see, and then *that*. Assimilation is the crude tool of the tribesman still facing the past.

Evidence that we have yet to disembark in this astounding new land is all around us. Communism collapses in Eastern Europe, freedom and democracy—our babies!—score one of the great moral triumphs in history, and we react as though the price of gasoline has just dropped a nickel. Where were the clowns and jugglers, the snake-dancing in the streets, the bonfires, the ecstatic month-long national holiday? Did the sight of liberated peoples pouring through the walls bring to light hidden doubts and fears about ourselves? Did those jubilant masses know something we once knew but that no longer echoes in our hearts? It is perhaps a small matter, but I have long been intrigued by the fact that three of our first five presidents died on the Fourth of July but that none has since. Has the life-and-death power which the meaning of that day once held over us faded into the irretrievable reaches of history?

Evidence is found, too, in our deplorable treatment of undocumented immigrants. In 1992 the human rights organization Americas Watch reported flagrant abuses of immigrants by INS agents along the Mexican border. Mistreatment included torture, sexual abuse, and unjustified shootings. Across the United States, thousands of unwelcome visitors languish in jails and detention centers, many suffering the kinds of humiliation and abuse to which the Leóns were subjected.

How do we explain our relentless contempt for these people? Does their valor embarrass us? Crossing oceans in leaky boats, plodding for days over trackless deserts, they do something few of us have done: they risk their lives to come to America. What voyages they make, and how they flatter us by their bravery! Each reminds us of the only bond we have as a people—that shimmering vision of an empty and beckoning land. We should celebrate the arrival of every one of these unexpected visitors, house them at the Hilton while they are here, and honor them with ticker-tape parades down Broadway. Those we must turn away we should fly home first class, armed with memories of fair and equal treatment while they were here. Witnesses not to empty words but to rigorous application of our loudly advertised principles of justice and equality, they will become permanent envoys of the ideals that may yet distinguish us from the rest of the world.

The melting pot is out, the salad bowl fast losing its crispness. How shall we model America?

To me, America is like the desert of southwestern New Mexico. It is vast and beautiful. It has a majesty too powerful to yield to a single will but generous enough to bend to an infinite number of small ones. It is quiet, so quiet that there is never a moment when one cannot pause and remember what it was like in the beginning, when one first grasped the possibilities of the land. It is empty, so empty that one readily understands that it is a work in progress and far from complete.

Populating this expanse are countless individuals, each secure on a carefully delineated plot of land. The variety of these specimens is endless. Each is unique, each armed with formidable capabilities. Some are tall and spindly; some display curious textures and hues. All are borne fiercely by the others. Each speaks plainly and guilelessly and attends with utmost care.

In those desert-wrought qualities of forbearance and honest regard lie the keys to our success. At the human level they are cultural values, collective and lasting responses to local sets of conditions. The foremost condition of America is a wildly diverse population, and it has arisen precisely because of the chaotic manner of our coming together. Our collective and lasting response must be to acknowledge that diversity and to attend with utmost care.

Which is to say, to treat one another with tolerance and respect. To do less is to deny our creation story and to lay the groundwork for our failure. We should teach those two cardinal values as we teach baseball and wiener roasts, and celebrate them as we celebrate our victories in war. They will lead us into a new country, one where we feel safe and content in each other's presence, confident that our personal borders are secure, and galvanized by the knowledge that we have shed the past at last and disembarked in this endlessly bountiful land.

One afternoon in 1990, Mimi López of the Albuquerque Border City Project received a frantic call from a man in the Valencia County jail.

"He was hysterical," López told me. "I could scarcely understand what he was saying. Finally I made out that he was in jail and that he didn't know where his family was."

López located Jorge León's family at the INS detention center in Nevada. "Immigration told me the family was going to be deported. Since their applications for asylum were still pending, that would have been illegal." López managed to secure the release of the two women and the children. The INS flew them to Albuquerque and, in López's words, "dumped them in a homeless shelter."

Jorge León spent the next two months in jail. The charge of transporting undocumented immigrants was dropped, but he was convicted of illegally entering the United States. Representatives of the INS attended his trial. As León left the courtroom following his conviction, an agent stepped forward and informed him that his application for political asylum had been denied.

León appealed his conviction. While a new case was being prepared, he was permitted to remain at liberty. Mimi López found a room for him and the others in an abandoned school building in Albuquerque. A local family donated a plot of land in Albuquerque's South Valley, and there the Guatemalans began raising some of their own food. Jorge found work with a roofing company.

And then, an astonishing development occurred. Five years earlier, a coalition of religious and civil rights organizations had brought suit against the U.S. attorney general, charging discrimination by the INS against Guatemalans and Salvadorans. Despite the slaughter of some two hundred thousand Guatemalans, mostly Mayan Indians, by the Guatemalan government, despite the disappearance of forty thousand more and the forcing of a million people from their land for resettlement in "model" government villages, the INS had approved less than one percent of the applications from Guatemalans seeking asylum here. (Approval rates for residents of the Soviet Union, China, Iran, and some Eastern European countries topped fifty percent.) There was a strong political reason for the INS's stinginess toward Guatemalans: a high rate of approval would have been tantamount to admitting that the United States was cooperating with a repressive government.

In 1990, while León's case was still under appeal, the government agreed to a settlement in the discrimination suit, tacitly admitting that the asylum process was biased. As part of the agreement, the INS agreed to stop all deportation hearings involving Guatemalans and Salvadorans, to readjudicate under liberalized guidelines all asylum denials issued since 1980 to Guatemalan and Salvadoran refugees, and to provide work authorizations to all applicants while their claims were being reconsidered. It was a shining example of justice, American-style, though it could never redress the injustice done to the thousands sent home, possibly to their deaths, to provide a pale gloss for a dirty little fact of U.S. foreign policy.

Jorge, Lupe, and Maria suddenly found themselves adrift quite happily in a sea of some five hundred thousand backlogged asylum applications. Immigration experts estimated that the INS would never catch up.

It had been nearly a year since I had last seen the Leóns. I wanted to find out how they were, so one brisk, early fall evening, I paid them a visit.

The apartment was bustling with activity. Albuquerque filmmaker Jim

Morrison, the producer of a film about the Leóns, was there to do some catching up of his own. Neighborhood kids piled in and out the front door. A woman I didn't recognize approached me and in a hesitant manner but with a broad smile introduced herself as Teresa León, Jorge's sister. Her hesitancy was understandable: recently arrived from Chichuamel, she not only did not speak English, she did not speak Spanish. Her shortcoming did not stop her from making a gracious effort to get to know me—from engaging in a long-standing family tradition of vanquishing a border before her.

Jorge and I excused ourselves and with Peter Simonson, who had joined me again that evening, left for a bite to eat. Over tacos, burgers, and beers at the Rio Grande Cantina, Jorge brought me up to date. He and his family were enjoying their lives. Both he and Maria had found full-time jobs working for a local jewelry manufacturer.

But seven years after arriving in the United States, Jorge, Lupe, and Maria were still awaiting hearings on their asylum applications. When I visited a year earlier, the three had been unwilling to speculate about their chances of success. On this visit, however, I heard a note of cautious optimism in Jorge's words. If they could make it for just two more years, he ventured, they might secure permanent residency at last.

I asked him to name the biggest difference between Albuquerque and Chichuamel. He answered without hesitation: "The education system is better here. My kids are in La Luz Elementary School. It's a good school and they will have advantages I never had." Earlier that evening I had learned a remarkable fact: the León children are fluent in four languages—English, Spanish, Kanjobal, and Chu.

Jorge recently visited relatives in Chichuamel. He told me that one of his most fervent wishes is for the people of the United States to learn about his village and about Guatemala. Closer to Washington, D.C., than is Salt Lake City, intimately tied to U.S. politics in recent decades, Guatemala remains unknown to most Americans. León regrets the neglect but refuses to dwell on the past. When we parted later that evening he seemed full of hope, a fox gazing at a line scratched in the dirt and wondering what might lie beyond.

ADRIFT IN THE PERMIAN SEA

Fear nothing. We shall overcome these, and many other difficulties. Besides, as we approach the Center, I expect to find it luminous.

—*Jules Verne*, A Journey to the Center of the Earth

Here at the end of history, having discovered everything worth buying or leasing, and understanding perfectly almost all that there is to know, we poke through the few remaining scraps of unfinished business in search of something we can confidently tag with the label "final frontier." Television has been a tireless ally in our search. Gene Roddenberry may have been the first to propose a candidate for the title: his ever-popular "space," playground of the starship *Enterprise*. Jacques Cousteau soon weighed in with his obsessive choice, the ocean. Practically weekly, *Nova* or some other PBS offering brings welcome tidings that the winner has been crowned at last—the atom, the gene, viruses, the tropical rain forest, the brain. The final final frontier.

Recently I flew back to New Mexico after a visit to New York City, which might itself be added to the list of uttermost boundaries. New Mexico enjoys more days of sunshine than any other state, but this was not one of them. At cruising altitude, to be sure, all was well. The plane sailed smoothly through roofless, easygoing sky, while at my shoulder the bare disk of the sun stood fast on the starboard wing.

But beneath the plane a commotion of nasty-looking clouds tumbled to the horizon. The clouds were dark and dense, modeled like a terrestrial landscape. They looked as impenetrable as the surface of the earth. Below them the world was nowhere to be seen.

Beginning its descent to the Albuquerque airport, the plane nosed down and sliced into the overcast. Beside me the sun flickered, then winked out. Darkness crept up my window. Groggy after the long flight, I had the sudden and rather intriguing notion that the pilot had decided to treat his passengers to a joyride through the earth's crust. Deeper and deeper we went, during each moment traveling not nearer to my terrestrial destination but farther from it.

For several minutes the aircraft burrowed through the blackness. Then with a jolt, as though it had broken through a stratum of rock, the plane popped out below.

I gazed down at the newly revealed underworld. A haunting ashen light lay over it, one that seemed to have been filtered through layers of dirt or sand. Tall prismatic buildings illuminated from within studded the landscape like stalagmites. The Rio Grande looked dark and menacing, like a noxious underground river. The Sandia Mountains formed an unending barrier in the east— a cavern wall.

As the plane hit the runway, a second jolt returned me to my senses. I was left with a freshly awakened curiosity about that mysterious and almost completely unexplored world which lies beneath our feet. Unlike space, the ocean, and New York City, this was a final frontier I had never thought much about, and then only in the unkindest of terms. To me (and I expect to most people), the underground is a repellent place where worms are among the handsomest citizens and where dirt is, ipso facto, the prevailing medium. The imaginative Tibetans have invented a funeral procedure called the sky burial which launches the deceased on what seems to me to be the correct heading. But the rest of us are likely to end up six feet in the opposite direction, a fact that does little to heighten the allure of the underworld.

At the public library I conducted a brief survey of books with the word *underground* or *underworld* in their titles. Among nonfiction works I turned up treatises on subways, the underclass, cemeteries, coal mining, toxic waste dumps, the Weather Underground, Neanderthals, the underground economy, guerrillas, the Warsaw ghetto, bats, moles, groundwater contamination, and garbage. A dim light illuminated a few appealing titles on alternative presses, spelunking, and the Underground Railroad. But for the most part my survey revealed a pretty grungy place.

The fiction landscape was no tidier. Dostoevski's *Notes from the Underground* epitomized the bunch. Written by the endlessly beleaguered novelist during his wife's final illness, the book deals not with the true underground but with that even messier inner world where we struggle against the squalidness of our darker selves. An early work on toxic waste, it offers little hope of cleanup.

With these rather bleak precedents informing my expectations, but with my eyes at least partially opened by the revelations at the conclusion of my plane flight, I set out on a tour of New Mexico's southeast quadrant. It is a place where what is underground is aboveboard and above contempt, and more a part of the scenery than in any other place I know. Southeastern New Mexico gives the underworld a good name.

Grant much of the credit for this achievement to an early version of Jacques Cousteau's ocean. During the Permian some 250 million years ago, a shallow sea rich in marine life overspread the region. Over eons the water evaporated, depositing deep layers of fossils. These were in turn paved over in rock and earth.

It's those fossil layers that distinguish southeastern New Mexico's underground. In some places the trilobites and brachiopods transmuted into petroleum, limestone, and other useful materials. Elsewhere the fragile layers disintegrated or split apart, leaving immense holes deep within the earth. Southeastern New Mexico resembles a big hunk of Swiss cheese. Geologically, it's a happening place.

The region borders West Texas, with which it shares topographic, economic, cultural, and linguistic ties. Indeed, the area is sometimes called Little Texas. The sobriquet rankles many New Mexicans, who suffer their lumbering and ill-bred neighbors to the east only out of native charity and mercy.

Both qualities are sorely needed to deal with Texans. Some residents of the Lone Star State have the unattractive habit of treating New Mexico as a colony, or a time-share, where they play in great numbers, overrunning ski resorts and mountain parks—neither of which they have had the good sense to establish at home—and conducting themselves importantly. During Indian dances and sunsets, Texans look at their watches and ask when there is going to be a commercial break. Much of the resentment toward undocumented aliens in New Mexico is directed not at Mexicans or Central Americans but at Texans.

The landscape of southeastern New Mexico is flat and barren, and spry with economic activity. Unlike the rest of the state, the region is not so much a celebration of mountains and deserts as it is a ringing tribute to commerce. Ubiquitous oil wells and drilling paraphernalia bestow a busy, purposeful look on the countryside. Cattle graze among the derricks. Monstrous gas flares corkscrew from vents by the road, out-blasting the sun by day and lighting the night like hungry dragons. Practically anywhere in Lea or Eddy County one can gaze out over the flats and count pumpjacks by the score, each drawing with every dip of its pail a few gallons of crude from one of those handy cavities in the underworld. New Mexico is the nation's fourth largest gas producer and seventh largest producer of oil. Much of the gas comes from the opposite corner of the state, but ninety percent of the petroleum is dug up here, in Lea and Eddy Counties.

The region's towns are dusty and earnest and smooth-rolling, if not terribly charming. Hobbs, with a population of thirty thousand, is the largest. In 1928, wildcatters from the Midwest Refining Company drilled a test well near Hobbs, then a tiny ranching community. On November 8 they struck a huge reservoir of petroleum, revolutionizing New Mexico's economy overnight. The famous well stands at the corner of Stanolind Road and South Grimes Street. It still produces oil.

Today, every major oil company has a branch office in Hobbs. Highway 62 leading west out of town is lined with businesses offering services to the petroleum trade—welding, blowout prevention, tank repair, truck rig-ups, oil-field supplies, pumping unit service, well service, bit service. A lot seems to be going on in Hobbs. Unemployment in the region stands well below the national average. The stores in Hobbs are full of shoppers. In the late afternoon, the main streets tie up in traffic. Many locals drive pickups, though older men and their wives—who have tall, rigid hair and the demeanor of beauty queens—favor Lincolns and Park Avenues.

Outside of Hobbs and Lovington, the other major city in the far southeast, the towns are mostly blink-of-an-eye places—Monument, Crossroads, Prairieview, Oil Center, Humble City, Nadine. Many are little more than storage fields or staging areas for oil-field operations. Driving the causeways between wide seas of bobbing pumpjacks, I sometimes saw a car or truck approaching from a distance. The vehicle would fly by, but not before the driver had invariably lifted a hand in greeting. I was treated to more waves in Lea and Eddy Counties than anywhere else in the state.

Oil and gas extraction are two uses for the flip side of the earth's surface in southeastern New Mexico, but not the only two. Potash—an ingredient in fertilizers, soap, and glass—is mined here. Water is mined, so to speak, in the town of Artesia, which sits on one of the largest rechargeable underground water basins in the country. Most of the pressure in the basin has long since been vented, but when Artesian farmers punctured it early in the century, gushers of water, sand, and rock shot ten feet into the air.

As if that were not enough to ensure Artesia a spot in the Underground Hall of Fame, the town is the site of the world's first underground school, an elementary school that doubles as a fallout shelter for two thousand people. President John F. Kennedy sent a telegram of congratulations when the Abo School opened in 1962, calling the construction of fallout shelters "a necessary step towards insuring the survival of this country."

In a related incident a year earlier, the Atomic Energy Commission (AEC) conducted the nation's first nonmilitary underground nuclear bomb test in salt strata southeast of Artesia, near Carlsbad. Project Gnome was undertaken to find out whether nuclear explosions could be used to generate electric power, dig harbors and tunnels, free underground rivers, and recover oil deposits.

Such were the dreams of long ago. Gnome got off to a bad start when gophers chewed up vital electrical cables. Then the bomb, advertised at five kilotons, went off with a bigger pop than anticipated. Nervous observers on the ground saw the earth ballooning upward ominously, threatening to turn what was supposed to be an underground test into an atmospheric one.

In fact, that is what happened. Instead of closing itself off in its tomb as it was supposed to, Gnome poked a narrow vent to the surface. Through the vent it shot a cloud of radiation—though how big a cloud no one could be sure, thanks to the gophers, who had put the radiation detectors out of action. As a precautionary measure, project officials threw up a roadblock and warned local drivers to hose down their cars. Gnome was pronounced a success, despite the mishaps. The AEC immediately announced plans to conduct an underground test in Nevada to explore the feasibility of using nuclear explosions to dig canals.

Inevitably, the underground mentality must descend to Dostoevskian depths. In blink-of-an-eye Eunice not long ago, a local man complained to neighbors that he had accumulated a mountain of trash and wasn't sure what to do with it. Soon afterward he was seen bringing in a backhoe and scooping a huge pit in his backyard.

A few days later the man's estranged wife disappeared. That night neighbors heard the backhoe laboring in the darkness. By sunup the pit had been filled.

The couple's distraught children began digging. At the bottom of the pit they found their mother's body; apparently she had been buried alive. The murder was the talk of Eunice when I went through. In southeastern New Mexico, the underground imagination, good or bad, is never less than inspired.

Because the region is big and mostly empty, requests arrive regularly from small, full places like Delaware and New Jersey to dispose of their garbage. One plan called for transporting sewage in railcars from fourteen New York City treatment plants and burying the sludge—some two thousand tons of it per day—on twenty thousand acres of rangeland in southeastern New Mexico. Nearby, the Mescalero Apaches are looking at a proposal to store nuclear waste—though aboveground—on their reservation. The details of the plans change, but not the aggravating problem: we are a nation of fouled nests. If the Midwest is America's breadbasket, New Mexico is fast becoming its wastebasket. Naturally there is money to be made in this unglamorous business, though at what cost to the land and to the people's health cannot be foretold with any accuracy.

The most controversial of the plans has produced acrimonious debate in New Mexico for more than a decade, splitting the state's citizens into two hostile and apparently irreconcilable camps. Under the proposal, low-level waste produced by the nation's nuclear weapons facilities over the past half-century would be buried in salt beds near where the Project Gnome bomb was detonated in 1961. Low-level waste means shoe covers, gloves, lab coats, test tubes, metal scraps, and other assorted by-products of nuclear weapons manufacture. Contaminated by plutonium and other transuranic elements that are deadly to humans, the refuse cannot simply be tossed into the garbage, though some of it undoubtedly has been. But exactly what to do with it is unclear, for no matter where it is placed (even if buried, like an unloved spouse), it will remain hazardous for 240,000 years. Unbelievable amounts of this stuff exist. Most of it is stored in fifty-five-gallon drums, hundreds of thousands of them. They wait at weapons facilities in six states for someone to come and cart them away.

During the 1970s the Department of Energy took a look—too perfunctory a look as it turned out—at those inviting Carlsbad salt beds and listened to impassioned sermons about layoffs in the local potash industry. Perhaps inspired by the memory of the Project Gnome triumph, the agency did what the designers of the Atomic Age have often done, casting its fate with New Mexico. Construction soon began on the so-called Waste Isolation Pilot Project plant (WIPP). Essentially a Brobdingnagian garbage can, WIPP is seven miles of passages and storage rooms carved out half a mile beneath the earth's surface. So far the project has cost a billion dollars, and not a barrel has been buried. Stymied by an endless succession of legal challenges, WIPP sits idle under the landscape, its opening postponed indefinitely. Opponents swear it will never open.

The problem stalling WIPP is the same one that has crippled the nuclear power industry in the United States: the facility has been run as though it were an illegal drug operation rather than as a sensitive public trust. It's easy to forget that during nuclear power's infancy, the grassroots environmental community, which today tosses wrenches into the nuclear works at every opportunity, stood solidly behind the industry. Nuclear power offered the bright promise of clean, inexpensive energy, if only the waste problem could be solved. No one knew then (or at least no one told the public) that the waste problem would never be solved, or that the industry would conduct itself so irresponsibly. Pro-nuclear forces like to blame environmentalists for their problems, but a better explanation is industry suicide—a carefully conceived, brilliantly executed, million-kiloton self-nuking. It was as if the industry had taken to heart singer Country Joe McDonald's stern atomic advice: "Go drop it on yourself."

Beginning in 1957, energy poured forth from nuclear power plants around the United States, eventually more than one hundred of them. But so did revelations of industry mismanagement, incompetence, negligence, cover-ups of accidents, criminal behavior, secret deals, lying to Congress, to the public, to whomever happened to be in the room at the time. Before long a guarantee of, say, safety by an official of the industry or a bedmate on the Nuclear Regulatory Commission was a warning to pile one's family into the station wagon and hightail it out of town. By the early 1970s many people had lost faith in the industry and its ability to solve its problems. The doubts and mistrust have only compounded in the years since.

Beginning its life as the unfortunate stepchild of this disreputable nuclear family, WIPP has done little to redeem the family name in the years since. Rather, the opposite has occurred; it has demonstrated a genetic predisposition to commit the same errors that crippled its forebears. Although WIPP is advertised as an ironclad, leakproof tomb for nuclear waste, construction of the plant began well before adequate geological tests on the salt beds had been performed, and the fact that they were neither ironclad nor leakproof has been apparent almost from the beginning. The first hint of trouble was the discovery of natural reservoirs of pressurized brine near the storage rooms. If punctured, the pools could spew plutonium into the local water supply. In 1981 WIPP workers narrowly escaped injury when they accidentally broke through one of the reservoir walls, releasing a geyser of brine.

In 1984 water began seeping into the storage rooms. Evidence began to accumulate that the salt walls, which were supposed to close in slowly to entomb the barrels, were closing at a rate three times faster than expected. In 1989 cracks began appearing in the walls. In 1990 an underground ceiling collapsed; since then ceilings have collapsed at a rate of better than one a year.

Meanwhile, concerns arose about the transportation of waste through New Mexico to the plant. Some citizen groups questioned the safety of the roads (the barrels will travel by truck) and the qualifications of the drivers. A survey of hospitals along the route revealed that medical personnel had not been trained to handle nuclear accidents.

Perhaps there were reasonable explanations for each of these embarrassments. Instead of discussing the problems openly and honestly, however, WIPP management adopted the self-destructive policies of its progenitors. Officials downplayed the 1981 brine accident. In a 1989 environmental impact statement, they neglected to mention the wall cracks. They insisted that transportation routes are safe and that the storage plan is above reproach. Early in 1992, energy secretary James Watkins blasted a lawsuit brought against WIPP by the state of New Mexico. "We're in litigation in my opinion for no good reason," said Watkins. "Why can't we move? This is some kind of extreme position taken by people who want to thwart progress."

As tax dollars poured into the facility by the hundreds of millions, the possibility that WIPP might be a bad idea that should itself be buried was rarely raised in WIPP circles or in Washington. Supporters reflexively met each challenge by denying its seriousness, then shifted blame to the opposition, which they portrayed as hysterical, meddlesome, uninformed, unpatriotic— anything but honestly concerned about the safety of the facility.

The strategy failed. Support for WIPP remains strong in Carlsbad, which reaps huge economic benefits from the dormant facility (even idle it employs nine hundred workers) and will reap considerably more if the plant opens. But statewide, enthusiasm for the project has waned steadily.

Somewhere in "southwest nowhere," as one New York–based writer covering the WIPP story put it, I turned at an unobtrusive sign and drove a few miles along a lonely road to the WIPP facility. Erected on flat, parsimonious ground, surrounded by chain-link fences and warning signs, the plant looks like an abandoned cement factory. It's an eerie place. Inside, I suppose, several hundred people were hard at work doing whatever they do to keep the place in tune. But in fifteen minutes of snooping around outside I saw not a soul.

As I was about to leave, a car rumbled down the road and turned in at the front gate of the plant. Unlike the back-road drivers I had encountered near Hobbs, neither of the vehicle's two occupants smiled or waved to me. Both emitted hollow-eyed stares. A ghost factory WIPP will remain until the day it opens its doors and begins the work it was designed, sort of, to do.

That day may come (currently the plant is scheduled to open in November 1997) if only because something has to be done with all those barrels, prudent or not, and because of the facility's astronomical price tag, projected at nine billion dollars over the life of the plant and rising sharply with each new estimate. Elephants that gross, white or not, usually are permitted to live.

But New Mexicans are a scrappy lot, and those who oppose the project won't give up easily. Many have promised that, should the plant open, they will use any means available to them—including civil disobedience—to shut it down again.

My own idea is that burying this junk is the worst thing we could do with it. Look at it this way: from primitive beginnings, nuclear weapons and nuclear power generators have evolved to levels of mind-bending sophistication. Today in a container the size of an orange crate you can tote a weapon that makes the Hiroshima bomb look like a firecracker. Power plants gleaming with the latest in computerized technology churn out electricity day and night and only occasionally threaten to blow up or melt down. For fifty years, the world's most brilliant scientists and engineers have pooled their talents to bring this extraordinary new world into being. Untold trillions of dollars have been spent in support of their efforts.

Though we don't like to discuss this part of the story, it happens that some very nasty stuff has been produced along with the miracles. What do the world's most brilliant scientists and engineers do with all of this nasty stuff? They cram it into barrels! Then they hammer on lids, slap skull-and-crossbones on the sides, and hide it in warehouses! Is that rich or what? (High-level waste at power plants is marinated in glorified swimming pools; like barrels, these merely conceal the problem.) Now we are going to bury this excreta in a hole in the ground, where we hope it will remain hidden until it is no longer dangerous—around the year 242,000. Or, failing that, put it safely out of sight until it becomes someone else's responsibility.

It seems to me that burying nuclear waste is like hiding a flask of bourbon under the mattress. It doesn't solve the problem, it's vulgar, and it disturbs one's sleep. My solution overcomes each of those shortcomings. I would draw up a list of the names and addresses of every politician, Department of Energy official, Nuclear Regulatory Commission member, Defense Department functionary, nuclear industry representative, scientist, engineer, and self-styled expert who has publicly sung the praises of nuclear power or downplayed the problems of nuclear waste disposal or ridiculed the promise of clean, renewable alternative energies at any time since it became clear that nuclear waste is an intolerable menace: say, during the past decade. (I'm being generous.)

Then I would gather up the crud—low level, high level, and every other level—load it onto jauntily marked eighteen-wheelers, transport it to the homes of the people on the list, and dump it in their front yards. I don't have the addresses of the winners of this sweepstakes, but I expect that most of them live in Connecticut and Virginia. In my view, their front yards are as desolate as "southwest nowhere," and no more necessary.

The recipients may do with the bilge what they please, so long as it stays on their properties. I'm confident that, stacked in artistic arrangements in gazebos and greenhouses, the faintly glowing drums, like the prospect of a hanging, will on each of these prophets have the effect of concentrating the mind wonderfully, to paraphrase Dr. Johnson. Wonderful concentration of mind has sometimes been absent from discussions in New York and Washington about what to do with nuclear scum. The idea that big, wide, empty, faraway, politically weak places like New Mexico are something like toilets is dreadfully simpleminded and needs to be reexamined by those who hold it.

Moreover, it is disrespectful. If the directors of the nation's nuclear weapons facilities will agree not to bury their waste in New Mexico, I will agree not to toss my empty beer cans onto their front porches. I am willing to bet that most New Mexicans will cheerfully sign similar agreements.

Crossing the flats toward the town of Jal I wondered: Suppose the plant opens. Suppose the softly singing drums are stacked in the big salty rooms. Suppose a panel of experts assures the world that all is well at WIPP. Is there anyone anywhere who will be surprised when, twenty years later, childhood leukemia rates skyrocket in Carlsbad?

On the radio it was Reba McEntire and Garth Brooks all the way. The road was smooth and swaying as a steel guitar leading waltzers to heaven. The sky was silky blue—Willie's voice, Loretta's smile. Country music makes sense on the road to Jal.

For several days I had been eyeing the wide fields of wigwagging pumpjacks. At last my curiosity got the better of me. I turned onto a side road and drove several hundred yards to a gate, where an unobtrusive metal sign informed me that I was about to enter oil company property.

I took stock of my surroundings: several hundred square miles of deadlevel planet. Here and there clumps of creosote and mesquite contradicted the general idea, but the vegetation was nowhere taller than I am, and it was everywhere so occasional that I could have listed it on the back of an envelope. I was trespassing and might have thought twice about continuing had it not been apparent that I was the only human being on earth. I checked the gate, found it unlocked, and drove in.

The month was July, and the temperature had broken three figures by midmorning. I parked in a bed of ruts, dodged several herds of cow chips, and stepped into a kind of power zone, a twenty-foot square of energy-producing earth. Before me stood a yellow-and-green Jones and Laughlin pump about the height and width of a goalpost, powered by an electric motor not much bigger than the one on a washing machine. A couple of frayed belts ran to the drive wheels on the pump, the broad beam of which rocked gently above me slowly and peacefully. The pump was old and rusty, notably deficient in the high-tech shine and sleekness of many of the newer models I had seen; but it seemed so faithful and earnest I couldn't help admiring it. I guessed it had been toiling in lonely isolation on its assigned pool of liquid trilobites for decades.

I sat on a chunk of cement and to the soothing *whirr* of the motor and *hiss-chuck* of the pump enjoyed a very musical time-out. There was no shade, naturally, and the heat was infernal. But I liked the hospitality. Every few minutes a car materialized on the main road. Observing the vehicle's resolute progress, I listened to an arching *whish* as the car sped by, then watched it angle away, shrinking steadily in size until it disappeared over the horizon. Pump and cars were my sole companions, and before long I had them working in tandem. The rhythm of the pump seemed to produce a related though slightly delayed and less insistent rhythm of cars. I imagined my pump grabbing a gulp of crude somewhere far below, then piping it out to the road, where drivers filled their tanks before hurrying off to the dry cleaners, the post office, the grocery store. The hissing of the pump began to sound like the breathing of the earth, and before long the labored breathing of the earth. Then I heard a gurgling sound, like the dreadful slurping of a respirator sucking bottom in a desiccated lung.

A day later I found myself atop an ancient barrier reef in the foothills of the Guadalupes, New Mexico's easternmost mountain range. The blistering heat of the previous day had given way to a cool and welcome wind. Wide limestone slabs cobbled the sky. A thunderstorm was forecast for late afternoon. Around midday I entered a cave discovered in 1901 by a nineteen-year-old cowboy named Jim White. Like many New Mexico discoveries, this one was really a rediscovery, for paintings and cooking pits found inside the cave proved that Indians had known of its existence more than a thousand years ago. But praise be to Jim White for following a flight of bats to the spot and entering under the great stone arch and recognizing the importance of what he saw. He became an indefatigable champion of the cave, the now world-famous Carlsbad Caverns.

Carlsbad Caverns seem to have been created to remind us that life and beauty and wonder are to be found in the darkest of places, whether we are there to appreciate them or not. This illumination runs counter to conventional wisdom, but so in many ways does New Mexico; the more I think about it the more certain I become that it is one of New Mexico's purposes to run counter to conventional wisdom. It is a commonplace devoutly preached from pulpit to living room to classroom to analyst's couch that we humans, like the earth beneath us, are a vile lot, rotten to the core. My own view—the Hitlers, Idi Amins, and monsters of the evening news and supermarket tabloids to the contrary—is that most members of our species are pretty decent souls most of the time. Of the many people I have known, some disappointed me, some angered me, and a few hurt me. But none, so far as I can tell, possessed a rotten core.

The merits of our fellow human beings are, of course, easy to overlook—it's our nature to do so. The unfortunate result of this habit is that we fail to appreciate that our abiding virtues usually far outweigh our occasional iniquities. This imbalance strongly suggests to me that, however Genesis would have it, human nature tends toward the good, not the bad. An afternoon in Carlsbad Caverns, where I found neither a tortured Dostoevskian psyche nor an evil essence but a bright and shining light, seemed to confirm that notion.

Carlsbad's magical caverns roll on and on, mile after mile of fantastical formations laid down drip by drip by drip over untold millions of years. Rooms the size of domed stadiums are jammed to the rafters with the most outlandish furniture—footstools like giant armadillos, chandeliers as big and rowdy as marching bands, filigreed howdahs saddled to blue whales. The profound patience and conviction of this generous act of creation reminded me of a few lines from a poem by Robinson Jeffers:

> We must uncenter our minds from ourselves;
> We must unhumanize our views a little, and become confident
> As the rock and ocean that we were made from.

Within this storehouse of tunnels stacked tall with curiosities there is not so much as an inch of territory one could not happily spend an hour admiring; in their entirety the caverns hold splendors one would need more than a lifetime to take in. Perhaps the greatest splendor, and surely the most difficult to comprehend, is this: deep within the caves there is life. Crickets. Worms. Beetles. Moths. Bats by the millions. The bats emerge at night, but the others spend their lives far below the surface of the earth, ignorant of sun, fresh air, and wide-open spaces, yet no less than grizzly bears or human beings fully engaged in the myriad processes of life.

One sees these wonders, or at least many of them, because the National Park Service has installed lights in the rooms and passageways. The effect of the illumination, paradoxically, is to destroy one's ability to fully appreciate what one is seeing. As necessary as the lights may be for showing off the breathtaking contents of the caves, they prevent the visitor from grasping the essential condition of Carlsbad, which is complete and utter darkness. Darkness blacker than anything the mind is capable of imagining: darkness, indeed, that suggests the unconscious. Electric lights, whatever their usefulness, obscure a crucial fact about the caverns; there was a natural radiance here—a brightness of moths and water droplets and limestone—for countless centuries before there were lamps on the walls or an audience to appreciate it.

As I wandered the passageways I became more and more troubled by the artificial illumination. I wanted the lights to be turned off so that I could see the caves aglow in their intrinsic brilliance. I wanted to see what the moth and the cricket see, what I know is to be seen in a million undiscovered caves around the world, at the bottom of the ocean, in the nucleus of the atom, and in the last final frontier that I know of, the deepest recesses of the human heart: a radiant and inextinguishable light. In consummate darkness I wanted to see what I knew to be true but had not observed with perfect clarity with my eyes. And that is that the soul of Carlsbad is not dead. It is gorgeously, joyously alive.

In late afternoon, returned once more to my familiar home aboveground, I was treated to one of those bravura feats of meteorology that New Mexico passes out offhandedly, as though they were travel brochures. Near park headquarters one can stand at the edge of the humpbacked reef and gaze out over the ancient waters, now planted in soil and rock. A light rain was falling. At three widely separated points, narrow storms slanted down against the tranquil sea. Between quavered aprons of saffron light. A gray mist overhung it all, pierced by a soft rainbow. In a rare feat of optical engineering, a ghostly second rainbow rose like a parasol over the first, as if to protect it from the rain.

Beneath these skies, New Mexicans have poked holes in their land and crowded the plains with derricks and sucked out their oil and gas, to be spent on powering cars and planes and heating America's homes. They invented atomic energy, unveiling it at Trinity Site and manufacturing it at Los Alamos and Sandia labs and discovering under their mountains uranium to make it run. They sent their people to mine the uranium. It was dangerous work, although those who labored did not know and were not told how dangerous until it was too late. Many died of their labors. Many who did not die are today gravely ill.

New Mexico has contributed mightily to the Age of Energy. The more they gave the more they were expected to give. Now they are being asked to bury the abominable refuse of the age in the luminous depths beneath their homes.

That is too much. It's tantamount to blinding a child with hot pokers. It's like corrupting a soul. Here's a different idea. Load the drums of nuclear waste onto flatcars. Tow them endlessly from city to town, from California to Maine, to haunt us all. Then travel to New Mexico. Stand atop the reef and close your eyes and imagine fresh, sweet-smelling air; cold, clear-running water; pure, life-giving soil. Then gaze out over the land into the falling light and imagine windmills, water wheels, and solar contraptions of every manner and kind reaching to the ends of the earth. Imagine not a final frontier but a new and promising one, a grand quest for the boundless energies of sun, wind, and water: energies we can use again and again without killing ourselves or our planet.

REBUILDING
THE CLOUDS

The deepest words
of the wise men teach us
the same as the whistle of the wind when it blows,
or the sound of the water when it is flowing.

—*Antonio Machado,* "*Rebirth*"

n this wondrous scientific age with its astonishing revelations that life is biology, the stars chemistry, the atom physics, and the mind a set of crisp instructions analyzable on a laptop computer, John Greenleaf Whittier's belief that nature speaks in symbols and in signs ought to seem as quaint as a husking bee. Strangely, it does not. Perhaps the most amazing thing about modern science is not the startling new view of the world it has given us but rather its failure to efface the old view. Church attendance and horoscope readings are up, psychics and channelers are doing brisk and lucrative business, afternoon television resounds with tales of near-death and out-of-body experiences, and a recent poll reveals that one out of five Americans not only do not understand that the sun is a thermonuclear reaction nearly a million miles in diameter, they believe that the sun revolves around the earth. "When has astrology not been popular?" Robertson Davies inquires. "When has the heart of man given a damn for science?"

Experts tell us that the science gap is one more lamentable consequence of our failed education system. As an avid reader of nature's symbols and signs, I'm not so sure; the science gap may reveal as much about the poverty of science as it does about the failure of our schools. Recently, a friend whom I know to be intelligent, informed, and sane described to me an encounter he had had with a coyote on sagebrush flats near Cuba, New Mexico. My friend called the incident "magical." For a few seconds he and the coyote stood no more than thirty feet apart gazing into one another's eyes. In that brief moment, my friend believes, a message of kinship, mutual respect, and good-will passed between the two creatures. Then they nodded to each other and the coyote trotted off. Science would have a hard time explaining the language of that remarkable communiqué or the manner of its transmission. John Greenleaf Whittier would not.

Not long ago I saw a dolphin leaping in the northern sky. The figure was a slim and muscular storm cloud a contrail in length. It leapt like a rainbow, its curve exactly matching that of the sky. In color the creature was hurricane gray, with a swash of tangerine splashed across its dorsal fin by the soft bristles of the late afternoon sun.

Far below, the month was April and springtime was in flood. Deep in thought, I tramped about in the backyard reconnoitering for tender shoots and sprouts, even as I crunched beneath my feet the pale remains of last year's greenery, as brittle as old bones. As I crunched I wondered over a mysterious illness which for more than a year had kept my wife in a state of constant and steadily worsening pain. In vain Carol had trudged from one practitioner to the next, collecting a steady stream of confident and expensive diagnoses, each one contradicting the last. We still hadn't even a name for the demon that had turned our lives upside-down, never mind a cure. I was weary and afraid: which is to say, a perfect candidate for a message from the sky.

When I glanced up and saw that graceful dolphin cavorting in the celestial sea, I understood its meaning at once. A meteorologist might have seen an altocumulus cloud and understood that rain was imminent; I saw a kind smile where the dolphin's mouth would have been and understood that there is a benevolent force in the universe and that it has the power to heal.

One's interpretation of the world is a function of the language that one speaks, and on this worrisome day my language was religion, a common tongue in lands of wide skies and yawning spaces like New Mexico. Historian Roderick Nash wrote of the Chinese Taoists of the fifth century B.C., who sought in wilderness glimpses of the unity and rhythm of the universe. He located the beginnings of the Jewish and Christian tradition of seeking God in big empty country in the Israelites' forty years of wandering in the desert. Before that, wilderness had been anathema to the Hebrews; but in the Sinai

Desert, wrote Nash, "wild country came to signify the environment in which to find and draw close to God."

The backcountry traveler in New Mexico finds an environment that has been put to just this purpose. Scattered throughout the state are mountains, mesas, and remote hideaways that are sacred to New Mexico's Indians. In hidden valleys, at bends in lonely roads, one stumbles upon Benedictine monasteries, Buddhist retreat centers, Tibetan stupas, Catholic churches of crumbling adobe. In sublime Chaco Canyon, the organizers of the 1987 Harmonic Convergence discovered one of the earth's cardinal energy points, a place to which they attribute enormous spiritual significance. Religions old and new have found a home in New Mexico, and even nonhumans seem to benefit from the rarified surroundings. Contemplating the crows over Christ in the Desert monastery near Abiquiu, Thomas Merton decided that the birds flew "at a greater psychic altitude, in a different realm" than other crows.

Paradoxically, New Mexico has another side, the antithesis of the one I have been describing. During the past sixty years this land of sacred mountains and adobe churches has evolved into one of the U.S. military's most spirited and devout partners. There has always been a taste for war here, of course, but it was usually small in scale, waged first with rocks and spears, later with grapeshot and Colt .45s. The state's weapons upgrade to Patriot missiles and Stealth bombers began in 1930 with the arrival in the town of Roswell of rocketry pioneer Robert Goddard. Booted out of Massachusetts as a fire hazard, dismissed by the army as a crank, Goddard discovered on New Mexico's parched southeastern plains the ideal laboratory for perfecting the science of liquid fuel. In the deep skies over Roswell there was cushion enough to absorb Goddard's occasional miscalculations, space enough to encourage even the myopic to envision a new and deadlier manner of war. The army came to its senses at last, and Goddard's flying pipe bombs became Pershing missiles and multiple independently targeted reentry vehicles.

World War II brought the Manhattan Project and the challenge of building an atomic bomb to New Mexico. The intricate network of connections between Washington and New Mexico that evolved during this period became the basis of a new economy. Beginning in 1945, military-based employment in the state skyrocketed. By 1990 New Mexico's population had more than tripled; Albuquerque's increased tenfold. Today, one in four jobs in the state is defense related. Two of the nation's premier weapons-research facilities—Los Alamos and Sandia national laboratories—are here. They employ some sixteen thousand New Mexicans. The combined area of the state's military bases is the size of Connecticut.

Whatever its spiritual heritage, New Mexico has never been a reluctant partner in its alliance with the military. During World War II, New Mexico suffered the highest casualty rate of any state, including some nine hundred deaths during the Bataan Death March and subsequent imprisonment. Car license plates are officially stamped with highlights of the driver's military career: "Purple Heart," "Ex-Prisoner of War," "Pearl Harbor Survivor," "Congressional Medal of Honor." Rarely a day passes when one of the state's newspapers or television stations fails to run a breathless story on a breakthrough at Sandia labs or a puff piece on the arrival in town of a new bomber or a party of Pentagon brass. Sonic booms are as common in Albuquerque as chile overdoses and are tolerated without complaint. A popular bumper sticker explains the public's forbearance: "Jet Noise—The Sound of Freedom." For many New Mexicans those six words define the state's purpose in life. They view this mission as no less important than that of serving as the spiritual capital of America.

New Mexico's military-based economy has paid off handsomely. Huge numbers of jobs and no small amount of capital have been created in exchange for a few minor inconveniences. An area the size of Connecticut is off-limits to wanderers and kite-flyers, it is true, but that still leaves an area the size of Arizona that is not. Albuquerque's exclusive Four Hills neighborhood has for several decades fronted on the nation's largest nuclear weapons stockpile. For most residents, however, that hollowed-out mountain of bombs is no more troublesome than jet noise—the occasionally queasy feeling of freedom. One study suggests that the residents of Los Alamos may be developing brain tumors at three times the national rate, probably due to happy-go-lucky nuclear waste disposal practices during the 1940s. But communities all over America suffer similar adversities.

Only once has New Mexico come close to paying more than it bargained for in its partnership with the Pentagon. That was on May 22, 1957, when a B-36 bomber crew accidentally dropped a hydrogen bomb on Albuquerque. The weapon was called the Mark 17, one of the nastiest ever built; it packed about six hundred times the punch of the Hiroshima bomb. As we all know, Albuquerque was not destroyed, so the air force simply pretended that the incident had not occurred and said nothing about it. Nearly thirty years passed before reporters from the *Albuquerque Journal* finally unearthed the story.

Looking back, the crew member who accidentally pulled the wrong lever readily admitted that he had been a little careless but, hey, the thing didn't go off, right, so what's all the fuss? Seeing Old Scratch slip from his moorings and take to the air over land owned by the University of New Mexico in southeastern Albuquerque, an excited crew member shouted "Bombs away!" The twenty-one-ton weapon plunged thrillingly through New Mexico's famed azure skies, singled out a nice open field for itself, made its potentially historic approach, and landed on a cow, killing it severely.

Fortunately for the city, the crew had been as negligent with the Mark 17's arming device as with the plane's bomb-bay doors. Conventional explosives on the weapon blasted out a small crater, but nothing you couldn't create just as easily by dropping a locomotive out of an airplane. The crew flew back to base, an air force team cleaned up the crater, and the citizens of Albuquerque went on with their lives, unaware of how close they had come to celebrity.

White Sands Missile Range, a thirty-two-hundred-square-mile slice of south-central New Mexico, is America's largest military installation. Practically everything that flies and that has an acronym for a name is tested at White Sands. Here modern warfare was invented, essentially antiquating bloody battles between ground troops and replacing them with desperate face-offs between electrical engineers. Inside range control, a computer jockey squeezing a Coke can in one hand and a joystick in the other zeroes in on a blip on a screen and fires. Another blip, the missile of the moment, streaks across the screen toward the first blip, usually a tank or a drone plane out on the range, but occasionally a herd of sheep or a carport on a ranch adjacent to White Sands. The blips square off, and the kill is made (or not, depending on the adequacy of congressional funding). And White Sands reloads for another test.

Most of the time the secrecy of these pocket wars and the dangers they present to observers keep the gates to White Sands tightly locked to outsiders. But two days each year—the first Saturdays in April and October—the army grounds its missiles, clamps a lid on its secrets, and opens its doors to the public. Several thousand come to visit the spot of the most famous test ever conducted at White Sands: Trinity Site, where the first atomic bomb was exploded on July 16, 1945.

It would be difficult to overemphasize the importance of that test to the future course of events in New Mexico. Were the drop at Trinity to have fizzled and the Manhattan Project team to have been thwarted in its efforts to correct the problem, New Mexico's spectacular growth since the war would never have occurred. The state's reputation sullied, its name forever-after uttered in scientific circles with scorn, this briefly glamorous and up-to-date place would have slunk quickly, quietly, and permanently back into the Dark Ages.

At first glance, the army's decision to build the bomb here may appear somewhat misguided. Of New Mexico's notable resources in 1942—peaceful isolation, heart-thumping beauty, and an old and distinguished culture—only the first was an obvious asset to the Manhattan Project team. But there were plenty of equally remote places where the bomb could have been built. Why, then, choose New Mexico? The answer was furnished by project director J. Robert Oppenheimer, and it turned on those very resources of beauty and culture that New Mexico had in such abundance.

Oppenheimer was a New Mexico kind of character—understated, rugged, sophisticated, an outdoorsman drawn to grand vistas and soul-searching ruminations. He did exquisite physics, he read Hindu philosophy, and he wore cowboy boots. He knew and loved New Mexico, having summered here for twenty years. With his brother he owned a ranch in the Pecos

Valley, not far from Los Alamos. Sizing up potential sites for project head-quarters, Oppenheimer was naturally drawn to New Mexico—not only be-cause of his personal experience of the state, but also because he knew that it offered aesthetic rewards that might sweeten ever so slightly the arduous work of the elite scientists and engineers who would be giving up several years of their lives to work here.

Oppenheimer was largely responsible for the choice of Los Alamos as headquarters for the Manhattan Project. Something of a Shangri-La set on the forested Pajarito Plateau among the graceful, rounded peaks of the Jemez Range, Los Alamos looks out on the bare, brown, deeply scarred floodplain of the Rio Grande, an Old Testament backdrop for Oppenheimer's mystic Hindu texts. Beyond the floodplain rise New Testament peaks: the Sangre de Cristos, mountains of the blood of Christ. Six centuries ago, aeries in nearby cliffsides provided homes for the long-vanished Anasazi. Hikers in the backcountry still stumble across pre-Columbian statuary and ancient petroglyphs depict-ing deer, eagles, and the wonderful hunchbacked flautist, Kokopelli.

In many aspects of their culture, Santa Clara and San Ildefonso Indians, whose pueblos border on Los Alamos, still marked the hours by Anasazi time. The day began with the sun, the night was lit by the moon. Music and dance were as essential to life as water and food. The calendar was a cycle of cosmic reminders. The Indians worshipped in secret but celebrated in public, and soon after Oppenheimer and his people arrived in New Mexico, white faces from the labs began appearing in the crowds attending the Puye ceremonial dances at Santa Clara and the Buffalo, Comanche, and Corn Dances at San Ildefonso. Some of the Manhattan Project team discovered New Mexican arts—Pueblo pottery, especially the stunning black pots by the renowned María Martínez at San Ildefonso; the woodcarvings of the master Hispanic carvers of nearby Cordova; and the weavings of Chimayo. In the evening a physicist could step outside his lab and smell provocations of piñon and juniper, and hear Tewa lullabies rising just beyond a smoky ridge of evergreen, and in the cold and glassy night see the lights of Albuquerque sixty miles distant, as cheerful and steady as campfires. Spring brought warm winds from the valley; summer wrought mild, easy days. In winter there was skiing in deep, dry powder on Pajarito Mountain. Most afternoons brought cottony clouds to solve along with differential equations.

Even today, fifty years after the Manhattan Project, the vast research labs that sprawl over the plateau remain overshadowed by the grandeur of their setting. My friend who works at Los Alamos speaks of browsing deer and dark mountainsides beyond his office window and blissful noontime runs on roller-coaster trails lined with ponderosa pine. Oppenheimer understood the importance to his team of amenities such as these. They could spell the difference between failure and success.

Seen in retrospect, work on the atomic bomb appears to have been driven by an irresistible moral and intellectual force. Success seems to have been assured from the start. And yet the success of the Manhattan Project was anything but inevitable. The technical problems presented by Fat Man and Little Boy were fiendishly difficult. Solving them required a new breed of weapons designer. Before Los Alamos, bomb builders were anonymous underpaid technicians who rode subways and slaved away in warehouses. Their job, crudely put, was to figure out new ways to cram more and more dynamite into smaller and smaller spaces.

By contrast, Manhattan Project team members were celebrated, princely. They collected Nobel prizes, appointments to presidential commissions, tenured university positions. They played cellos and wrote poetry. Together they constituted perhaps the brainiest, most accomplished group of people ever joined in common cause. They brought a new aesthetic to the theretofore somewhat distasteful business of weapons design. Old-time bomb builders were tinkerers, plodders, pyromaniacs. Bomb builders on the Pajarito Plateau were artists.

For obvious reasons, there is a sizable danger in allowing such people to write their own press releases. On the day of Trinity, the Manhattan Project team created not only a bomb but a cloak for it as well, an almost impenetrable linguistic cloud concealing the true nature of their invention. Physics and engineering became prayers and incantations; New Mexico once again became big, empty, God-fearing country. Here is J. Robert Oppenheimer quoting the Bhagavad-Gita as the fireball lit up the New Mexico dawn: "Now I am become death, the destroyer of worlds." Another source gives him this line: "If the radiance of a thousand suns were to burst forth at once in the sky, that would be like the splendor of the Mighty One." (We are not told whether Oppenheimer lowered his voice for this reading or embellished it with primitive dance steps.) Said physicist Isador Rabi: "It was a vision which was seen with more than one eye. It was seen to last forever." Said physicist Robert Serber: "The grandeur and magnitude of the phenomenon were completely breathtaking." Said chemist George Kistiakowsky: "I am sure that at the end of the world, in the last millisecond of the earth's existence, man will see what we have just seen."

And on and on. What the poets of Los Alamos observed was glorious, terrible, uncanny, unearthly, apocalyptic—anything but more dynamite in a smaller space. The bomb was pure science, but the idiom of the bomb was religious to its plutonium core. It was as if the true nature of New Mexico could not be destroyed, not even by a nuclear weapon. At exactly the moment when spirit appeared doomed, it revealed itself more clearly than ever.

The kyries of Trinity are truly soul stirring. Given their suspect origins, however, one is well advised to treat them as warily as one might treat a physics text by Robert Lowell or calculus theorems by Allen Ginsberg. As guides to understanding the events at Trinity they are too riddled with ecstasy to be trusted. Add the oversimplifications of a fawning and thoroughly addled press attempting to whittle the bomb down to column size: inevitably, the Manhattan Project team was said to have "unlocked the secrets of nature." Factor in the workaday obfuscations of the military: General Thomas Farrell, an observer at Trinity, said, "The effects could well be called unprecedented, magnificent, beautiful, stupendous, and terrifying."

The result is a mythology as profound, as sweeping, and as grand as Wagner's Ring Cycle. It was only a bomb, but one would have thought it the Holy Grail. One might as well come to know Trinity through these hosannas as study the history of Germany by attending a performance of *Parsifal* at Bayreuth. On the wide and fearful desert of New Mexico, the sands are white and J. Robert Oppenheimer is a Heldentenor in cowboy boots. Behind the chorus a black and terrible cloud rises toward the heavens, and we raise our opera glasses to see. . . .

On the road to Trinity I resolved to stay sober. I would indulge in no ornamentation, no reflection—just the facts. The setting was not ideal for attempting such a stunt. From the town of San Antonio the highway struck east into a vertiginous scrubland that pitched and rolled like a choppy sea. Low on the horizon floated the Oscura Mountains, bare and sullen as tramp steamers. The sky was weary, the wind mean. At a dip in the road I came upon a textbook dust devil, a complete meteorological event scrunched into a space the size of a barnyard. The twister lurched to and fro drunkenly, dust and debris flying about like squabbling chickens. At every turn the landscape conspired toward mindscape, and I feared that before long I would be seeing a mushroom cloud rising over the Oscuras.

But I resolved to stay sober. Here, barely expanded, are the notes I made during the remainder of my journey to Ground Zero.

San Antonio, a dusty crossroads but nonetheless home of three inter-nationally famous celebrities—the Owl Cafe, the World's Finest Green Chile Cheeseburger, and, somehow, Conrad Hilton. Drive twelve miles east on Highway 380 to the White Stallion turnoff. Take a right.

White Sands Missile Range.

A couple of cars ahead of me, one behind. Straight south over Jornada del Muerto, the dead man's march. I'm on the military base now, technically, though there's no way of telling by looking around. Nothing military about it. Looks like a big ranch. No sand, certainly no white sand. The white sand of the name is gyp-sum, and it's eighty miles from here, at the south end of the range. Here it's dirt and rocks. Big, wide, scrubby—nothing. It's easy to see why they chose this place.

Pickup truck ahead of me, family in a van ahead of the truck. It still looks like a ranch, but now things are changing. Low hills. Tracking dishes. Little backyard observatories, little Palomars, a whole hill of them. Trailers, Quonset huts, army-green vehicles zipping around like jackrabbits. A huge plateau, like a Chinese military base in Tibet.

Check-in at a kind of toll booth or border-crossing station. The M.P. is formal but friendly. He smiles and hands me a sheet of regulations: no photography, no demonstrations, no picketing, no sit-ins, no protest marches, no political speeches, no weapons of any kind (I read this one twice), no alcohol, no drugs, no wandering about in a silly manner, no eating or drinking at Ground Zero, no taking of souvenirs, no motorcycle riding without a protective helmet.

Pretty much nothing.

I ask him for directions.

"Thirteen miles south, hang a left and another four."

In a minute I'm doing eighty; it doesn't say, "No doing eighty." Vegetation tearing across the road, tumbleweeds, UFOs. Wind blazing like retroburners, clouds chugging like freight trains. Surroundings dreadful, nothing but yucca, black, cracked, sucked dry. Van half a mile ahead. Not much to see except twenty miles of not much to see. Patches of mesquite. More yucca. Wretched mountains. The scenery is Neptune without the fun.

Sign: "High explosive test area."

Sign: "Missile impact area. Do not enter without permission."

A line from Loren Eiseley comes to me: "Certain coasts are set apart for shipwreck."

More cars. Hang a left. Here's where the road comes in from the town of Alamogordo. More cars. More cars. Military buses full of visitors. People all over the place. Ahead, straight-topped and striated, a low wall of mountains. The road readies, aims, fires straight at 'em.

M.P.'s, male and female. The parking lot is full of cars, hundreds of them. At one end stands a row of buses. Visitors mill about in the parking lot. I park and join the crowd. There's a feeling of tension and excitement, as though we're on our way to a ball game. Churning winds, thickening clouds. Somehow it's as bright as hell.

Near the entrance, vendors hawk books, hot dogs, T-shirts. The crowd drifts by: lots of retired folks and families with kids. I hear German and French. I pass a party of Japanese.

A dirt path leads two hundred yards to Ground Zero. The wind is cold and nasty. Sheets of dirt fly parallel to the ground, forcing me to squint even behind sunglasses. People on the path walk slowly, talk in undertones. Everyone has a camera, despite the regulation. What brought them here? I'm nervous, sick to my stomach. Warning: "The use of eating, drinking, chewing and smoking materials and the application of cosmetics is prohibited within this fenced area, per AMC *regulation 385-25." There's an M.P. answering questions. There's a woman with a Geiger counter. There's a man with a Lhasa Apso.*

Oppenheimer was at S-10000, a concrete-and-earth-covered wooden shelter ten thousand yards south of Ground Zero. General Leslie Groves, the military director of the Manhattan Project, was ten miles southwest. Most of the witnesses were twenty miles northwest at a place called Compañia Hill. During the night there were thunder and lightning. Groves and Oppenheimer considered calling off the test. Groves threatened the project meteorologist, who promised a break in the weather at dawn.

The rain stopped at 3:15 A.M. Groves phoned the governor of New Mexico and told him to get ready to declare martial law. At 3:45 breakfast was served at the ten-mile shelter. At 4:00 the wind shifted, and observers could see the stars. At 5:09:45 the automatic timing sequence was started at T-minus-20. At T-minus-1 Oppenheimer said: "Lord, these affairs are hard on the heart."

End of the path. On July 16, 1945, no one was here, of course, no pounding pulses.

Come in, come in!

I expect a crater; but there is none, not even a saucer. The area is as flat as the surrounding countryside. The blast scooped out a hole eight feet deep, but afterward a mop-up crew filled it to keep down the radiation.

Fenced area the size of a skating rink. Still some radioactivity here but not enough to hurt: a whole-body exposure of half a milliroentgen per hour, about what you get during a coast-to-coast jetliner flight. Even so, ten times the amount of natural background radiation, after fifty years. Silver-green grass. Yellow twisted blades. Mats of dead and trampled gray. Flecks of glassy Trinitite, Coke-bottle green, a compound of blast-fused sand. Shadowy mountains, dark clouds in a sky rapidly going bad. Small clusters of people scattered throughout

the enclosure. A cold wind. A bookstore hush. A scent of dry, baked, barren earth.
A mangled section of one leg of the tower, all that was left. A hideous monument
of black lava. A Japanese woman. A sound of weeping.

TRINITY SITE, WHERE THE WORLD'S FIRST NUCLEAR DEVICE WAS EX-
PLODED ON JULY 16, 1945.

Carol is sick. Please, God.

Following a visit to Trinity Site, it is difficult to look into any of the
countless efforts to explain the origins of religion without thinking of the
Manhattan Project team and their worshipful responses to the events of
July 16, 1945. William James saw the divine as a "primal reality" to which the
individual responds "solemnly and gravely." Religion is "the feelings, acts, and
experiences of individual men in their solitude, so far as they apprehend
themselves to stand in relation to whatever they may consider the divine."
Sir James Frazer found that religion arises in primitive cultures when magic
fails and people discover themselves powerless. Malinowski's Trobriand Is-
landers cast a spell to quell a storm at sea—one thinks of Oppenheimer
spinning Hindu at S-10000. Jung wondered at our yen for worshiping "repellant things" and found the cause, not surprisingly, in our heads: repellant
gods "are of the substance of the psyche." Did the great minds of Los Alamos
suffer from rotten psyches along with the rest of us?

Then there is this sentence, which leaps out from Huston Smith's introduction to his grand survey, *The Religions of Man:* "Authentic religion is the
clearest opening though which the inexhaustible energies of the cosmos can
pour into human existence." Clearly, Smith was not thinking of the atom, but
his observation helps explain our reverence for the bomb and our difficulty in
renouncing it, a difficulty that has often led Americans to denounce as here-
tics those who oppose nuclear weapons.

I observed that the fenced enclosure at Trinity Site has the area of a
skating rink and, during my visit, the hush of a bookstore. Perhaps I should
have said that the confine has the size and stillness of a cathedral. Like the
classic cathedrals of medieval Europe, Trinity Site is laid out along an east-
west axis. Entering by the south door, one traverses the south transept to the

crossing, the intersection of the transept and the nave. To the right stands Ground Zero, exactly where the altar would be. Most visitors begin here, then in respectful silence pay homage to the statues and relics located elsewhere in the interior—the tower footing, a bomb casing like that of the Nagasaki bomb, beads of Trinitite sparkling beneath the glass of a shelter erected to protect a small section of the original crater floor.

Along the north fence hang several dozen historical photographs—Stations of the Cross. In a long solemn line visitors file past. Base Camp. Assembling the bomb. Hoisting the bomb into the tower. A copy of the Santa Fe *New Mexican,* dated August 6, 1945, which reveals what had been going on up on the plateau: "Los Alamos Secret Disclosed by Truman," "Atomic Bomb Drop on Japan," "Deadliest Weapons in World's History, Made in Santa Fe Vicinity." Hiroshima, one learns, was "an important Japanese army base." There is no mention of suffering or death; there are no photos of charred bodies. (Nor at Chartres are there depictions of the dead of Constantinople, Dalmatia, or Jerusalem.)

The display ends with a series of photographs of the blast itself. Like all such photos, they are failures. The light is too brilliant, the silver nitrate too worldly to record the unearthly transfiguration. One sees a flat, featureless, bloated cloud—a horrible egg, or a massive tumor, or the grotesque distended belly of a fish brought up from the black depths of the sea. So ghastly are the images that they evoke terror in an instant—not the terror of death by vaporization, for it is nothing to die in a microsecond, but nuclear terror, the terror of slow, silent, helpless, wretched death by radiation poisoning. The vomiting, the creeping blindness, the snapping off of the skin like tree bark. The kind of terror only a god could devise. An Old Testament terror, delivered by the wrathful God of the Seventh Plague.

The deity created in New Mexico moves by clouds and kills by shadows. For fifty years it has been omnipresent yet, amazingly, almost totally unseen, for not one in a thousand of us has witnessed a nuclear explosion. Like the god of the medieval mystic, it is a cloud of unknowing. Created in secrecy on the Pajarito Plateau, shrouded in metaphor, photographed surreally, venerated in prayer, understood abstractly or not at all, tested beneath the ground, stored in hollowed-out mountains, denied by those who make it and those who guard it: the bomb has ascended Christlike into a heaven of incomprehension, not as the big, ugly, glorified stick of dynamite that it is but as the central theological mystery of our time. Not communism, not totalitarianism, not even the peerless joy of making a buck can explain the permanent state of war that has existed in the United States since nuclear weapons were invented; only nuclear religion can account for the condition. We have a president, whether Republican or Democrat, whose powers are truly papal, allowing him to mount crusades against demons real or imagined, openly or clandestinely, with or without the consent of Congress. We accumulate state secrets faster than Abraham and Jeremiah accumulated wisdom and truth; only the Word of God could mount with such fury. Our arms salesmen venture to the ends of the earth, spreading the gospel of weaponry with the zeal of missionaries. Meanwhile, at the doors to the Pentagon, obedient members of the fourth estate stand watch with the solemnity of Swiss guards at the Vatican, heralding fabulous press releases as though they were encyclicals.

Like archangels we discover infidels worthy of our awesome power. Before World War II our enemies were treacherous or villainous or detestable, but they were never evil or mad. Beginning with Hitler they have been nothing but. The satans of the Evil Empire, of course, are readily identified—Stalin, Mao, Ho Chi Minh, Khrushchev, Castro. Qaddafi, the mad Libyan. Khomeini, quite mad. Aidid, evil. Noriega, mad. Hussein, evil and mad. Like Christian soldiers we slay the dragon and march on, oblivious to the silent dead, the shattered lives, the burning flesh—the human faces behind the cloud. No souvenir photos of Nagasaki or Baghdad or Panama City adorn our fences. War is hell or evil or shadow or madness or hypothesis or God or blips on a screen. But it is not something we believe ourselves capable of understanding, and so we do not even try.

The mystery of Trinity clouds our view of the world; it is an element of the "awful smog" of which Daniel Berrigan speaks. Berrigan challenges us to see through the veil, through "a duplicitous leadership, an inert Congress, a morally cloudy church, and the jingoistic media." Even today, fifty years after the blast, something unnamed and powerful conspires to obscure the events at Trinity Site. Tramping back and forth over that tiny circle of earth, my emotions conflicted, my thoughts confused, I could make no sense of what I saw or felt. It was as though I were trying to understand the Virgin Birth.

Utterly defeated, I was about to return to my car, when on a hunch I decided to visit the wall of photos one last time. There my perseverance paid off and I found the piece of the puzzle that had been missing. The key photo shows not the blast, not the front page of the *New Mexican*, but J. Robert Oppenheimer sometime after the event. He stands at Ground Zero inspecting the mangled strut of the tower.

I gazed at the familiar figure—pale, skinny, almost emaciated—and the baggy clothing, and the signature porkpie hat. Behind him runs a long low shape of mountains. Looking more closely at the shape, I realized I had seen it before.

I studied the photo, memorized the angles and shadows of the mountains behind Oppenheimer. Then I set out toward the spot where the photographer must have stood. As I moved I trained my eye on the fluid geography of the horizon. With each step that I took, the shape changed minutely, melting toward the profile of mountains I had memorized from the photo. After I moved a few more steps, the two slipped together: a perfect fit. Those old dusty hills became my link to Trinity. They were there to witness the events of July 29, 1945, and they were there for me half a century later, to see with my own eyes.

The cloud lifted at once. Before me stood the project director—a physicist, not a priest. I understood that a great scientific experiment had taken place on this spot, and that what lit up the New Mexico desert that July morning was not a thousand suns or the splendor of the Mighty One or a vision of the last millisecond of the earth's existence: it was an explosion triggered by the compression of a subcritical mass of plutonium into a high-density supercritical mass.

A healer—I don't remember whether it was the neurologist or the Tibetan lama—divined a diagnosis, and to Carol it seemed right. Another cloud began to lift. As it did, we read of the appearance of nuclear weapons in more and more alarming places. At the same time, peaceful, clear-eyed men and women signed disarmament treaties and made plans to sign more.

It's a beginning. The world is full of Fat Men, Little Boys, and all their jolly obese cousins, but some at least are being disarmed. At Sandia labs there is talk of conversion. At Los Alamos there is work for people like plutonium chemist Joe Marz, who spends much of his time working on problems of disarmament. Los Alamos schoolchildren are raising money to erect a children's peace statue in their town. Through the awful smog we see the faint outlines of the faces of individual men, women, and children again. And we begin to wonder if the god may be false, or mortal at least—a silly wizard pressing buttons behind a curtain.

Through fifty years of war the fundamental peaceableness of New Mexico, its habit of addressing the deepest concerns of people through the language of mountains and deserts, has not vanished; it has merely been overshadowed. Many New Mexicans remain committed to the old-time religion, and in every community there are churches to serve them—the Rural Alliance for Military Accountability, Citizens Against Nuclear Threats, the Santa Fe Community Peace Forum, the Society of Friends. There is a long list of such organizations. A few years ago the Dalai Lama brought his message of compassion and nonviolence to Santa Fe, and five thousand turned out to hear him.

One afternoon in 1991 I dropped in to the Albuquerque Peace Center in search of a way to register my opposition to the Gulf War. I struck up a conversation with a man who looked vaguely familiar, a grayer, bulkier version of someone I had seen before. When he told me his name I needed a few moments to retrieve it from a quarter-century of dusty memories. Mark Rudd, the anti–Vietnam War activist and firebrand of Columbia University, now quietly teaching mathematics in New Mexico. He's milder and cheerier than he was in 1968 but no less committed to the goals that motivated him then. There are many like him, for (mainstream propaganda to the contrary) the ideals of the 1960s and the somewhat grizzled veterans who embraced them are as alive today as ever.

It is argued that we have come too far, that the bomb is here to stay and that history cannot be reversed. Nonsense. Ridding the world of nuclear weapons presents an enormous challenge, but so did the building of the first atomic bomb. Eliminating its descendants will require men and women with the intellect, the determination, and the poetic vision of the team that J. Robert Oppenheimer gathered around him at Los Alamos. Such men and women exist in great numbers. Knocking about in the backyard on a lusty April afternoon, snooping after rabbit tracks and cherry blossoms, I had no difficulty picturing a day when the brightest and best of our time will be brought in secret to some lofty and beautiful spot in New Mexico and there put to work on this urgent and difficult problem. And I envisioned the morning, perhaps years later, when we will witness the shining success of their efforts rising in the East—not a thousand suns but one again, the old and good and best one, sign and symbol of the human capacity to light the world.

INTO THE
SECRET
MOUNTAINS

Stones here are dream rooms
With answers to my questions.

—Jimmy Santiago Baca, "What's Real and What's Not"

A good many miles ago, I set out to discover New Mexico. I had two goals in mind. First, I wanted to know New Mexico's land and its people and to make at least a beginning toward understanding how they affect one another. Second, and far more difficult, I hoped to rediscover a bracing sense of promise about America that I had once known but had long since lost sight of.

How I would accomplish those rather conquistadorean missions I had only the vaguest of notions. I decided to do what Charles Darwin said every good researcher should do once in a while—conduct a damn fool experiment, like blowing a trumpet at a bed of tulips, just to see what happens. Forsaking itinerary, motel reservation, and list of recommended restaurants, I climbed into my car, stuck the key in the ignition, and waited to see what would happen. A few minutes later I was on my way to Gallup. As time passed and the miles mounted, I worked out a plan: drive slowly with the windows down, choose the road with the fewest lanes and the worst surface, explore on foot when the road ends, climb hills and wade streams, get lost regularly, picnic widely, avoid anything advertised on a billboard, talk to people who pop up unexpectedly, check things out at odd hours and in peculiar conditions. I tooted my trumpet often, eventually performing with the gusto of a mariachi band. In so doing, I learned that damn fool experiments are risky and occasionally lead to undesirable results, as when a Volkswagen-sized rottweiler came after me on the wrong side of a fence near Columbus, New Mexico.

But they pay off, too, in ways I could never have imagined. Things happened. Hot springs and yellow aspens in the Jemez Mountains. A wondrous visitation of snow geese at Bosque del Apache. Rosy twilight, a vast emerald field, the scent of grass, and eternal softball on a summer evening in Taos. One chill November morning before the sun had crested the horizon, I sipped coffee on a curb outside the Snappy Mart in the town of Deming, listening to a symphony of Spanish and studying through the steam rising from my cup the solemn faces of a hundred workers as they waited to board buses that would take them to the cotton fields. One afternoon with my friend Dave Hertz, I walked onto the long, hauntingly empty Rio Grande Gorge Bridge, one of the highest spans in the world. We peered over the edge at the stomach-turning 650-foot plunge to the river and listened to the screech of the wind as it fiddled on the girders beneath us. Suddenly a grandstanding golden eagle skidded out of the sky, banked hard, and soared beneath our feet. These occasions and others like them allowed me to experience the mystery and romance I had hoped to find on my journey. Only at road's end did I realize how intimately connected those experiences had been to the achievement of the other goals I set for myself when I began my travels.

One summer day I made my way into New Mexico's northern mountains along a road that passes through many of the principal villages of the region. It is an exuberant and magical place possessing a simple but awe-inspiring beauty. The spirit of old New Mexico lives on here, gravely threatened by the forces of progress but staunchly holding its own. Each time I visit I come away with renewed wonder at the resilience of the human animal and rekindled belief in the power of land and tradition. Here blood and water run thick with the wisdom and confidence of time.

The towns nestle in steep-sided valleys and along ridgetops at altitudes of six to eight thousand feet in the Sangre de Cristo Mountains. At the lower end, near the town of Chimayo, the wrinkled countryside of pink marl and juniper has the wide-open, defiant quality that is characteristic of much of New Mexico. Northward the road ascends a steep hogback with breathtaking views on all sides—deep gulches and green sinews of mountains in one direction, the distant and often misty Rio Grande valley in the other.

Beyond the village of Truchas the sides close in, the river valley drops out of sight, and the sense of openness vanishes. The feeling grows that one has left the world behind and entered a new and intriguing country. The land is corduroy; the odor, mountains and ponderosa. A creamy filling of thirteen-thousand-foot peaks is sandwiched between earth and sky. Tousled settlements pop up on the intervales. They look as ragged as boom towns—short-lived, one judges, till closer inspection reveals earthen homes and log barns bound to the soil like spruce trees.

New Mexicans say that one disappears in time on this tattered road. The observation is true but greatly misunderstood. The time a visitor enters here is, paradoxically, the present, not the past. One feels isolated and slightly out of sync because one misses the gray, undifferentiated wash of urban time. A loudly ticking second hand orbits the Sangre de Cristos. Here the twinkling of an eye is a long and engrossing gaze. Time is not forgotten; rather, it is heeded as scrupulously as the first snow of winter.

Hispanic wanderers from Santa Fe and points south came to these mountains three centuries ago. They founded scores of settlements that flourish to this day. By removing themselves from a barely settled New Mexico province that was itself woefully isolated from Mother Spain, they practically ensured their disappearance from the world. What they created by absenting themselves was an indigenous culture of dazzling unity and splendor. They constructed fat-walled adobe houses and churches that still stand. They dug their hands into the difficult land and cleared it and made it work. They raised horses, cattle, sheep, and goats and planted beans, corn, chiles, squash, and varieties of vegetables and fruits as rare as themselves.

With the products of the earth they fashioned the requisites of their lives—bread of corn, clothing of wool, shoes of leather, art of wood, walls of stone, music and dance of wind and pine. They learned to make a few inches of rain behave like a deluge. The streams were pathetic trickles, but the people worked them like dough. Certain men could make the waters rise at a touch and spill over the fields, following the rows like grasshoppers.

The men and women of the northern mountains practiced a fierce Catholicism. It guided them dependably through the seasons of the year and the chapters of their lives. Some of the men answered to a higher call: they became obsessed by the mystery of Christ's passion. Farmers, shopkeepers, family men, they joined the Penitente Brotherhood, a lay order of uncertain origins but with clear links to medieval religious fraternities that offered salvation through suffering. The Penitentes strove to lead exemplary lives, to practice good works, and to understand the agony of Jesus. In deep mountain retreats they prayed through the night and sang *alabados*—sacred refrains— first heard a thousand years before in monasteries in Italy and France. They did penance. They had visions and experienced raptures. One *alabado* summarized their faith:

> From the earth I was made
> And the earth shall eat me.
> The earth has sustained me
> And at last earth I shall be also.
> Goodbye for the last time
> Those who see me on this earth.
> Place me in the sepulcher
> Which is truly my house.

Good Friday was the most solemn day of the year. Singing, praying, bleeding from self-inflicted wounds, the Penitentes trudged over backcountry roads to the villages. Some dragged carts bearing macabre figures of death. Others struggled beneath life-sized wooden crosses. In calvary fields on mountainsides, the cross-bearers donned hoods, planted their burdens, and ascended to the crossbeams. Legend has it that some members of the order died of their divine interpretations.

For those not of the brotherhood, life was scarcely less eventful or numinous. Mary appeared. Crucifixes materialized in gardens. Fields were planted unexplainably. Animals spoke. Spirits roamed the countryside.

As nothing intruded, a perpetual calendar evolved. Spring was serene and diaphanous; summer a time of great labor and primrose; autumn the slow, sad closing of the bloom; winter the trial. The people were philosophical, lithic; they acquired the patience and understanding of mountains. Together they fashioned a unique and sustaining culture. Because they were distant from the world, they were able to keep tradition burning, like the flame of a candle cupped vigilantly in the hand, even as the winds of change blew harder and harder through the hidden valleys of the Sangre de Cristos.

The flame burns yet. In a tumbledown church I paused in tranquil shadows to admire massive and ornate vigas and a magnificent painting by an artist of the hills whose work has outlasted his name. On a winding, unpaved street I heard lilting Spanish and nodded to an earthenware grandmother and stole a glance at her teenage granddaughter, whose brown eyes and barely perceptible smile momentarily stopped my heart. Between houses, robust stalks of corn elbowed for breathing space. Above town, artisans fine-tuned the irrigation ditch. In spring the citizens of the town will patch the walls. Now in late summer, by a familiar and intoxicating aroma, I knew that they had begun to roast the chiles. On certain days they will open glass cases in the old church and bring down their Holy Mother and their saints and parade them through the streets. The whole town will turn out to solemnize these occasions. At Christmas they will kindle their farolitos and luminarias, and the town will be starlight come to earth. The entertainment will be a medieval religious play, the fare *empanaditas, biscochitos, posole,* and chiles. On Good Friday many will make the pilgrimage to the *santuario* at Chimayo. On mountain roads you will hear them singing and see them coming—the children, the men with their crosses, the elderly shuffling, some barefoot, a few on crutches, some over the final lengths humbly on their knees. At the church they will worship and in a small room at the rear push their hands into a vessel of sacred and healing earth. On their pilgrimages they will find confirmation, peace of mind, and release. A few will leave their crutches behind. They will return home and the fields will be plowed and the animals will speak. There is God or magic still in these venerable hills. Whatever it is may be all that can save this place.

In Cordova I stopped at the studio of woodcarver George López. López carries the surname of a distinguished family of Cordova artists, one seen on several of the signs that dot the town's streets inviting visitors to view the carvers' work. During the mid nineteenth century, family patriarch Nazario López began creating life-sized statues of Lady Death for the Penitente chapels and Holy Week processions. His son José Dolores López was New Mexico's first artist to gain an international reputation. José Dolores's unpainted, severely stylized cottonwood figures established the Cordova style, one that recalls El Greco and Velázquez. López carved what he saw around him— hummingbirds and squirrels, saints, trees of life, the Garden of Eden. Like his surroundings and his religion, his works were stark, direct, uncompromised. He saw life as something that was simultaneously raw and grand, tragic and beautiful. Especially through the carvings known as *santos* (after the saints they depicted), he strove to portray this mysterious paradox. Expressionless, world-weary, they bear an impossible weight, yet with dignity and perfect understanding.

José Dolores fathered three woodcarving sons. George is the best known of the now-passing generation of Cordova artists. He was a railroad worker, thirty-seven years old, when he carved his first significant piece; he was fifty-two before he was able to devote himself fully to his art. Today he is something of a national treasure: López was one of the first fifteen American folk artists to receive National Heritage Fellowships from the National Endowment for the Arts. In 1982 the governor of New Mexico presented him with the Governor's Award for Excellence and Achievement in the Arts. His works grace collections around the world.

Tiny and gaunt, crisply dressed in dark trousers and a white long-sleeved shirt, López sat at the open door of his studio taking in the sun that poured down on a bright August morning. At ninety-three he no longer possessed the eyesight or the strength to fashion his saints and his birds. His wife, Silvianita, had died recently; and he had moved beyond art into quiet watchfulness, for which Cordova seems perfectly designed. Most of his work he had turned over to his niece Sabinita Ortiz, who began carving at his knee when she was only eight.

Glancing up, López noticed that I had entered the room. His eyes twinkled as he smiled and in a strong voice welcomed me to his studio. In my hand his fingers felt rough grained and spindly, so frail that I feared they would snap if I squeezed too tightly. His thin, pale arm jutted from his sleeve like a seedling poking through a protective mantle of snow.

Symmetry comes to those who cooperate with trees. The carver's arms and fingers were all bone and length, unpainted, become cottonwood.

I drove up the yawning ridge to Truchas, a village of a few hundred residents perched on a ramp that extends from the mountainside at an altitude of nearly eight thousand feet. The feeling of foreverness is distinct here. Truchas seems carved from the mountain by wind and storm. It isn't much—small adobe homes, stone walls, tin roofs, a few stores, sheep and horses, log stalls. For the farsighted, the panorama extends for 150 miles, to be enjoyed from anywhere in town.

Despite the feeling of foreverness, change is coming. During the past few years, bed-and-breakfasts, art galleries, and realty offices have opened. Anglos from Santa Fe and Albuquerque have purchased second homes in Truchas. The change is part natural evolution, part a consequence of celebrity acquired when Robert Redford came to town a few years ago to film his adaptation of John Nichols's novel *The Milagro Beanfield Wars*.

Practically everyone in town worked on the film. Truchas resident Max Córdova showed me a photo of Redford and the cast posing with several hundred valley residents. Córdova is a traditionalist who does volunteer work with young people. His observations were unsettling.

Into this remote country where change was practically unknown for centuries, something new and disturbing has made its way. One cannot label it simply progress or development, which in the right proportions are desperately needed here, or materialism, or the violent culture of our time, though all are clearly involved. What is new to the mountains is a withering doubt that the mysterious paradox which José Dolores López strove to portray in his carvings can still nourish and give meaning to existence. For many of the young people of the region, life is not simultaneously raw and grand, it is merely raw; if it was ever both tragic and beautiful, it long ago lost its radiance. These youngsters bear an impossible weight. Unlike López's santos, however, they do so with neither dignity nor understanding. Max Córdova described rudderless kids, failure of nerve, fear to stare challenge in the eye, apathy, disrespect, hopelessness. Many of the young people are leaving, though they depart with no known destinations. Some are turning to drugs and crime.

Córdova's words reminded me of a common theme on my travels: an old and honorable New Mexico beset by a new and sinister force. Looking more closely I had usually discovered that the old New Mexico was not always so honorable, the force not so new. The raw and the grand, the tragic and the beautiful have commingled here for as far back as I have been able to see. The dignity and understanding of this place, and the ultimate hope, lie in the fact that New Mexico is still mostly earth and sky. Whatever adversities I have found, I have also found standing staunchly against them a quiet and unshakable confidence rooted in the natural world—an indomitable penstemon tugging at my sleeve, a quenchless light deep within the earth, a desert dawn, a river without measure, a silvery night for lost souls. The importance of New Mexico is that in this age of rootlessness and uncertainty, it stands as an immutable affirmation, a sacred text where we can read of our common birth and gain knowledge of our connection to the stars. That, I am convinced, is the truth I was searching for, the wind of possibilities and dreams.

Approaching the one crossroads in Truchas I faced a decision—which way to go, south to Santa Fe or north to Taos? In the midst of my deliberations I heard a shout. Glancing in the rearview mirror I saw a man running toward me in the middle of the street. He was waving his arms and calling for me to wait.

He made a curious and somewhat disconcerting picture, this obviously troubled figure, racing along that deserted byway and crying out in alarm. Compounding his difficulties was the burden that he carried: an acoustic guitar that instead of being tucked comfortably into its case was slung over his shoulder, as though he were about to perform. As he ran, the instrument swung and bounced, nearly banging him on the chin on every upswing.

Panting heavily, the troubadour came up to the window on the passenger side of the car and peered in. For a moment I thought he expected me to recognize him. He looked to be about thirty, a short and stocky man with thick, jet-black hair, narrow brown eyes, and beads of sweat glistening on his forehead. We shook hands. In a weary voice he said that his name was Eddie Montoya and that he needed a ride down the hill to the village of Cordova.

Clutching his guitar, Montoya crawled into the front seat beside me. We shared a few pleasantries and then, with no urging on my part, he began to tell me a story, one he clearly needed to tell.

His tale was one that is all too familiar in our sorrowful times, yet no less disheartening for its familiarity, or its banality. It concerned a sturdy, broad-shouldered young man, a mountain juniper—twenty-three years of age, a friend of Eddie's since childhood. He grew up among these ancient hills, played here, dreamed here, lost heart and direction here. A few hours earlier as dawn shattered over the Sangre de Cristos, and Eddie despaired, and I came awake with bright sunlight streaming through the window of my rented room, the young man died of an overdose of drugs.

On that warm and serene August day my passenger's revelation hit me with crushing force. We talked for a while, about loss and friendship, about what would come next. Then in the hope of lifting both our spirits, I asked Montoya to play his guitar.

He smiled sheepishly. "It's not mine," he said. "It belongs to my friend. Anyway," he added, "I don't know how to play the guitar."

He gazed out the window for a moment. Glancing down, he touched the instrument tentatively. Suddenly, with a flourish of his fingertips, he struck the strings, finding among them a deep and resonant chord. He ran his hand gently over the lustrous curves of the guitar and picked out phantom melodies between the frets. Then, with the surehandedness of a virtuoso, he lifted the instrument to his chest and rocked it softly in his arms.

Mourning doves and yellow daisies stood by the road as we descended the long hill to Cordova. Near the turnoff a group of kids played ball in a tree-lined field. We passed a young couple walking hand-in-hand beside the road. In golden sunlight, George López watched over the world from the open door of his studio. We stopped at a tiny family-owned grocery store, where Eddie bought me a soft drink. Later in the dirt street outside the store we shook hands and wished each other well. I climbed into my car and drove away.

I have been told that in the years to come, those of us who survive war, famine, violence, and disease will inhabit dimly lit rooms, where we will worship at computer terminals and communicate by video phone and grow wise from the genius of a thousand channels. Products will fulfill us and hatreds divide us, and poisons will darken the sky.

I don't believe it. I believe we will sit side-by-side in the bright sunlight and speak trustingly of our hopes and fears, and tell stories about our children, and carve for one another squirrels and hummingbirds of cottonwood. All that we will ever need is here today, as it has always been—kindness, love, gentleness, earth, beauty, family, sky. We must learn to play them. We must press them to our hearts like timeless guitars and never let them go.

SOURCES OF QUOTATIONS

Introduction

Barry Lopez, *Arctic Dreams: Imagination and Desire in a Northern Landscape* (New York: Charles Scribner's Sons, 1986).

Book Epigraph

Jimmy Santiago Baca, "In My Land," in his *Immigrants in Our Own Land* (Baton Rouge: Louisiana State University Press, 1979). Reprinted by permission of Jimmy Santiago Baca.

Tumbleweeds

Willa Cather, *Death Comes for the Archbishop* (New York: Vintage Books, 1971).

D. H. Lawrence, *Posthumous Papers* (New York: Viking Press, 1936).

Journeys through Space and Time

For much of the historical background in this chapter, I am indebted to Dee Brown's *Bury My Heart at Wounded Knee* (New York: Holt, Rinehart & Winston, 1970); quotations not attributed to other sources below can be found in this splendid and indispensable work. For the extensive recollections of the Long Walk, I've relied on *Navajo Stories of the Long Walk Period*, ed. Ruth Roessel (Tsaile, Ariz.: Navajo Community College Press, 1973). Reprinted by permission of the publisher.

Many of the statistics I've cited were supplied by the Indian Health Service and the University of New Mexico Bureau of Business and Economic Research. The statistics on highway fatalities appeared in the *Albuquerque Journal*, March 11, 1992.

Leonard Crow Dog's retelling of the hopeful Brule Sioux creation story is from *American Indian Myths and Legends,* ed. Richard Erdoes and Alfonso Ortiz (New York: Pantheon Books, 1984).

G. K. Chesterton, *What I Saw in America* (New York: Dodd, Mead and Company, 1922).

John Hay, "The Nature Writer's Dilemma," in *On Nature,* ed. Daniel Halpern (San Francisco: North Point Press, 1987).

Thomas Merton, *Woods, Shore, Desert* (Santa Fe: Museum of New Mexico Press, 1982).

Annie Dillard, *Living by Fiction* (New York: Harper & Row, 1982).

John Steinbeck, *The Grapes of Wrath* (New York: Penguin Books, 1986).

McCabe's letter is reprinted in Lawrence C. Kelly, *Navajo Roundup* (Boulder, Colo.: Pruett Publishing Company, 1970).

Andy Rooney quoted in Jim Belshaw's column in the *Albuquerque Journal,* April 21, 1992.

Vincent Scully, *Pueblo: Mountain, Village, Dance* (New York: Viking Press, 1975).

Lupita Johnson, writing in the fall 1991 edition of the quarterly *Americans Before Columbus,* published by the National Indian Youth Council.

Herraro Grande quoted in Lynn R. Bailey, *The Long Walk* (Pasadena, Calif.: Westernlore Publications, 1978).

Barboncito, Ganado Mucho, and Castañeda quoted in John Upton Terrell, *The Navajos* (New York: Weybright and Talley, 1970).

Letter by Randolph G. Runs After, *Albuquerque Tribune,* October 2, 1992. Reprinted by permission of the author.

Rudyard Kipling, *Something of Myself and Other Autobiographical Writings,* ed. Thomas Pinney (New York: Cambridge University Press, 1990). Reprinted by permission of the publisher.

A Shelter in the Sky

For the New Mexico history that I discuss in this chapter I turned to many sources, principally Paul Horgan's monumental *Great River: The Rio Grande in North American History* (New York: Holt, Rinehart and Winston, 1954).

Rainer Maria Rilke, "Initiation," in his *Selected Poems,* ed. and trans. C. F. MacIntyre (Berkeley: University of California Press, 1940). Copyright © 1940, 1968 C. F. MacIntyre. Reprinted with permission.

Henry Moore quoted in Roger Berthoud, *The Life of Henry Moore* (New York: E. P. Dutton, 1987).

D. H. Lawrence quoted in Arrell Morgan Gibson, *The Santa Fe and Taos Colonies: Age of the Muses* (Norman: University of Oklahoma Press, 1983).

Paul Horgan, *Approaches to Writing* (New York: Farrar, Straus and Giroux, 1973).

William Kennedy, *Ironweed* (New York: Viking Press, 1983).

V. S. Pritchett, preface to *The Sailor, The Sense of Humor, and Other Stories* (New York: Alfred A. Knopf, 1965).

Phil Gramm quoted in David S. Broder's syndicated column, *Albuquerque Journal*, March 1, 1995.

John Kluge, interview, *Albuquerque Journal*, October 14, 1990.

Death on a Distant Plain

W. Eugene Hollon, *Frontier Violence: Another Look* (New York: Oxford University Press, 1974).

National Commission on the Causes and Prevention of Violence, *To Establish Justice, To Insure Domestic Tranquility* (Washington, D.C.: Government Printing Office, 1969).

Richard Hofstadter, *American Violence* (New York: Knopf, 1970).

Arthur Koestler, *Darkness at Noon* (London: Longmans, 1968).

George Orwell, "Shooting an Elephant," in *The Collected Essays, Journalism, and Letters of George Orwell* (New York: Harcourt, Brace & World, 1968).

James Baldwin, *Nobody Knows My Name* (New York: Dial Press, 1961).

The Voice of the Flower

Edmund Wilson quoted in Jeffrey Hogrefe, *O'Keeffe: The Life of an American Legend* (New York: Bantam Books, 1992); Lewis Mumford quoted in Laurie Lisle, *Portrait of an Artist* (New York: Seaview Books, 1980).

Georgia O'Keeffe quoted in Anita Pollitzer, *A Woman on Paper* (New York: Simon & Schuster, 1988); Lisle, *Portrait of an Artist;* O'Keeffe, *Georgia O'Keeffe* (New York: Viking Press, 1976). Reprinted with the permission of Simon & Schuster from *A Woman on Paper: Georgia O'Keeffe* by Anita Pollitzer. Copyright © 1988 by The Estate of Anita Pollitzer. All quotations from Georgia O'Keeffe © 1998 The Georgia O'Keeffe Foundation/Artists Rights Society (ARS), New York.

John Marin quoted in Lisl Dennis, *Santa Fe* (Houston: Herring Press, 1987); Frederic Remington quoted in Van Deren Coke, *Taos and Santa Fe: The Artists'*

Environment, 1882–1942 (Albuquerque: University of New Mexico Press, 1963); adjacent quotations about New Mexico's qualities are from Gibson, *Santa Fe and Taos Colonies.*

Lincoln Steffens quoted in Gibson, *Santa Fe and Taos Colonies.*

Pablo Picasso quoted in Françoise Gilot and Carlton Lake, *Life with Picasso* (New York: McGraw-Hill, 1964).

Judy Chicago, *Through the Flower* (Garden City, N.Y.: Doubleday, 1975).

John Gardner quoted in the *New York Times Book Review,* February 20, 1977.

Material on the UDC affair summarized from Lucy R. Lippard, "Uninvited Guests: How Washington Lost 'The Dinner Party,'" *Art in America,* December 1991, from which all of the quotations in this section (and Hilton Kramer's comment) are taken.

Samuel Johnson quoted in James Boswell, *The Life of Dr. Johnson* (New York: Oxford University Press, 1980).

For Georgia O'Keeffe's comment on color see *New Mexico: A New Guide to the Colorful State* (Albuquerque: University of New Mexico Press, 1984).

Sir Michael Tippett quoted in Andrew Porter, *Music of Three More Seasons, 1977–1980* (New York: Knopf, 1981). Originally published in the *New Yorker,* September 19, 1977. Reprinted here by permission of the publisher.

Jacobo Timmerman, *The Nation,* June 13, 1981.

Alexis de Tocqueville, *Democracy in America* (New York: Harper & Row, 1966).

River of Wings

Loren Eiseley, "The Flow of the River," in *The Immense Journey* (New York: Random House, 1957).

John Muir, *John of the Mountains: The Unpublished Journals of John Muir,* ed. Linnie Marsh Wolfe (Boston: Houghton, Mifflin, 1938); Henry David Thoreau, "Walking," in *Excursions: The Writings of Henry David Thoreau* (Boston: Houghton, Mifflin, 1893) and *Walden* (Boston: Houghton, Mifflin, 1995); Gary Snyder, *The Practice of the Wild* (Berkeley: North Point Press, 1990).

Ronald Reagan's comment on Shangri-La was widely quoted during the 1980 presidential campaign.

Henry David Thoreau, *Journal* (Princeton: Princeton University Press, 1981).

Antoine de Saint-Exupéry, *Wind, Sand, and Stars* (New York: Harcourt, Brace, 1949).

Jack Kerouac, *On the Road* (New York: Viking Press, 1957).

Desert Genesis

Walt Whitman, "Pioneers! O Pioneers!" in his *Leaves of Grass* (New York: Modern Library, 1993).

Frederick Jackson Turner, *The Frontier in American History* (New York: Holt, Rinehart and Winston, 1962); de Tocqueville, *Democracy in America*.

Richard Rodriguez, "Does America Still Exist?" *Harper's*, March 1984.

Walt Whitman, "Song of Myself," in his *Leaves of Grass*.

T. S. Eliot, "East Coker," in his collection *The Complete Poems and Plays* (San Diego: Harcourt Brace Jovanovich, 1980).

Eskimo paean to daybreak is in *Wilderness USA* (Washington, D.C.: The National Geographic Society, 1973).

For John Jay's notion of who should govern a country see Lewis Lapham's editorial "Storm of Words," *Harper's*, June 1992.

Bill Evans, "Improvisation in Jazz," liner notes for the Miles Davis recording *Kind of Blue*, Columbia Records, 1959.

Walt Whitman, "Song of the Open Road," in his *Leaves of Grass*.

John Donne, "Hymn to God my God, in My Sickness," in *The Complete Poetry and Selected Prose of John Donne* (New York: Modern Library, 1994).

Adrift in the Permian Sea

Country Joe McDonald, from the song "Thought Dream," published by Joyful Wisdom Music, recorded by Country Joe and the Fish on *I-Feel-Like-I'm-Fixin'-To-Die*, Vanguard Records, 1967. "Don't Drop That A Bomb on Me," words & music by Barry Melton and Joe McDonald © 1967, renewed 1995 Joyful Wisdom Music Co., BMI. Used by permission.

James Watkins quoted in the *Albuquerque Journal*, January 30, 1992.

Samuel Johnson quoted in Boswell, *Life of Samuel Johnson*.

Robinson Jeffers, "Carmel Point," in his *Selected Poems* (New York: Random House, 1987).

Rebuilding the Clouds

Antonio Machado, "Rebirth," in his *Times Alone*, trans. Robert Bly (Middletown, Conn.: Wesleyan University Press, 1983). Copyright 1983 by Robert Bly. Reprinted with his permission.

John Greenleaf Whittier, "To Charles Sumner," in *The Complete Poetical Works of Whittier* (Boston: Houghton Mifflin, 1894).

Robertson Davies, "A Few Kind Words for Superstition," in *75 Readings: An Anthology,* ed. Santi V. Buscemi and Charlotte Smith (New York: McGraw-Hill, 1991).

Roderick Nash, *Wilderness and the American Mind* (New Haven, Conn.: Yale University Press, 1967).

Thomas Merton, *Woods, Shore, Desert.*

J. Robert Oppenheimer quoted in Peter Wyden, *Day One* (New York: Simon and Schuster, 1984) and Bartlett's *Familiar Quotations* (Boston: Little, Brown and Company, 1968); George Kistiakowsky quoted in Wyden, *Day One;* Isador Rabi and Robert Serber quoted in Richard Rhodes, *The Making of the Atomic Bomb* (New York: Simon and Schuster, 1986).

Thomas Farrell quoted in Dan Kurzman, *Day of the Bomb* (New York: McGraw-Hill, 1986).

Loren Eiseley, "The Star Thrower," in his collection *The Unexpected Universe* (New York: Harcourt, Brace & World, 1969).

J. Robert Oppenheimer quoted in Kurzman, *Day of the Bomb.*

William James, *The Varieties of Religious Experience* (New York: Modern Library, 1936); Sir James George Frazer, *The Golden Bough* (New York: Macmillan, 1940); Bronislaw Malinowski, *Magic, Science, and Religion, and Other Essays* (Garden City, N.Y.: Doubleday, 1954).

Carl Jung, *Modern Man in Search of a Soul* (New York: Harcourt, Brace & World, 1933).

Huston Smith, *The Religions of Man* (New York: Harper & Row, 1958).

Daniel Berrigan, "The Empire Lurches Downhill," *The Progressive,* March 1991.

Into the Secret Mountains

Jimmy Santiago Baca, "What's Real and What's Not," in *Black Mesa Poems* (New York: New Directions, 1986). Copyright © 1986 by Jimmy Santiago Baca. Reprinted by permission of New Directions.

CAROL DIMMICK REID

ABOUT THE AUTHOR

Robert Leonard Reid is the author of *Mountains of the Great Blue Dream* and editor of the anthology *A Treasury of the Sierra Nevada*. He has taught creative nonfiction and nature writing at the University of New Mexico and Western Nevada Community College. He is married to Carol Dimmick Reid, with whom he has a son, Jake.